Your Art Heritage

Your Art Heritage

OLIVE L. RILEY
Director of Art
Public Schools of the
City of New York

McGRAW-HILL BOOK COMPANY, INC.

New York · Toronto · London

YOUR ART HERITAGE

x

52925

CONTENTS

PREFACE   xix

1. INTRODUCTION   I

What Is Art? Common Qualities in Great Art; Meaning of Art; Selection and Use of Media; Relation of Form to Use; Are We Always
in Agreement? The Search for Beauty; Practice Is Essential; Your
Part in Art.

2. PRIMITIVE AND EARLY ART   15

The Will to Survive; Art Is Born; Primitive Painters; Forerunners of
Architecture; The Egyptian, Master-Builder of Tombs; Religion Affects Building; Egyptian Temples; Egyptian Mural Painting; Significance of Egyptian Building.

3. PRIMITIVE AND EARLY SCULPTURE   37

The Sculptor as Maskmaker; The Sculptor as Stone-Carver; Mesopotamian Art; Aegean Culture; Cypriote Sculpture; Other Early Sculptors; The Maya Sculptor; Accomplishments of Early Sculptors.

4. EARLY MINOR ARTS   57

First Women Artists; Art of Pottery; Art of Weaving; Coptic and Indian Textiles; Egyptian Woodcarving; Carvers of the Northwest Coast
of America; Eskimo Art; Pueblo Maskmakers; Spirit of Early Craftsmen.

5. BIRTH OF EUROPEAN ARCHITECTURE   79

The Greek Way of Life; The Greek Temple; Design of the Parthe-
non; The Grandeur That Was Rome; The Pantheon; Other Examples
of Roman Architecture; The Roman Basilica; Early Christian Archi-
tecture; Byzantine Art; Santa Sophia; Mohammedan Architecture;
The Venetian Church of St. Mark; Coming of the Middle Ages to
Europe; Romanesque Architecture; Gothic Cathedrals of the Middle
Ages; Chartres Cathedral; Notre Dame de Paris; Amiens and Rheims
Cathedrals; Ste. Chapelle, a Glory of Glass; Gothic Cathedrals of
England; Significance of Gothic Architecture.

6. DEVELOPMENT OF SCULPTURE   III

Early Greek Sculpture; Climax of Greek Sculpture; Roman Sculpture;
The Far-Eastern World; China of the Past; Religions of China; Early
Indian Art; The Hindu Sculptor; Hindu Sculpture; Gothic Sculpture;
Sculpture and the Spiritual Life.

v

7. EARLY PAINTERS   137
The Painter Offers His Services to the Church; Fra Angelico's Paint-
ings; Italian Renaissance; Paintings of Masaccio; Other Early Renais-
sance Painters; Pageant Painters; Da Vinci, Genius of the Renaissance;
Michelangelo, the Titan; Raphael, the Beloved Painter; Renaissance
Painting in Venice; The Bellini Brothers; Titian, Master of Venetian
Painting; Chinese Painting.

8. ENRICHMENT OF THE MINOR ARTS   163
Egyptian Writing; Phoenician Alphabet; Medieval Manuscripts;
Oriental Calligraphy; Block Books; Art of Printing; Early Engravers;
Importance of the Minor Arts.

9. DEVELOPMENT OF PAINTING   183
Painting in Germany; Painting in Spain; Painting in Holland; Eng-
lish Painting; French Painting; Daumier, the Crusader; Degas, the
Innovator; Impressionists; Renoir, the Colorist; Neo-Impressionists.

10. DEVELOPMENT OF ARCHITECTURE   211
Civic Building; Baroque Architecture; French Renaissance Architec-
ture; English Renaissance Architecture; Building in Colonial America;
Spanish-American Architecture; Eighteenth-Century Architecture;
Later American Architecture.

11. MODERN PAINTING   229
Accomplishments of Cézanne; Paintings of Van Gogh; Paintings of
Gauguin; Early Expressionists; Paintings of Matisse; Other Expres-
sionist Painters; Rousseau, the Primitive; Picasso and the Cubists;
Paintings of Kandinsky; Surrealists; Directions of Modern Painting.

12. DEVELOPMENT OF SCULPTURE   249
Beginning of Modern Sculpture; Revival of Stone Carving; The All-
around View; Further Experiments in Sculpture; Mobiles; Significance of Modern Sculpture.

13. PAINTING IN THE AMERICAS   269
Arrival of the Trained Artist; Pioneer Painters; Painters of the Amer-
ican Scene; Painting Loses Its Boundaries; Paintings of Marin; Other
Important Painters; Painters of the Social Scene; Experimental Paint-
ers of Today; Painting in Mexico; Painting in Cuba and Brazil;
Meaning of Modern Painting.

14. MODERN ARCHITECTURE   289
Design and Materials; The Skyscraper; The Slab Skyscraper; Modern
Houses; Interiors; Problems of City Planning; Zoning the City; Com-
munity Planning; What Plans for the Future?

TOPICS FOR DISCUSSION AND THINGS TO DO   307
INDEX

ILLUSTRATIONS

1. THE GOURMET *Picasso (Color)*   *Facing*   I
   Courtesy, The Art Institute of Chicago, Chicago, Illinois; The Chester Dale
   Collection—loan
2. RCA BUILDING, ROCKEFELLER CENTER New York, N.Y.   3
   Courtesy, Standard Oil Company of New Jersey, Parks, photographer
3. MOSES *Michelangelo*   3
4. MME. CHARPENTIER AND HER CHILDREN *Renoir*   4
   Courtesy of The Metropolitan Museum of Art, New York, N.Y.
5. THE NATIVITY *Fra Angelico*   4
6. WOMAN OF THE OLD TESTAMENT France   8
7. CIRCUS GIRLS *Gross*   8
   Courtesy, the artist
8. HEAD *Modigliani*   II
   Courtesy, The Museum of Modern Art, New York, N.Y. Donor, Mrs. John
   D. Rockefeller, Jr.
9. THE CITY *Léger*   13
   Courtesy, Philadelphia Museum of Art, Philadelphia, Pa.
10. TUGENDHUT HOUSE Brno, Czechoslovakia   13
11. CORAL REEF CAVES South America   16
   Courtesy, Standard Oil Company of New Jersey, Collier, photographer
12. BRI-BRI KING'S HOUSE Central America   16
   Courtesy, Museum of the American Indian, New York, N.Y. Heye Foundation
13. CAVE PAINTING Spain   19
   Courtesy, The Museum of Modern Art, New York, N.Y. and the Frobenius
   Collection
14. ROCK PAINTING Africa   19
   Courtesy, The Museum of Modern Art, New York, N.Y. and the Frobenius
   Collection
15. MURAL PAINTING North America   22
   Courtesy, Peabody Museum, Harvard University, Cambridge, Mass.
16. CHILD'S PAINTING England   22
   Courtesy, British Information Services, New York, N.Y.
17. CLIFF PALACE North America   24
   Courtesy, The National Park Service, Mesa Verde National Park, Colorado

18. STONEHENGE   England   24
19. INNER COFFIN OF TUTANKHAMEN   Egypt   26
20. THE SPHINX OF GIZEH   Egypt   28
    Ewing Galloway photograph
21. MODEL OF PYRAMID OF SAHURE   Egypt   28
    Courtesy of The Metropolitan Museum of Art, New York, N.Y.
22. MODEL OF TEMPLE OF HATSHEPSUT   Egypt   30
    Courtesy of The Metropolitan Museum of Art, New York, N.Y.
23. TEMPLE OF RAMSES II   Egypt   30
    Courtesy, The University of Chicago, Chicago, Illinois, The Oriental Institute
24. MODEL OF HYPOSTYLE HALL, TEMPLE OF AMON   Egypt   31
    Courtesy, The Metropolitan Museum of Art, New York, N.Y.
25. SECTION OF A PAINTED BOX   Egypt   31
26. NOBLEMAN HUNTING   Egypt   32
    Courtesy, The University of Chicago, Chicago, Illinois, The Oriental Institute
27. SEACOAST MAYA VILLAGE   Mexico   34
    Courtesy, Carnegie Institution of Washington, Washington, D.C.
28. EL CASTILLO   Mexico   34
    Courtesy, Carnegie Institution of Washington, Washington, D.C.
29. WAR GOD   Hawaiian Islands   36
    Courtesy, Peabody Museum of Salem, Salem, Mass.
30. KORWAR   New Guinea   36
    Courtesy, The University Museum, Philadelphia, Pa.
31. TIKI   Marquesas Islands   38
    Courtesy, The University Museum, Philadelphia, Pa.
32. STONE PIPE   North America   38
    Courtesy, Ohio State Museum, Columbus, Ohio
33. HEAD   North America   40
    Courtesy, Museum of the American Indian, New York, N.Y. Heye Foundation
34. SOUL BIRD   New Guinea   40
    Courtesy, The University Museum, Philadelphia, Pa.
35. MASK   Africa   41
    Courtesy, The University Museum, Philadelphia, Pa.
36. MASK   Africa   41
    Courtesy, The Brooklyn Museum, New York, N.Y.
37. QUEEN HATSHEPSUT   Egypt   42
    Courtesy of The Metropolitan Museum of Art, New York, N.Y.
38. QUEEN HATSHEPSUT   Egypt   42
    Courtesy of The Metropolitan Museum of Art, New York, N.Y.
39. QUEEN NOFRETETE   Egypt   44
    Courtesy of The Metropolitan Museum of Art, New York, N.Y.
40. RAMSES II   Egypt   44
    Courtesy of The Metropolitan Museum of Art, New York, N.Y.
41. SUMERIAN PRIEST   Mesopotamia   46
    Courtesy of The Metropolitan Museum of Art, New York, N.Y.
42. WINGED BEING   Mesopotamia   46
    Courtesy of The Metropolitan Museum of Art, New York, N.Y.

43. KING ASHURBANIPAL AND HIS QUEEN   Mesopotamia   48
Courtesy of The Metropolitan Museum of Art, New York, N.Y.
44. TRIBUTE BEARERS   Mesopotamia   48
Courtesy, The University of Chicago, Chicago, Ill., The Oriental Institute
45. HEAD   Island of Cyprus   51
Courtesy of The Metropolitan Museum of Art, New York, N.Y.
46. PRIEST WITH A DOVE   Island of Cyprus   51
Courtesy of The Metropolitan Museum of Art, New York, N.Y.
47. HEAD OF A MAIZE GOD   Central America   53
Courtesy, Peabody Museum, Harvard University, Cambridge, Mass.
48. CARACOL TOWER   Central America   53
Courtesy, The Brooklyn Museum, New York, N.Y.
49. PORTRAIT OF A MAYA ASTRONOMER   Central America   55
Courtesy, The Brooklyn Museum, New York, N.Y.
50. TWINED BASKET   North America   56
Courtesy, The Denver Art Museum, Denver, Col.
51. COILED BASKET   North America   56
Courtesy, The University Museum, Philadelphia, Pa.
52. POTTERY JUGS   Island of Cyprus   60
Courtesy of The Metropolitan Museum of Art, New York, N.Y.
53. CERAMIC JAR   Egypt   60
Courtesy of The Metropolitan Museum of Art, New York, N.Y.
54. POTTERY DRUM JAR   North America   62
Courtesy, The Taylor Museum, Colorado Springs, Col., and the Museum of
Modern Art, New York, N.Y.
55. EFFIGY VASE   South America   62
Courtesy, the permanent collection of the Fine Arts Department, The International Business Machines Corporation, New York, N.Y.
56. TEXTILE   South America   64
Courtesy of The Metropolitan Museum of Art, New York, N.Y.
57. WOVEN BAG   South America   66
Courtesy, The Museum of the American Indian, New York, N.Y. Heye Foundation
58. WOVEN BLANKET   North America   67
Courtesy, The Museum of the American Indian, New York, N.Y. Heye Foundation
59. WOVEN SHOULDER BLANKET   North America   67
Courtesy, The Museum of the American Indian, New York, N.Y. Heye Foundation
60. BUCKSKIN DRESS   North America   68
Courtesy, The Brooklyn Museum, New York, N.Y.
61. BEADED MOCCASINS   North America   68
Courtesy, The Museum of the American Indian, New York, N.Y. Heye Foundation
62. HORSE AND RIDER   Egypt   70
Courtesy of The Metropolitan Museum of Art, New York, N.Y.
63. OFFERING BEARER   Egypt   70
Courtesy of The Metropolitan Museum of Art, New York, N.Y.

ix

64. BOAT MODEL   Egypt   71
Courtesy of The Metropolitan Museum of Art, New York, N.Y.

65. HARP OF QUEEN SHUB-AD   Mesopotamia   71
Courtesy, The University Museum, Philadelphia, Pa.

66. TOTEM POLE   North America   72
Courtesy, The Museum of Natural History, New York, N.Y.

67. HOME POST   North America   72
Courtesy, The Brooklyn Museum, New York, N.Y.

68. POTLATCH DISH   North America   74
Courtesy, Portland Art Museum, Portland, Ore.

69. ARTICULATED DANCE MASK   North America   74
Courtesy, Portland Art Museum, Portland, Ore.

70. FISH EFFIGY MASK   North America   76
Courtesy, Portland Art Museum, Portland, Ore.

71. SEATED WHITE MAN   North America   76
Courtesy, Museum of the American Indian, New York, N.Y. Heye Foundation

72. MASK OF SAIYATSHA   North America   77
Courtesy, The Brooklyn Museum, New York, N.Y.

73. KATCHINA DOLLS   North America   77
Courtesy, Museum of the American Indian, New York, N.Y. Heye Foundation

74. PARTHENON   Athens, Greece   82

75. PORCH OF THE MAIDENS   Athens, Greece   82

76. PONT DU GARD   Nîmes, France   84
Philip Gendreau photograph

77. PANTHEON   Rome, Italy   84

78. COLOSSEUM   Rome, Italy   86

79. BATHS OF CARACALLA   Rome, Italy   86

80. ST. APOLLINARE IN CLASSE   Ravenna, Italy   90

81. MOSAIC, ST. APOLLINARE IN CLASSE   Ravenna, Italy   90

82. SANTA SOPHIA   Istanbul, Turkey   92
Ewing Galloway photograph

83. INTERIOR, SANTA SOPHIA   Istanbul, Turkey   92
Ewing Galloway photograph

84. TAJ MAHAL   Agra, India   94

85. CATHEDRAL OF ST. MARK   Venice, Italy   94

86. CAERNARVON CASTLE   Wales   97
Courtesy, British Information Services, New York, N.Y.

87. MONT ST. MICHEL   France   97
Courtesy, French National Tourist Office, New York, N.Y.

88. PORTE DES ALLEMANDES   Metz, France   98
Ewing Galloway photograph

89. CARCASSONNE   Carcassonne, France   98

90. ST. TROPHIME   Arles, France   99

91. CLOISTERS, ST. TROPHIME   Arles, France   99

92. CATHEDRAL OF PISA   Pisa, Italy   101

93. PLAN, CATHEDRAL OF CHARTRES   Chartres, France   101

x

94. CATHEDRAL OF CHARTRES   Chartres, France   102
    Ewing Galloway photograph
95. CATHEDRAL OF NOTRE DAME   Paris, France   102
    Ewing Galloway photograph
96. ROSE WINDOW, CHARTRES   Chartres, France   104
97. DOORWAY, CATHEDRAL OF AMIENS   Amiens, France   104
98. CATHEDRAL OF RHEIMS   Rheims, France   106
    Ewing Galloway photograph
99. STE. CHAPELLE   Paris, France   107
100. CATHEDRAL OF SALISBURY   Salisbury, England   109
101. INTERIOR, WELLS CATHEDRAL   Wells, England   109
102. HERA OF SAMOS   Greece   110
103. BIRTH OF APHRODITE   Greece   110
104. STATUETTE OF A HORSE   Greece   113
    Courtesy, The Metropolitan Museum of Art, New York, N.Y.
105. CHARIOTEER OF DELPHI   Greece   114
106. ARCHER   Greece   114
    Courtesy, Clarence Kennedy
107. HEAD OF A YOUNG MAN   Greece   116
108. HEAD OF ATHENA   Greece   116
109. DIANA FASTENING HER CAPE   Greece   117
110. DANCING GIRL   Greece   117
    Courtesy of The Metropolitan Museum of Art, New York, N.Y.
111. STRIDING WARRIOR   Italy   119
    Courtesy of The Metropolitan Museum of Art, New York, N.Y.
112. PORTRAIT OF CAESAR   Italy   121
    Courtesy, Ludwig Goldscheider, Phaidon Press, Oxford University Press
113. WINE VESSEL   China   122
    Courtesy, The Art Institute of Chicago, Chicago, Ill.
114. STATUETTE OF A BEAR   China   122
    Courtesy, City Art Museum of St. Louis, St. Louis, Mo.
115. LAO TSE ON A WATER BUFFALO   China   124
    Courtesy, The Worcester Art Museum, Worcester, Mass.
116. BODHISATTVA   China   124
    Courtesy of The Metropolitan Museum of Art, New York, N.Y.
117. BODHISATTVA ON A DOUBLE LOTUS LEAF   China   126
    Courtesy, The Smithsonian Institution, Freer Gallery of Art, Washing-
    ton, D.C.
118. BAWON TEMPLE   Java   128
119. BUDDHA   Ceylon   128
120. BRAHMA   India   130
    Courtesy of The Metropolitan Museum of Art, New York, N.Y.
121. DANCING SIVA   India   131
    Courtesy, William Rockhill Nelson Gallery of Art, Kansas City, Mo.
122. KALI WITH CYMBALS   India   131
    Courtesy, William Rockhill Nelson Gallery of Art, Kansas City, Mo.

123. NORTHERN PORTAL, CHARTRES France   133
124. SHEPHERDS OF THE NATIVITY, CHARTRES France   135
125. ANGEL OF NOTRE DAME, CHARTRES France   135
126. THE THREE KINGS Christian Byzantine Mosaic   136
127. MADONNA AND CHILD Christian Byzantine Mosaic   136
128. THE VIRGIN ENTHRONED *Giotto*   138
129. ADORATION OF THE MAGI *Giotto*   140
130. THE ANNUNCIATION *Simone Martini*   140
131. JOURNEY OF THE MAGI *Sassetta (Color)*   *Facing* 141
     Courtesy of The Metropolitan Museum of Art, New York, N.Y.
132. PARADISE, DETAIL *Fra Angelico*   143
133. FLIGHT INTO EGYPT *Fra Angelico*   143
134. THE TRIBUTE MONEY, DETAIL *Masaccio*   144
135. VISIT OF THE QUEEN OF SHEBA *Piero della Francesca*   144
136. MADONNA ADORING THE CHILD *Fra Filippo Lippi*   146
137. THE VIRGIN, INFANT JESUS, AND ST. JOHN *Botticelli*   148
138. ADORATION OF THE MAGI *Da Fabriano*   150
139. JOURNEY OF THE THREE KINGS *Gozzoli*   150
140. THE VIRGIN AND CHILD WITH ST. ANNE *Da Vinci*   152
     Courtesy, Ludwig Goldscheider, Phaidon Press, Oxford University Press
141. MONA LISA, DETAIL *Da Vinci*   153
     Courtesy, Ludwig Goldscheider, Phaidon Press, Oxford University Press
142. DELPHIC SYBIL *Michelangelo*   155
143. MADONNA OF THE GOLDFINCH *Raphael*   155
144. MIRACLE OF THE HOLY CROSS *Bellini*   157
145. DOGE LEONARDO LOREDANO *Bellini*   157
146. THE STROZZI CHILD *Titian (Color)*   *Facing* 158
     Courtesy, Kaiser-Friedrich Museum, Berlin, Germany
147. LANDSCAPE *Tung Yüan*   160
     Courtesy, Museum of Fine Arts, Boston, Mass.
148. TIGER BY WATERFALL *My Ch'i*   160
     Courtesy, British Museum, London, England, and Tom Nash
149. WRITING: PICTOGRAPH TO CUNEIFORM Mesopotamia   162
     Courtesy, The Pierpont Morgan Library, New York, N.Y.
150. INSCRIPTIONS, CYLINDER SEALS Mesopotamia   162
     Courtesy, The Pierpont Morgan Library, New York, N.Y.
151. STELE OF SENU Egypt   165
     Courtesy of The Metropolitan Museum of Art, New York, N.Y.
152. PAGE, BOOK OF KELLS Ireland   166
153. INITIAL LETTER, BOOK OF KELLS Ireland   166
154. COVER, MANUSCRIPT OF THE GOSPELS France   168
     Courtesy, The Pierpont Morgan Library, New York, N.Y.
155. PAGE, WINDMILL PSALTER England   170
     Courtesy, The Pierpont Morgan Library, New York, N.Y.
156. PAGE, CHOIR BOOK Italy   171

157. PAGE, HOURS OF THE VIRGIN   Portugal   171
Courtesy, The Pierpont Morgan Library, New York, N.Y.
158. PAGE, THE KORAN   Persia   172
Courtesy, The Pierpont Morgan Library, New York, N.Y.
159. MANUSCRIPT   Persia   172
Courtesy, The Pierpont Morgan Library, New York, N.Y.
160. BAMBOO IN THE WIND   *Wei Chû*   174
Courtesy, Museum of Fine Arts, Boston, Mass.
161. PAGE, BLOCK BOOK   Netherlands   176
Courtesy, The Pierpont Morgan Library, New York, N.Y.
162. PLAYING CARDS   France   176
Courtesy, The New York Public Library, New York, N.Y.
163. PAGE, GUTENBERG BIBLE   Germany   178
Courtesy, The Pierpont Morgan Library, New York, N.Y.
164. PRINT SHOP   Germany   179
165. PAGE, CANTERBURY TALES   England   179
Courtesy, The Pierpont Morgan Library, New York, N.Y.
166. TEMPTATION OF ST. ANTHONY   *Schöngauer*   180
Courtesy, The New York Public Library, New York, N.Y.
167. ST. EUSTACE   *Dürer*   181
Courtesy, The New York Public Library, New York, N.Y.
168. GIOVANNI ARNOLFINI AND HIS WIFE   *Van Eyck*   184
169. PORTRAIT   *Van der Weyden*   186
Courtesy, National Gallery of Art, Washington, D.C., Mellon Collection
170. PEASANT DANCE   *Breughel the Elder*   186
171. SUZANNE FOURMONT   *Rubens*   187
172. SELF-PORTRAIT   *Dürer*   189
173. CATHERINE HOWARD   *Holbein the Younger*   189
Courtesy, The Toledo Museum of Art, Toledo, Ohio
174. THE HOLY FAMILY   *El Greco*   190
Courtesy, The Cleveland Museum of Art, Cleveland, Ohio
175. VIEW OF TOLEDO   *El Greco*   192
Courtesy of The Metropolitan Museum of Art, New York, N.Y.
176. INFANTA MARGARITA   *Velázquez*   194
177. EXECUTION OF THE MADRILEÑOS   *Goya*   194
178. YOUNG GIRL AT A HALF-OPEN DOOR   *Rembrandt*   196
Courtesy, The Art Institute of Chicago, Chicago, Ill.
179. WOMAN WEIGHING GOLD   *Vermeer*   198
180. BLUE BOY   *Gainsborough*   200
Courtesy, Huntington Art Gallery, San Marino, Calif.
181. HAMPSTEAD HEATH WITH A RAINBOW   *Constable*   200
Courtesy, The Worcester Art Museum, Worcester, Mass.
182. SAYING GRACE   *Chardin*   202
183. THE UPRISING   *Daumier*   202
Courtesy, The Phillips Gallery, Washington, D.C.
184. REHEARSAL OF BALLET ON STAGE   *Degas*   204
Courtesy, The Metropolitan Museum of Art, New York, N.Y.

xiii

185. THREE GEISHA *Utamaro*   204
Courtesy, The Art Institute of Chicago, Chicago, Ill.
186. BAR AT THE FOLIES BERGÈRE *Manet*   206
187. BOULEVARD DES ITALIENS *Pissarro*   206
Courtesy, National Gallery of Art, Washington, D.C.
188. LUNCHEON OF THE BOATING PARTY *Renoir*   208
Courtesy, The Phillips Memorial Gallery, Washington, D.C.
189. SUNDAY ON GRANDE JATTE ISLAND *Seurat*   208
Courtesy, The Art Institute of Chicago, Chicago, Ill.
190. CATHEDRAL OF FLORENCE Florence, Italy   210
191. PAZZI CHAPEL Florence, Italy   210
192. MEDICI-RICCARDI PALACE Florence, Italy   212
193. CA D'ORO Venice, Italy   212
194. ST. PETER'S CATHEDRAL Rome, Italy   214
195. INTERIOR, ST. PETER'S Rome, Italy   214
196. PALACE OF VERSAILLES Versailles, France   216
197. GALLERY OF MIRRORS, PALACE OF VERSAILLES Versailles, France   216
198. ST. PAUL'S CATHEDRAL London, England   218
199. JOHN WHIPPLE HOUSE Ipswich, Mass.   221
200. MOUNT VERNON Mount Vernon, Va.   221
201. SAN FRANCISCO Quito, Peru   223
Courtesy, The Library of Congress, Washington, D.C.
202. CATHEDRAL OF HAVANA Havana, Cuba   223
Courtesy, The Library of Congress, Washington, D.C.
203. MISSION OF SAN XAVIER Tucson, Arizona   224
Courtesy, The Library of Congress, Washington, D.C.
204. MISSION OF SAN JOSÉ Y SAN MIGUEL DE AGUAYO San Antonio,
Texas   224
Courtesy, The Library of Congress, Washington, D.C.
205. NATIONAL CAPITOL Washington, D.C.   226
Courtesy, The Museum of Modern Art, New York, N.Y.
206. LINCOLN MEMORIAL Washington, D.C.   226
Courtesy, National Park Service, Washington, D.C.
207. CARD PLAYERS *Cézanne (Color)*   *Facing* 229
Courtesy, Stephen C. Clark
208. STILL LIFE WITH FRUIT DISH *Cézanne*   231
209. MONT SAINT-VICTOIRE *Cézanne*   231
210. COUNTRY ROAD BY NIGHT *Van Gogh*   232
211. LA MOUSMÉ *Van Gogh (Color)*   *Facing* 233
Courtesy, National Gallery of Art, Washington, D.C. Chester Dale Collection
—Loan
212. THE WHITE HORSE *Gauguin*   234
213. VASE WITH POPPIES *Matisse (Color)*   *Facing* 236
From Faber Gallery, London, England
214. PIERROT *Rouault (Color)*   *Following* 236
Courtesy, Agnes Rindge Claflin

xiv

215. GIRL IN PINK   *Modigliani (Color)*   *Facing* 237
Lewisohn Collection
216. PORTRAIT OF DR. TIETZE AND HIS WIFE   *Kokoschka*   238
Courtesy, The Museum of Modern Art, New York, N.Y. Mrs. John D.
Rockefeller, Jr. Purchase Fund
217. RAIN IN THE JUNGLE   *Rousseau*   238
Courtesy, Reinhardt Gallery, New York, N.Y.
218. VASE OF FLOWERS   *Redon (Color)*   *Facing* 239
Courtesy, William S. Paley
219. STILL LIFE: THE TABLE   *Braque*   240
Courtesy, The Art Institute of Chicago, Chicago, Ill.
220. STILL LIFE: LE JOURNAL   *Gris*   240
Courtesy, The Museum of Modern Art, New York, N.Y.
221. THREE MUSICIANS   *Picasso*   242
Courtesy, Philadelphia Museum of Art, Philadelphia, Pa.
222. LIGHT FORM   *Kandinsky*   244
Courtesy, Museum of Non-Objective Painting, New York, N.Y.
223. PERSISTENCE OF MEMORY   *Dalí*   244
Courtesy, The Museum of Modern Art, New York, N.Y.
224. PEOPLE IN THE NIGHT   *Miró*   246
Courtesy, The Miller Company Collection, Painting Toward Architecture,
Miller Company, Meriden, Conn.
225. ACTOR'S MASK   *Klee*   246
Courtesy, Sidney Janis Collection and The Museum of Modern Art, New
York, N.Y.
226. COLLEONI   *Verrocchio*   248
227. LA PIETÀ, DETAIL   *Michelangelo*   248
Courtesy, Ludwig Goldscheider, Phaidon Press, Oxford University Press
228. LORENZO DE' MEDICI, DETAIL   *Michelangelo*   250
229. BALZAC   *Rodin*   252
230. HEAD OF A YOUNG GIRL   *Maillol*   252
Courtesy, Collection of The Museum of Modern Art, New York, N.Y., Mrs.
John D. Rockefeller, Jr., donor
231. SINGING MAN   *Barlach*   254
Courtesy, Collection of The Museum of Modern Art, New York, N.Y., Mrs.
John D. Rockefeller, Jr., donor
232. MISS EXPANDING UNIVERSE   *Brancusi*   254
233. FIGURE   *Lipchitz*   255
Courtesy, Collection of The Museum of Modern Art, New York, N.Y., Van
Gogh Purchase Fund
234. THE CITY   *Grippe*   255
Courtesy, Collection of The Museum of Modern Art, New York, N.Y.
235. AFFECTION   *Zorach*   258
Courtesy, The Downtown Gallery, New York, N.Y.
236. CRYING WOMAN   *Salerno*   258
Courtesy, the artist

XV

237. HORSE AND RIDER *Marini*   260
Courtesy, Collection of The Museum of Modern Art, New York, N.Y., Lillie
P. Bliss, donor

238. YOUNG MONK *Rox*   260
Courtesy, the artist

239. FAMILY GROUP *Moore*   262
Courtesy, Collection of The Museum of Modern Art, New York, N.Y., Lillie
P. Bliss, donor

240. THE COSDEN HEAD *Hepworth*   262
Courtesy, British Information Services, New York, N.Y.

241. HENRY *Dlugosz*   263
Courtesy, Collection of The Museum of Modern Art, New York, N.Y.

242. HEAD *Belling*   263
Courtesy, Weyhe Gallery and The Museum of Modern Art, New York, N.Y.

243. LINEAR CONSTRUCTION, VARIATION *Gabo*   264
Courtesy, The Phillips Gallery, Washington, D.C.

244. HANGING MOBILE *Calder*   266
Courtesy, Collection of Mrs. Meric Callery and The Museum of Modern Art;
Herbert Matter, photographer

245. HANGING MOBILE IN MOTION *Calder*   266
Courtesy, Collection of Mrs. Meric Callery and The Museum of Modern Art;
Herbert Matter, photographer

246. HENRY GIBBS *Unknown Artist*   268
Courtesy, Mrs. Alexander Quarrier Smith and The Worcester Art Museum,
Worcester, Mass.

247. THE PEACEABLE KINGDOM *Hicks*   268
Courtesy, The Museum of Modern Art, New York, N.Y.

248. LITTLE ROSE OF LYME REGIS *Whistler*   270
Courtesy, Museum of Fine Arts, Boston, Mass.

249. THE BATH *Cassatt*   270
Courtesy, The Art Institute of Chicago, Chicago, Ill. The R. A. Waller Memorial Collection

250. THE RACE TRACK *Ryder*   272
Courtesy, The Cleveland Museum of Art, Cleveland, Ohio. Purchase from the
J. H. Wade Fund

251. ALBERT P. RYDER *Hartley*   272

252. STORM AT THE BAHAMAS *Homer*   274
Courtesy of The Metropolitan Museum of Art, New York, N.Y.

253. WHITE HORSE *Bellows*   274
Courtesy, The Worcester Art Museum, Worcester, Mass.

254. MAINE COAST *Marin*   276
Courtesy of The Metropolitan Museum of Art, New York, N.Y.

255. PERTAINING TO YACHTS AND YACHTING *Sheeler*   276
Courtesy, Earl Horter

256. BOY STEALING FRUIT *Kuniyoshi*   278
Courtesy, Ferdinand Howland

257. APRIL SHOWERS *Rattner*   278
Courtesy, A. P. Rosenberg & Company, Inc., New York, N.Y.

xvi

258. DON'T CRY, MOTHER *Evergood*   280
     Courtesy, The Museum of Modern Art, New York, N.Y.
259. THE RED STAIRWAY *Shahn*   280
     Courtesy, City Art Museum of St. Louis, St. Louis, Mo.
260. GARAGE LIGHTS *Davis*   283
     Courtesy, The Permanent Collection of the Memorial Art Gallery, University
     of Rochester, Rochester, N.Y. and Encyclopedia Britannica Films, Inc., Wil-
     mette, Ill.
261. TRANSFLUENT LINES *Pereira*   283
     Courtesy, The Miller Collection, Painting Toward Architecture, Miller Com-
     pany, Meriden, Conn.
262. ZAPATISTAS *Orozco* (*Color*)   *Facing* 284
     Collection of The Museum of Modern Art, New York, Anonymous Gift
263. LANDSCAPE WITH WILD HORSES *Enríquez*   286
     Courtesy, Collection of The Museum of Modern Art, New York, N.Y., Donor,
     Dr. C. M. Ramírez
264. BARBER SHOP *Bermudez*   286
     Courtesy, Collection of The Museum of Modern Art, New York, N.Y.
265. WOMAN AND CHILDREN *Portinari*   287
     Courtesy, the permanent collection of the Fine Arts Department, The Interna-
     tional Business Machines Corporation, New York, N.Y.
266. OFFICE, JOHNSON WAX FACTORY Racine, Wis.   290
     Courtesy, Frank Lloyd Wright
267. U.S. FOREST SERVICE BUILDING Madison, Wis.   290
     Courtesy, U.S. Forest Service, Forest Products Laboratory photograph
268. FRAMEWORK, ESSO BUILDING New York, N.Y.   292
     Courtesy, Standard Oil Company of New Jersey, Libsohn, photographer
269. BAYTOWN REFINERY Baytown, Texas   292
     Courtesy, Standard Oil Company of New Jersey, Corsini, photographer
270. PHOENIX UNION HIGH SCHOOL Phoenix, Arizona   294
     Courtesy, Architectural Forum, The Magazine of Building; Julius Shulman,
     photographer
271. LEA COUNTY COMMUNITY HOSPITAL Hobbs, New Mexico   294
     Courtesy, Architectural Forum, The Magazine of Building; Julius Shulman,
     photographer
272. WOOLWORTH BUILDING New York, N.Y.   295
273. DAILY NEWS BUILDING New York, N.Y.   295
     Courtesy, The Museum of Modern Art, New York, N.Y.
274. ROCKEFELLER CENTER New York, N.Y.   297
     Courtesy, Rockefeller Center, Inc.; Thomas Airviews
275. SECRETARIAT BUILDING, UNITED NATIONS New York, N.Y.   297
     Courtesy, United Nations
276. FALLING WATER Bear Run, Pa.   298
     Courtesy, Frank Lloyd Wright and The Museum of Modern Art, New
     York, N.Y.
277. SAVOIE HOUSE Poissy, France   298
278. SHATTUCK HOUSE Seattle, Wash.   300
     Courtesy, Architectural Forum, The Magazine of Building; Charles R. Pear-
     son, photographer

xvii

279. HAINES HALL HOUSE   Marin County, Calif.   300
    Courtesy, Architectural Forum, The Magazine of Building; Minor White,
    photographer
280. CLOVER LEAF   New York, N.Y.   305
    Courtesy, Paul J. Woolf, photographer
281. FRESH MEADOWS   Long Island, N.Y.   305
    Courtesy, New York Life Insurance Company, New York, N.Y.

PREFACE

THIS book is written especially for the adolescent. The purpose of the book is to arouse, and to aid in sustaining, a direct and lively interest in all forms of art by presenting its various phases in a way that will attract and hold the youthful reader.

A limited amount of historical background has been included, together with various social and economic factors that have had direct bearing on the type of art created in a particular period. The major stress, however, of *Your Art Heritage* is placed upon the development of two concepts: the esthetic relationships to be found among the works of artists widely separated by space and by time, and the understanding of art as an important element in the cultural development of mankind throughout the ages.

Method of Use

Although this book may be used in a variety of ways, it is designed essentially as a textbook to be placed directly in the hands of the student. Topics for discussion and suggestions for activities in connection with each chapter are to be found at the end of the book.

The vast wealth of material available for illustration has made selection difficult. Examples have been chosen on the dual basis of being representative of their times and of having potential interest for students. Occasionally a well-known work of art with which students may already be familiar has been omitted in favor of another one, less well known, but equally interesting.

Teachers and students, naturally, will have additional illustrations of their own choosing to amplify the text and to add interest to class discussion. In addition, there is the art of contemporary life that may be found close at hand: the paintings, sculpture, and crafts that we or our friends create, or that may be seen in shops or local collections. The very buildings and the communities that serve our everyday needs are admirable starting points for personal exploration.

Encouragement should be given the students to take self-directed excursions to augment their class work. The assignments at the end of each chapter may be used as the starting point for discussions which should be made vital and lively through personal contributions by each student. Through personal exploration of and personal contact with art of the past and present, the student will arrive at a more vivid realization of his own creative impulses.

Establishment of Standards

As every art teacher knows, there are controversial issues in the teaching of art. Quite naturally, the individual teacher's attitude colors her teaching. One point in question is in the realm of esthetics. When we look at a work of art, is our primary reaction emotional or intellectual? Should students first be taught to look for certain art qualities in order that their intellectual understanding of them may aid their appreciation, or should they forego previous instruction because it tends to detract from the spontaneity of their emotional and purely esthetic reactions?

Since the adolescent needs help in broadening the range of his appreciation so that it may encompass more than his likes and dislikes, and in sorting out the relevant from the irrelevant factors that clutter his mind when seeing a work of art, a few simple and generally accepted standards for judgment are presented in the first chapter of this book. It should be understood that these suggested standards are flexible and cannot be rigorously applied, for often the qualities in a work of art are unique and cannot be measured in terms of other works of art.

Art and Education

Educational philosophy now strongly stresses art as an important factor in the development of the adolescent. Such practical subjects as the three R's, languages, science, and social studies were established long ago in the curriculum, but art, until comparatively recent times, was considered a luxury in daily living. The present-day educator believes that art has a definite and significant task to perform for the welfare, self-adjustment, and happiness of all. He knows that art is related to the life and needs of every student, and that a study of art is particularly essential to the development of the adolescent; for it is at this age that he begins to sense the need for solo flights into unexplored realms. The adolescent feels a restless longing for new experiences. The awareness of the beauty of art expressions of other ages and of our own, together with the development of his own creative impulse, supply the sought-for experience. As the adolescent matures, he carries with him these essentials of future inner happiness. Perhaps the present-day insecurity felt by our young people most of all, may be somewhat alleviated by an acquaintance with something permanent, his heritage of beauty.

Scope of Art Education

A wide sector of the general educational program is devoted to the development of concepts. Another sector is based on memorization of factual material, the accumulation of layer upon layer of concrete knowledge. Both the development of concepts and the mastery of facts are of vast importance, but they do not complete the circle needed to make the student "well rounded." The missing sector, the development of perception, is aided by art education. While linked in some degree to both conceptual thinking and factual knowledge, art education concentrates directly on personal reactions to the visible world. Art training, through its emphasis on the training of the senses, opens the eyes of students to things to be seen, to be felt, and to be remembered. With this deepening of perception and the development of visual memory comes a greater realization of the essential aspects of the world, both immediate and past.

It would be an exaggeration to say that each art student leaves his classroom with an identical and added quota of awareness of the world around him for the power to perceive, which is both inherited and acquired, varies in each individual. It has, however, been demonstrated in our own classrooms that the majority respond to our teaching and that they develop in awareness, in sensitivity, and in power of judgment with gratifying speed.

The Art Program

The ideal program of art in the high school is student-centered, not subject-centered. This program, which is concerned primarily with the general development of the adolescent, strives to show him how to live harmoniously with his society and its broad cultural pattern. Carefully planned courses of study linked to the student's natural interests are necessary to achieve this aim.

For all students, the acquisition of a background of art is far more important than the tangible art results they may obtain. For every student who may become a practicing artist, there are several hundred who may not continue with art training, but who may use art as an avocation. This interest will contribute to and enrich the inner life of the individual so that he may seek enjoyment in further contacts with creative expressions. In selecting objects for use in his daily surroundings, he may apply some of the precepts that have been presented to him. Thus his daily life may express his inner awareness of art.

Those who love art cherish all its manifestations, from the apparently unimportant to the sublime. It is hoped that *Your Art Heritage* will foster this love through adolescence into maturity, where it may become even more rewarding. This awareness of the heritage that is his, will widen the scope of each individual's educational progress and cultural growth, and will give to him that precious gift—a deep and abiding love of beauty.

Great tribute should be paid the teachers of art for their contribution to present-day philosophy of art education. Impetus for the development of this new philosophy has come directly from their classrooms, which have been the proving ground for the value of art in the mental and moral development of the adolescent.

Acknowledgments

Your Art Heritage owes many debts of gratitude. It was inspired by the incomparable spirit and the creative philosophy of Miss Virginia Murphy, late Director of Art in the Public Schools of the City of New York, and a widely recognized leader in her field. The author sincerely hopes that this book will aid in realizing her enlightened ideals of education through art.

Ideals must be implemented, as art teachers know, by an administrative policy that gives constant and practical support to the art program within the school. The author wishes to acknowledge the wholehearted coöperation given both by Dr. Mary E. Meade, Principal, and by the Administrative Staff of Washington Irving High School. Through their coöperation, they have enabled their Art Department to make significant contributions toward the goal of the self-realization of the student through personal experience in the field of art.

If *Your Art Heritage* has achieved clarity, it is due to the perception and the consistent efforts of Miss Louise Gurren, its editor, and of Miss Muriel Macarthy, its "best friend and severest critic." Both have read and reread the text in manuscript form and again in proof. The author is indeed grateful to them for their sustained interest and for their professionally constructive suggestions.

This list would be incomplete without an acknowledgment of the unfailing interest taken in this book and the always fascinating supply of information given the author by an enthusiastic student of history, James Howard Savage.

Olive L. Riley

1. **THE GOURMET** *Picasso*

1.

Introduction

THE love of art is a characteristic that all of us have shared since the days of the first man. The heritage of art that has come down to us since the earliest days of man's attempt to create beauty is our link with all the artists of bygone days. In the long course of time, there have been great changes in our physical life, in our way of thinking, in our ideals and in our religious beliefs, and in our customs and institutions. Fortunately, however, the strongly forged and common bond of art enables us to travel back mentally to past eras and through vast spaces, to overcome all kinds of barriers so that we may add to our understanding of mankind and to our appreciation of his accomplishments. Through the universal language of art, human beings have always spoken vividly to their fellow men. Their message, even though recorded long ago, is clear and vital, for its spirit is timeless.

Many a dimly-lit cave, sunny cliffside, lowly hut, glorious palace, stately church, temple, and tomb bears eloquent testimony to man's conscious use of art to record in permanent form the ideas most important to him. For this reason, a study of art is, in actuality, a study of man. Man's turning to art as an instrument of expression is no mere impulse. Its long and glorious history reveals the fact that the love of art is one of man's strongest instincts.

We all have within us this precious gift, this instinctive love of art, to be cherished and to be strengthened. Each generation receives this personal heritage directly from its forebears. Each in turn bequeaths it directly to its descendants.

Today we hear a great deal about modern art, just as we hear about modern youth. Neither can be thought of as arriving or existing by itself, for each is firmly rooted to its past. You, for example, are the product of your parents, as they of theirs, and so on back into the remote spaces of time. You like to think of yourselves as modern, just as your parents did when they were your age, and you are certain that your generation has many unique accomplishments to its credit. It is true that teen-agers are especially proud, as well they may be, of their contribution to their particular times. However, it should be remembered that the very achievements on which youth prides itself are often the fulfillment of an ideal for which its predecessors strove long ago.

So it is with art. Each generation contributes certain elements to its development that are logical outcomes of the life and the thought of the times. Little by little, each successive contribution becomes part of the great tradition of art that has been built by gradual accumulation and by a continuous flow of the creative energies of mankind. Art serves each successive generation as an instrument of expression and as a servant to its needs. It has performed this service for millions of our predecessors and will continue to play the same important role in the lives of generations to come.

It is important, therefore, that we think of art as a living and continuing force, and as one that brings eternal life to its creators. To contribute during our own life to the heritage of art, to appreciate it, to strengthen it, and to help it serve humanity in every way, is to share fully in the universal culture of man.

What Is Art?

How do we decide what is art and what is not art? Why, for example, are many of Rembrandt's paintings thought to be master-pieces while the works of many of his contemporaries are not so regarded? For what reason do many lovers of art praise Greek, rather than Roman sculpture? Why are the Gothic cathedrals in France thought to be finer than those in Italy? Is there any single

The pattern created by the play of light and shadow on recessed surfaces emphasizes both the height and the greatly simplified form of this modern building.

2. **RCA BUILDING,**
   New York, N.Y.

3. **MOSES** *Michelangelo*

Arresting and dynamic, this powerful figure of *Moses* shows Michelangelo's amazing ability to make his statues seem composed of living flesh rather than cold marble.

4. MME. CHARPENTIER AND HER CHILDREN *Renoir*

The figures in this beautifully composed painting are united by glance, by gesture, and by line and pattern movements into a compact and harmonious group.

The story of the birth of Christ has been told by many artists. Fra Angelico describes it here in a humble, reverent, and emotionally moving way.

5. THE NATIVITY   *Fra Angelico*

standard by which we judge works of art, or do we use a different one for each individual piece?

It seems logical to assume that all of the things that we call great works of art share similar qualities that can be seen, felt, and understood.

Common Qualities in Great Art

Is it possible for a building, a piece of sculpture, and a painting to have something in common? Look at Illustrations 2, 3, and 4. You will find that each one of them affects you emotionally. The swift upward movement of the *RCA Building,* the majestic force of the sculptured figure of *Moses,* and the serenity of *Mme. Charpentier and Her Children* are quickly felt.

All great works of art have the magnificent power of arousing the beholder. The resulting emotion, which is a source of ever-increasing pleasure for so many of us, is called the esthetic emotion. It is not dependent on time or place, for just as we share with all mankind our instinctive love of art, so we share the emotional, or esthetic, response to it.

Another quality, common to all great works of art, in addition to their power to move us emotionally, is that of order—the result of a carefully planned whole. To some of us, order may mean tidiness. The two should not be confused. It is possible to have order in what seems to be, at first glance, disorder. For example, you may think that your own room is in perfect order because you know where everything is and can find it quickly; however your mother, surveying it, may think it disorderly. Similarly, an artist may organize his work of art in such a way that his scheme is not apparent at first glance. Nevertheless, all great works of art, simple as well as complex, have been planned with care. Their orderly arrangement and their wholeness, or unity, have been achieved. On closer study of the work of art, the organization or order is soon apparent.

Meaning of Art

All great art conveys a message. Since the language of art is universal, the message can be understood by all. We have only to look with a sensitive eye and an inquiring, unprejudiced mind to discover what the artist wishes to say. It may be something about the creator himself: his loves, his interests, or his emotional responses to people and to things about him. Often it is his impression of the actual world in which he finds himself. His thoughts may be philosophical, spiritual, idealistic, militant, fantastic, humorous, kindly, or bitter. They may run the full range of physical and emotional experiences, both fleeting and constant. Countless thoughts and emotions have been expressed and have been made eternal in some tangible, concrete form of art. For example, Fra Angelico was moved to paint *The Nativity* shown in Illustration 5. Through this painting his devotion to his Maker is immediately made apparent to us. He pictures the story of the birth of Christ and also conveys an unmistakable, intense message of his own love for Him.

The message, we know, is the motivating force of a work of art. The means that the artist uses to convey his message are the structural elements of art with which all students are familiar, and that all artists have at their disposal: line, tone, shape, pattern, texture, color, space, movement, and volume. All of these elements may be used freely to serve the artist's purpose. Look at Illustration 1, *The Gourmet*, by Picasso, the well-known modern artist. Color plays an especially important part in this painting. Large areas of yellow-green, green, and blue-green are effectively contrasted with subtle, warm tones which encircle the little figure and its head and hands.

The truly creative artist realizes, of course, that he must bring to his work an intense and personal vision. In great works of art we find no slavish imitation of nature, God's creation, for the mere recording of appearances seldom interests a true artist. The camera mechanically records surfaces; the eye of the artist seeks to penetrate them and to create, through his discoveries, a man-made work of art.

Selection and Use of Media

The materials, tools, and processes selected by the artist affect the nature of his design. A hard stone, for example, forces the sculptor to work in large masses, with little detail, as we may notice in Illustration 6. The steel girders used in modern building require no actual

6

support from the enclosing walls so that a present-day architect may plan for a building almost completely enclosed by glass. Watercolor, a painter's medium, requires a simplified and bold technique and cannot be used for subjects that must be shown in detail.

As we go deeper into the study of art, we become conscious of the fact that the artist has considered the possibilities and the limitations of his medium; in other words what he can and cannot do with it, and that, in some cases, he has allowed his design to spring from the very nature of the medium in which it is composed. When a sculptor, for example, looks at the piece of wood that he is going to carve, its natural shape and its graining often suggest a subject to him. Study, for a moment, the *Circus Girls* by Chaim Gross seen in Illustration 7. By looking at the base, we can see that the pole-shaped block of figures has utilized much of the cylinder of wood, and that in some places the figures touch its outer original limit. The natural grain of the wood appears to great advantage in its suggestions of both form and texture.

When there is an attempt to make one material look like another or to force a material into a form of construction that is essentially foreign to its nature, the result cannot be called art. Painting plaster to look like wood or bronze, or printing wallpaper to look like marble are examples of forgeries done under the guise of art. An honest and logical use of materials is demanded of every artist worthy of the name.

Relation of Form to Use

Essentially, art is designed for a particular reason or use, or to fill a particular need. Buildings are essential to man; painting and sculpture add to his esthetic and spiritual well-being; and the Minor Arts contribute to his daily life, both practically and esthetically.

When the element of practicability enters into the forming of a work of art, we should be aware of how successfully the artist has met its demands. This thought may best be illustrated by two extreme examples. No matter how beautiful a new tall office building might appear, we could not think of it as well designed if it lacked a way of carrying its occupants quickly from one level to another. Similarly, a

This sculptured head from a figure on the exterior of the *Cathedral of Chartres* shows us that the stone carver works in a highly simplified way. The compact quality of this head reveals the fact that its sculptor understood and respected his medium.

6. **WOMAN OF THE OLD TESTAMENT** *France*

7. **CIRCUS GIRLS** *Gross*

The living, growing quality of wood is suggested in this piece of sculpture by all of its movements, which seem to grow naturally upward, like those of a tree.

coffee pot might be highly interesting and novel in form, and be made beautifully from unusual materials, yet if coffee could not easily be poured from it, we could not consider it satisfactory in design.

On the other hand, there are some designers who believe that function alone should determine design. If it is useful, they say, and if its functioning is satisfactory, that is all that is needed to make the object an esthetically satisfying form. If we are to subscribe to this belief, an object, let us say a chair, might be comfortable to sit upon, yet be barren of beauty of line, of form, or of texture. Since man has always striven for beauty in the things he has made, it hardly seems possible that the majority of us would believe in a strictly utilitarian standard of judgment.

To sum up the relationship between form and function, let us say that a work of art must be both efficient in the performance of its functions and fine in form.

Are We Always in Agreement?

You are undoubtedly wondering about personal differences in reactions to art. Jack Smith, for example, greatly admires a certain painting and Mary Jones cannot understand why he does; she positively dislikes it. Many a newly erected building is praised by some critics and condemned by others. Newspapers and magazines are full of controversies about current exhibitions of works of art. If we have standards, why do they not serve all of us as a definite means of measurement so that we can arrive at uniform judgments?

The answer is simply this: it is possible to have common standards and yet disagree about individual art expressions. Just as Jack Spratt would eat no fat and his wife would eat no lean, we cannot escape from our personal preferences. Each person who looks at a work of art brings to it the sum total of his likes and his dislikes, and especially, the ideas of his generation about particular phases of art.

For example, you may see a black and white reproduction of a painting in this book and you may not admire it as much as the person who has seen the original in color. An individual who has been brought up in a New England town feels at home with Colonial architecture; to him a modern and strictly functional home might seem strange and

9

unattractive. Each generation tends to appreciate one style of art much more than another. Our particular generation, for example, considers El Greco, a sixteenth-century Spanish painter, to be one of the outstanding painters of all times, although in our grandfather's day, he was given very little recognition.

The fact that all of us do not agree is natural and stimulating to further learning. One who has had very limited experiences in appreciating art is unable to see in it all that a more experienced observer does; so he may reject some things simply because he does not understand them, or because they convey no particular message to him. Yet all of us, fortunately, can be taught to search for significant things, and can acquire the capacity to look for real, rather than for surface meanings. We can become sensitive to genuine and varied expressions of art especially when we add to our knowledge of their background and the people who produced them. All of us are capable of working toward a more solid judgment, increased insight, and heightened enjoyment.

The Search for Beauty

If we are to work toward a goal of esthetic appreciation while we are young, enthusiastic, and full of creative energy, we should free ourselves of the heavy load of prejudice and equip ourselves with one lighter than air, open-mindedness.

No one likes to be thought of as a prejudiced person for we know that prejudice and ignorance are synonymous. Even so, we are all tempted to arrive at hasty judgments, or to dismiss quickly from our minds something, non-objective painting, for example, for which we feel no sympathy, or which we do not understand. Are you capable of looking at works of art without prejudice, with an open mind, and with the curiosity to seek the artist's meaning? Have you a genuine interest in the way he communicated his message?

If you think you can meet this challenge, study the work of various artists shown in Illustrations 8, 9, and 10. Try to analyze your reactions to each one of them. The first, a *Head* by Amadeo Modigliani, both redesigns human features and simplifies them. Do you find it

8. **HEAD** *Modigliani*

What qualities do you think the artist wished to impart to this head? Try to describe them in your own way.

satisfying because of its simplicity and power of form or do you think that it is merely ugly and grotesque?

The next illustration, *The City* by Fernand Léger, is a semi-abstract painting. The artist has combined certain selected shapes that to him symbolize the striking features of a city. Do you admire the strikingly bold quality of the dark and light pattern, or do you dislike the painting because it does not clearly represent a city scene?

What do you think about the modern house shown in the third of these illustrations? Would you like to live in it or do you think it looks too odd and unlike a comfortable home?

Initial attempts at esthetic appreciation are necessarily timid. They are reminiscent of a person who is first learning to swim. He hesitates, struggles, is fearful. Gradually, courage, strength, and skill come. Finally he swims with confidence. The exhilaration of the trained swimmer may be compared with that of the person who has acquired enough knowledge to plunge confidently into the stream of art for a pleasurable excursion.

Practice Is Essential

Unfortunately, in our everyday world, we are surrounded by things that are utterly lacking in any of the qualities essential to art. We find them in the places in which we live, in the stores where we buy things, in the movies that we see, and in the magazines that we read. All too frequently, smart, flashy, slick products clutter up our homes and our lives. Any one of these elements of our environment is an excellent starting point for the practice of discriminating judgment. To reject bad taste in our homes, in our surroundings, in our personal possessions, and in our form of entertainment, is to start upon the road to a cultivated judgment.

Once we reject things, we must either search for others to take their place or find ways of improving what we have. All of us should strive for substantial, rather than shoddy building; for clean, community-minded neighborhoods rather than unpleasant, uncoöperative ones; for well-designed and carefully selected, rather than trashy possessions; and for entertainment, movies, clubs, hobbies, and reading, that can lead to a lasting, rather than a momentary pleasure. All of

9. THE CITY *Léger*

The spirit of a city may impress us in countless ways. It may seem sad or gay, colorful or drab, forbidding or inviting, depending on our mood. The appearance of its structures, too, is changed by personal vision. Do you think that this artist was successful in describing his particular reactions to a city?

10. TUGENDHUT HOUSE *Brno, Czechoslovakia*

Living in an almost completely glass house would certainly keep its inhabitants aware of the charms of their natural surroundings.

us must realize that art can be found everywhere about us, not just in museums and galleries.

Your Part in Art

Your esthetic and cultural progress is dependent on you alone, on the intensity of your desire to achieve it. The cultural progress of all mankind is equally dependent on individuals; that means each and every one of you. It is within your power to see that culture is sustained and enriched, that it does not sink to a low level through indifference, neglect, and the pressure of economic forces. Each one of us, therefore, as an individual and as a member of a group must assume a personal responsibility for the maintenance and development of our cultural heritage. A united group, no matter how small, can accomplish wonders. To cherish, to uphold, to add to this cultural heritage is to ensure for all of us better standards of living, greater happiness, and an increased respect for our fellow men.

2.

Primitive and Early Art

FEW of us are satisfied with the way in which we live. We sigh for larger homes, wish we had more new clothes, and often complain about the nourishing food that is available to us. However, if we were to compare our lot with that of our ancestors who lived in the Stone Age, about twenty thousand years ago, we would appreciate the modern comforts that we take for granted.

Imagine, for a moment, how they fared in those days. Could they buy or rent a home as we do today? Indeed not, as well you know! Primitive man had to improvise one with only the help of his instincts and the few primitive implements that he could make. To furnish his home he collected stones to cook over or to sit upon. For his bed he spread out a few animal skins. When any kind of container for food or for storage was needed, primitive woman had first to collect materials, then make it.

The garments worn by the primitives may have been in the latest style, but few of us would admire them. Made from the pelts of animals, such as the bison or the reindeer, they were far from the sleek, soft, pleasant-smelling furs that are worn today. Furthermore, a single garment probably served for all occasions until it was worn out. No sport costumes or "formals" were even dreamed of for the men, women, or teen-agers of those faraway days; all they had were work clothes.

Millions of years ago the shorelines of Peru were altered by earthquakes. Coral reef caves and the fossilized ocean bottom that were raised from the seas by volcanic action formed shelters for primitive man.

11. **CORAL REEF CAVES** *South America*

12. **BRI-BRI KING'S HOUSE** *Central America*

A scrutiny of the space to the right of the doorway of this cone-shaped Costa Rican hut shows us how it was constructed. In tropical countries the skeleton of poles was often thatched with leaves.

When mealtime came, your ancestors could not "come and get it"; they had to "go and get it." It was the difficult and dangerous task of the primitive man to track and to slay a wild animal lurking in a forest, streaking over a plain, or crouching in frozen drifts; or to catch some fish; or to bring to earth the fast-flying birds so that his family might eat and maintain strength to survive a rigorous life. It could not have been pleasant to have to search for edible roots and grasses, wild berries and corn, when the fury of the beast was always a menace to him, or to travel for days over the plains or deserts without fresh water. Perhaps some of these hardships will remind you of a hiking or a camping experience you have had, when you lived for a brief time what seemed to you a Spartan and self-reliant existence. However, you must agree that all of us live a life of luxury compared with that enjoyed by our ancestors, the Cavemen, and the other hardy folk who led primitive and rigorous lives.

The Will To Survive

Have you ever wondered what would happen to you if you were to be shipwrecked on a desert island, hopelessly lost in a forest, or even miraculously transported to another planet? What would you have to do in order to survive? Your problem would be, of course, to maintain yourself by your own hands and through your own resources.

First of all, you would immediately need to find something to eat and to drink. After taking care of the "inner man" you surely would look for some kind of shelter as a protection from the heat or the cold, from the rain or the snow, and, most important, as a defense against an unknown and possibly dangerous foe.

You might find a cave, make sure no animals were lurking there, clean it out, and bar the entrance. Thus you would have a snug spot to which you could retreat in time of need. If no caves were available, you might build a house high up in a tree as the imaginary Swiss Family Robinson did. If you found yourself in a country where there were no caves or tall trees, doubtless you might make a hut by binding low trees together at the top and by interweaving them with stout vines or reeds, then covering the whole with turf or leaves. Even stones and mud could be shaped into a dwelling. If stranded on plains,

17

you might decide, as the American Indian did, that the tepee would be the perfect shelter since you could take your home along with you if you wanted to move. On the other hand, if you found yourself in a glacial territory, you might make an igloo of ice blocks, in Eskimo fashion.

All these varieties of man-made shelters have been used, as you know, by primitive man throughout the centuries. Oddly enough, they have one thing in common: all of them have been round. Not until a later period in his development did primitive man learn to square the circle and to construct his buildings on a rectangular plan. Furthermore, there is a marked similarity between the types of shelter he used and those used by animals and birds. Through necessity, he was a keen observer of his world, and he probably imitated their instinctive building for protection.

Art Is Born

You can easily appreciate the ingenuity of primitive man when you observe the great variety of shelters he devised. Seeing his dwellings, his crude weapons, and the household utensils he made, helps to create a picture of his physical life. In addition, however, to the things related to his struggle for survival, there is definite evidence of the fact that primitive man was not only a craftsman but also a highly creative artist.

To realize this, you have only to see the paintings of the men of the Stone Age. How many centuries it took man to develop his artistic capabilities we shall perhaps never know. Yet it is certain that he did attain remarkable heights in his time, for paintings which mark the beginning of his career as a conscious and purposeful artist were discovered in caves deep in the earth of France and Spain.

There is a frequently related story about the first discovery of these cave paintings. A man interested in exploring a certain cave in Altamira, Spain, took his five-year-old daughter along with him. While he was digging up the floor of the cave to find some evidence of man's early occupation of it, she wandered about, candle in hand, in search of adventure.

Suddenly her father heard her cry, "Bulls, bulls up there." Looking

18

13. CAVE PAINTING *Spain*

How vividly the primitive artist has captured the arrested power and cautiousness of the bison! The formidable bulk and strength of the body and the wary glance of the eye have been recorded with amazing power.

This lively scene with its fast-flying arrows shows a fight between rival groups for the possession of a bull. Even though they remind us of "stick figures," the silhouetted warriors are dramatic in movement. Notice how the path traced by the fallen arrows unifies the group.

14. ROCK PAINTING *Africa*

upward in amazement, he saw that the ceiling of the cave was decorated with extraordinarily lifelike figures of animals.

Since this discovery, many more caves have been found with the figures of animals and men painted or incised by means of a sharp cutting instrument upon the walls and ceilings. While it is possible that the prehistoric artist decorated a cave for the sheer pleasure of making it attractive, just as we might decorate a clubroom today, it is far more probable that the figures he painted there were a part of his religious beliefs. To appease and to glorify the animals he had slain, perhaps to gain further power over them, and to introduce them into his magical rites were, in all likelihood, some of the reasons that motivated his work. Painted under the light of a torch or a crudely contrived lamp, with brushes of reeds, and paint of earth substances mixed with animal fat, these cave paintings reveal to us the desire of the early artist to express his spiritual ideas in some visual form of art.

As for the paintings themselves, an example is Illustration 13. One can only marvel at the keenness of observation, the intimate knowledge of anatomy and of movement, and the power with which the essential characteristics of the animals have been so vividly recorded. Usually done with black and a single color, red, brown, or ochre, the gradations, or shadings, build solid forms of strength and fleetness.

Other Primitive Painters

After seeing the art of the Caveman, it is interesting to compare it with that of another primitive group, that of the natives of the Libyan Desert in Africa. Look at one of their paintings (Illustration 14) which was discovered there with countless others, painted on rock. It, too, was done, it is estimated, during the Stone Age. You see that the African artist also was concerned with the hunt; his paintings of animals are as lively, as keen, and as intense as those of the Caveman. In some respects the African artist was somewhat more ambitious, for he used several figures in his painting and composed them in a highly effective way. One more thing to be noticed about the painting from the Libyan Desert is its suggestion of depth, or distance.

20

How do you think the artist achieved this? As a clue to the answer, note the comparative sizes of the figures.

Another example of the painting of primitive man is the restored mural (Illustration 15) done by a Pueblo Indian painter of the Southwest in about the sixteenth century. Notice that the artist did not first observe his subject keenly, and then record it. Rather, he painted his concept, or mental image of it. This is characteristic of primitive painters. In general, they do not confine themselves to what they see, but prefer to paint what they know to be true about their subject.

Primitive art, as you will more and more realize, is not a question of time or of place, of race or of religion. It is an art that emerges when man has conquered nature sufficiently to free himself from her demands. This form of art, which is based on certain impulses, is being created even today. As you continue your study of it, you will find many examples of the work of primitive artists who might possibly be your neighbors and who are certainly of your time.

Primitive painting is said to have a childlike quality. This description is by no means derogatory. The painting of a youthful artist (Illustration 16) has the confident vigor that characterizes all primitive work. You may have painted just as forcefully when you were a child and, as some people would say, uncivilized.

Forerunners of Architecture

In order to understand how architecture developed, let us return briefly to the Caveman. As time passed, there came a change in his mode of life because of two important factors: his becoming an agriculturist and his learning to domesticate such animals as dogs, sheep, goats, cattle, and pigs. Since he was no longer dependent on the trophies of the hunt for food, the wanderer could become a permanent member of a small community. As one area could now feed many people, communities were able to survive and to develop tribal customs and practices. Buildings became more permanent and were constructed with greater skill. This communal mode of life was also adopted by other primitive groups, almost within our own time. The Navaho Indians of the Southwest, for example, settle down for the

21

15. MURAL PAINTING *North America*

16. CHILD'S PAINTING *England*

This mural painting from northwestern Arizona, a restoration of one done in the early part of the sixteenth century by an Indian painter, reveals the unhesitating directness of the artist. It represents a warrior at the moment when he has been pierced by an arrow. Forceful and dramatic murals such as this were painted on the plaster walls of kivas, or meeting rooms.

This six-year-old city child was so impressed with the sunshine of the countryside that she included five suns in her picture. In addition to showing her cottage, her mother, her father, and herself, she painted two dogs "that like to smell the grass."

winter in a community building, a great advance over their former mode of life. The early white settlers of America, forced into primitive living, also adopted its pattern and built crude log cabins and stockades for the protection of their communities. Perhaps the most interesting of the community buildings of men in this period of their civilization are those of the Indians of the Southwest, made as early as the tenth century and used almost to the present day. They hollowed out and built up pueblos, or community dwellings (Illustration 17), on the mountain side for as many as 250 people. Their multiple dwellings were, for their time, as complete as the housing projects of today.

Preoccupied as man always was with his after-life, it was only natural, as he became more securely established, that he applied his ever-increasing ability to the building of tombs to protect and to mark the site of his mortal remains. One of his first efforts, the dolmen, was erected by placing a horizontal stone slab on top of two upright stones. This construction looked somewhat like the frame of a doorway. A later development, the tumulus, was constructed in the same way but, in addition, was covered with an earthen mound. A somewhat more complicated structure, the stone kist, had a burial chamber beneath its superstructure.

These tombs and other early structures, like the famous *Stonehenge* in England (Illustration 18), thought to have been erected for use in religious rites, were not consciously designed works of man and therefore we do not speak of them as architecture. However, they point the way to structures similar in purpose, but far more organized and definite in plan.

The Egyptian, Master-Builder of Tombs

In Egypt, at the beginning of the period known as the Old Kingdom, about 4500 B.C., the Egyptian had been building for some time the tombs that we have just described. At this time in history the story of man was beginning to be recorded in word as well as in deed; so it is known that conscious planning both entered and dominated the mind of the master builder.

History has shown that the Egyptians achieved a high degree of

23

17. CLIFF PALACE *North America*

Cliff Palace at Mesa Verde, Colorado, is a timeless monument to the intelligent planning and to the industry of its primitive builders. Over a thousand feet above the river, within the tremendous cave, stretches a long row of many-storied houses. Beneath the connecting courtyards are countless kivas.

18. STONEHENGE *England*

This strange, rugged structure was probably used by the ancient Britons for religious rites. The rough and massive stones mark one of ancient man's first purposeful though mysterious constructions.

civilization. Egyptian life and thought have been extensively revealed through the efforts of archeologists; our museums are full of evidences of its existence. What were the factors, you may ask, that produced a rich, continuous flow of art and allowed man to practice it as naturally and as consistently as he ate and drank? What was responsible for the pattern of Egyptian life, and what made this pattern so constant for thousands of years?

For one thing, life in Egypt was stable; its form of government was unchanging. Rule by Pharaohs, by nobles, and by priests provided definite formulas for every phase of life. As long as the ordinary man did not question his lot, and you may be sure that he seldom dared to, he was secure and well fed. His land was fertile and rich in natural resources. By virtue of its location, it was well protected from invaders.

It is true that the working man was, in effect, a slave, and that during the time that the Nile overflowed its banks and so made agriculture impossible, his services were commandeered by his rulers for building the vast temples, tombs, and palaces designed to reflect and to add to the royal power and glory. On the whole, however, his life could not have been an unhappy one, for Egyptian mural painting and the work of its craftsmen tell us of a people who seemed to take pleasure in their daily occupations.

If the Egyptian painter, sculptor, or craftsman wanted to make a more individual type of art than that prescribed by tradition, we have no evidence of his desire. As you study the art of the Egyptian, it becomes evident that the goal of his ambition was magnitude. The reigning king and his master-builder never thought, "Let's build a smaller or a different type of tomb." Instead, they thought, "Our next building must be larger than all those previously built. It must have much more impressive sculpture, and contain many more rooms than ever before." This attitude, imposed by the will of king upon subject, coupled with unquestioning acceptance of tradition, made Egyptian art a servant of the state. Individual expression, as we know it today, was almost unknown.

It has been noted above that the dolmen and the kist were the early types of tombs. In addition to these, the Egyptian constructed another, flat-topped type known as a mastaba. The mastaba, however,

19. INNER COFFIN OF TUTANKHAMEN *Egypt*

After the mummy case of this Pharaoh was excavated, an inner coffin of gleaming gold was revealed. The pattern of the Pharaoh's garments and the symbols of his royal office, such as his whip, crook, and beard, make this an interesting relic.

was not sufficiently impressive for the rulers of Egypt, who were not only the kings but also the gods of their subjects. The Pharaohs, naturally, had to have the strongest, the most elaborate, and the largest tombs: the strongest to protect the royal body, the most elaborate to befit their great majesty, and the largest to impress upon their subjects the vast difference between a king and a common man. Hence a new form arose, the pyramid.

Religion Affects Building

Due to the Egyptian religion, there was an additional reason for so elaborate and so enduring a tomb as the pyramid. As you probably know, the Egyptian people believed in reincarnation, which meant to them that the spirit of the deceased would spend three thousand years in the company of the god Osiris, then return to its mortal body. To preserve this body, therefore, was most important. It was embalmed, carefully wrapped in stiffened linen, placed in a sarcophagus, or coffin, and left within a sealed tomb. Beside the body were placed food and countless material things to sustain the spirit on its journey.

The body of a king, of course, received unusual attention. The resplendent coffin of gold which contained the mummy of King Tutankhamen, a ruler of Egypt, is shown in Illustration 19.

The pyramids, the early tombs of the Pharaohs, are excellent examples of how the Egyptian related power to size. Because they are breathtaking for sheer monumentality, as well as for the effort involved in their construction, some facts concerning them are well worth knowing.

Of the three large pyramids, the *Great Pyramid* to be seen in Illustration 20 is the largest. It was built almost five thousand years ago by the Pharaoh Cheops in the Fourth Dynasty (2900–2750 B.C.). It is about 480 feet high and covers an area of thirteen acres, or twelve city blocks. This enormous structure is so large that it takes about three-quarters of an hour to walk around it. In its present state it seems rough and unfinished, but at one time it was completely covered with polished limestone. The entire mass is solid, except for the burial chambers and apartments.

Many conjectures have been made as to where the vast amount of

27

20. SPHINX OF GIZEH *Egypt*

Cut from natural rock, the sphinx has the body of a lion and the head of a man. Between huge stone paws you may see a small temple, brought to light by recent excavation. Beyond the sphinx are the three most famous pyramids of Egypt.

21. MODEL OF PYRAMID OF SAHURE *Egypt*

See how elaborate the later Egyptian pyramids became. In addition to the pyramid, there were other structures, such as an adjoining chapel and a long, covered causeway which led down the cliffs to a valley temple below, on the bank of the Nile.

stone needed to build the pyramids came from, as to how it was transported to its present location, since many of the blocks weighed fifty tons and measured thirty feet in length, as to how the massive blocks were lifted into place, and, especially, as to how many men and how long it took to build so massive a monument. Concerning the latter question, a Greek historian recounts that one thousand men labored twenty years to build it, but modern architects doubt that it ever could have been accomplished in so short a time.

A model of a restored pyramid, that of Sahure, built in the Fifth Dynasty, shows that the pyramid was the central feature of several structures (Illustration 21). Within the royal tomb, which was concealed in the heart of the pyramid, all of the things thought to be needed for the comfort of the departed spirit were placed. They included food, utensils, furniture, jewelry, effigies of household servants and of animals, and even models of the royal boats and apartments. Some of these interesting things are discussed in the following chapter. The interior of the tomb-chamber was enriched, as an additional act of devotion, with mural decorations and sculptural images of the deceased.

Egyptian Temples

In time, the Old Kingdom civilization, which lasted from about 4500 B.C. to 2475 B.C., gave way to that of the Middle Kingdom. The pyramid was supplanted by the rock-cut tomb and temple which were hollowed out of the rocky cliffs along the Nile. The actual tomb, in those days, was concealed deep in the rocks on one side of the Nile, and the temple was erected on the other side, directly across from it. In this way, the cautious Pharaohs hoped to thwart both the robbers and those of their successors who might seek to plunder their tombs.

Of these rock-cut temples, two of the most impressive are the *Temple of Queen Hatshepsut,* seen in Illustration 22, and the *Temple of Ramses II,* shown in the following illustration.

From the time of the Middle Kingdom onward, the power of the kings declined while that of the priests grew stronger. It is not surprising, therefore, to find that fewer monuments were erected to kings

22. MODEL OF TEMPLE OF HATSHEPSUT *Egypt*

You see here a beautifully planned temple in a model reconstructed by experts in archeological studies. A series of stately terraces are connected by ramps with the sanctuary which extends deep into the heart of the cliff towering above the Nile.

23. TEMPLE OF RAMSES II *Egypt*

The rugged and masculine quality of this huge temple is an interesting contrast to the delicate and elegant *Temple of Queen Hatshepsut*. Four gigantic statues of Ramses II guard the entrance. Note their size in relation to the tent pitched below.

24. MODEL OF HYPOSTYLE HALL, TEMPLE OF AMON *Egypt*

The hall of this famous temple had 134 columns which supported a flat, two-tiered roof. Made entirely of stone, including its richly painted columns, this temple was erected without the use of cement to hold the blocks in place.

25. SECTION OF A PAINTED BOX *Egypt*

Egyptian love of decoration is evident in this painted box which has a richness of design and detail that is fascinating. A powerful line movement unites the figures of the triumphant Pharaoh, the richly arrayed horses, and the trampled Asiatic enemy.

26. NOBLEMAN HUNTING *Egypt*

In this mural painting, you will notice an immensely rich surface decoration and a flow of line and pattern that result in the lively movement characteristic of a hunting scene. The nobleman stands alert, boomerang in one hand and three captive birds in the other. His wife and child, shown smaller than he, since to the Egyptian mind they were not so important, are riding in a skiff, holding lotus blossoms. A hunting cat, perched on a bent papyrus plant, has secured three victims. Some other interesting details are the alarmed birds and the fish, all painted with quite a degree of realism. Notice the consistent use of the concept figure, which was the Egyptian's idea of clarity of representation.

In addition to painting a significant description, the artist seems to have been interested in conveying the idea of human beings moving confidently down a stream of life toward a future existence. The pose of the woman, the strong forward movements balanced by the plants and the backward glance of the child, contribute to this idea.

and many more temples were built to add to the glory of the gods and, of course, to their priests as well.

Of the many temples erected, the best known and the most elaborate are those at Karnak and Luxor. While these temples followed the plan dictated by religious conventions, it is interesting to discover that each generation of kings, priests, and master-builders added to them, embellished and ornamented them anew, so that while they all have the same general plan, each one expressed in some way a growth in thought and in artistic expression.

The hypostyle, or inner, hall of the *Temple of Amon* at Karnak (Illustration 24) is constructed in the post-and-lintel, or upright and crossbeam, type of building and shows again the Egyptian's skill in the use of building materials. The wide columns are lavishly decorated with motifs derived from the lotus flower, the palm tree, and the papyrus plant with which Egypt was so richly endowed. Monumental sculpture formed an impressive entrance as well as an important part of the interior.

The walls of the Egyptian temples were covered with murals, as were the tombs. Beautifully designed, rich in color, and lively in subject, they show scenes from the life of the people, both rich and poor. You see them hunting, fishing, reaping grain, and feasting. The murals suggest that the Egyptians were a happy people who enjoyed what life offered them.

Egyptian Mural Painting

As you know, the Egyptian artist was bound by convention. When the master-artist was called upon to design a mural for a tomb, he consulted the *Book of the Dead,* which was not a book in our sense of the word but a collection of prescribed subjects deemed suitable by the priests for this purpose. From these he made a small sketch on clay or plaster which was then enlarged and painted by an artisan. Naturally, some workers were more gifted than others, and this fact accounts for the noticeable difference in the quality of Egyptian mural painting.

Convention demanded, for example, a highly stylized figure, such as you see in *Nobleman Hunting* (Illustration 26). Notice that it is

27. SEACOAST MAYA VILLAGE *Mexico*

If you look carefully at this mural from the *Temple of Warriors,* you will find many things painted in the direct way in which a child paints. The activities of daily life in this community are painstakingly portrayed above, while below, all kinds of undersea creatures are to be seen on the surface of the carefully rippled sea.

28. EL CASTILLO *Mexico*

This structure, built in about the fourteenth century at Chichen Itza, was originally the principal temple of Kukulcan, the "Feathered Serpent" and patron deity of the city. Covering an acre of ground, with exterior stairways leading to the sanctuary on its summit, it is an amazing tribute to the perseverance of its untrained builders.

a concept figure, that is one that shows a mental rather than a visual image. The head and the lower part of the body are shown in profile view, while the eye and the upper part of the body are in front view. The actual result of this twisting and turning of the body is the creation of a significant and beautiful shape.

It is interesting to contrast this Egyptian mural with one painted many years later, in about the fourteenth century by a Maya Indian artist (Illustration 27) on a wall of the *Temple of Warriors* in Mexico. The figures are shown here in an apparently conventional profile view but we sense a freedom and a personal, rather than a restricted kind of expression, that is refreshing to find. As the Maya artist, in contrast to the Egyptian, was evidently allowed to include as much background space as he wished in his picture, he boldly, and in a childlike way, filled it up with several rows of figures, one on top of the other.

Significance of Egyptian Building

Do you think of the pyramids, tombs, and temples of the Egyptian only as stupendous feats of engineering and man power, or do they have other and more important qualities? Should they be considered an outstanding type of building simply because they are very large? This conclusion is a possible one, yet, on the other hand, some of the finest buildings in the world are comparatively small.

It might be well for us to formulate some standards for judgment at this time. In order to judge any building, you must look for four things: its reflexion of the life and the spirit of its times; its appeal to the esthetic emotions; its solution of practical needs; its use of structural materials.

In the light of these standards, it seems undeniable that the early building of the Egyptian may be considered notable. It showed, above all, that the master-builder was well on his way toward becoming an architect, one who would eventually combine his creative powers with an increasingly practical knowledge of his art.

Perhaps the greatest tribute we may give to Egyptian building is this: it was a loyal and enduring servant of its builders.

The elaborately pierced shield behind which the figure stands is a definite and interesting contrast to the slight body and the compact head. It is amazing that this wooden figure can be so grotesque in proportions and yet express such great dignity and authority. He might be a captain on the bridge of his ship, a preacher addressing his congregation, or an oracle for primitive man to consult.

29. **WAR GOD**

Hawaiian Islands

This towering wooden idol is both terrifying and bestial, as its maker doubtless intended it to be. The elaborately carved and expressive head, which resembles a huge mask, appears much too large for the plump, childlike body. Possibly it is this striking difference that makes the primitive figure so effective.

30. **KORWAR** *New Guinea*

3.

Primitive and Early Sculpture

MANY of you have seen the stone arrowheads used by the American Indians and other primitive tribes in hunting. Perhaps you even have had the thrill of finding one in a country field. If so, you may have thought, "Imagine killing a wild animal with a thing like that!" Or you may have wondered how an arrowhead could be made from stone without tools of any kind.

Anthropologists believe that primitive man made his stone weapons by striking one stone against another until one became pointed and sharp-edged. As he gained in skill and in resourcefulness, primitive man produced a greater variety of weapons for hunting, fishing, and other practical purposes, most of them of stone, some from bone and ivory. These he fashioned with loving care, shaping, polishing, and often carving beautiful designs on them to satisfy his innate love of beauty.

Primitive man, however, had an urge to do more than make and decorate practical things. His emotions of hope, of fear, and of reverence prompted him to carve from various hard materials, such as stone, wood, and bone, representations of the more-than-human spirits so closely tied up with his life. Thus his weapons and implements, first designed for killing, became sculptor's tools.

The islands in the South Seas, between the Pacific Coast and Australia, have produced many rich and varied forms of native arts. This stone carving, even though very small, has considerable dignity. Its compact body and expressive head show how effectively a good sculptor can work with a medium as difficult as hard stone.

31. **TIKI** *Marquesas Islands*

32. **STONE PIPE**

North America

The Indian sculptor, even when carving as commonplace an object as a pipe, could make his work remarkable for its power. This small figure, as in previous illustrations, shows the primitive artist's custom of emphasizing the head of a figure by making it abnormally large.

The images he carved, some tall as towers, others tiny as pebbles, are equally impressive, regardless of size. The Hawaiian *War God,* shown in Illustration 29, is almost seven feet high and must have greatly awed its primitive worshipers when they beheld it within the dimly lit temple where it originally stood. The *Tiki* from the Marquesas Islands, shown in Illustration 31, is an equally vigorous figure. Although it appears here to be as tall as the *War God,* actually it is only eight inches high and was originally worn as a neck ornament by a native chief. Whether large or small, delicate or rugged, conventional or personal in expression, the images of primitive and early man are notable for their inspired vividness.

Illustration 30 shows us an interesting example of a phase of primitive religion, ancestor worship, which is part of the religion of the natives of New Guinea. This small figure was carved to receive the spirit of a man after his death. Since all primitive sculptors emphasize the head of a figure, it is not surprising to find it so important a feature of this carving. An additional reason for its size, however, is the fact that the head of this type of mortuary figure was often hollowed out to receive the skull of the deceased.

It is interesting to note that the early wood-carvers could keep the natural roundness of the wood, even when they hollowed it out or cut all the way through some sections. If you were to attempt your first carving of a head from a section of a tree trunk, you would probably work very much as the Seneca Indian did when he carved the simple but majestic face seen in Illustration 33. After you had made a number of carvings, however, you would probably become more inventive in your treatment, like the sculptor who carved the small wooden *Soul Bird* shown in Illustration 34. Notice that although some of the forms are partly detached from the body, the figure as a whole is still strongly cylindrical in character.

The Sculptor as Maskmaker

Most of us have made and worn masks at a party not only to conceal our identities, but also to assume new ones. This practice is a survival from earliest days. Countless primitive ceremonies, many of which survive today among certain tribal groups, feature masked dancers who are accompanied by chanting and by bold rhythms of

You have but to look carefully at this carving, roughly hewn from a section of a tree trunk, to see how much a sculptor can count on shadow to suggest and to emphasize planes. The eyes of the masklike face have a definite and majestic expression, yet you will notice that they are suggested only by scooped-out sockets, carved without detail, and that it is the light and shadow contrast that makes them so effective. The marks left by the chisel of the Seneca Indian sculptor add to the rugged quality of the head. Even the crack in the wood suggests sternness of character.

33. **HEAD** *North America*

34. **SOUL BIRD** *New Guinea*

This small figure seems possessed of magic-making powers. The fantastic quality of its imagery, the large and strongly marked oval eyes, and the prolonged beak make it appear weird and unearthly. The lower part of the body, a hollowed-out cylinder, furnishes an interesting contrast to the cone-shaped, solid head. If you place your hand over the lower part and visualize a different shape there, you will probably find that it will not seem nearly so satisfactory as the one already there.

An expression of compelling majesty and age-old wisdom distinguishes this African mask. The design of its forms, their simplicity and rhythmic repetitions, and the richly contrasted surface treatments all contribute to make the mask a highly spiritual and sensitive expression of a religious belief.

35.   MASK   *Africa*

Strong rhythms of line, of form, and of pattern give movement and vitality to this antelope mask. Painted bands of color emphasize its distinguishing feature, the horns. Do you recall seeing other examples of art that showed how primitive man deified and worshipped animals?

36.   MASK   *Africa*

37. QUEEN HATSHEPSUT

Egypt

You have seen the impressive tomb of this famous queen on page 30. In those days it was the custom to place within the tomb a portrait statue of the deceased. This one of red granite, much larger than life-size, shows the queen wearing her ceremonial wig and holding in her hand a lion's tail.

Another portrait of this queen is distinguished by the compactness and simplicity of its form. Although part of a kneeling figure, it retains the queenly aspect of its subject. The broken chin indicates that the queen originally was wearing the false beard which, like the lion's tail, symbolized her power as a Pharaoh.

38. QUEEN HATSHEPSUT

Egypt

drums and other primitive musical instruments. By wearing a mask in such a ceremony primitive man has felt in close contact with his gods, his ancestors, and the innumerable spirits that controlled his world.

Of the many maskmakers who have practiced this art for centuries, none are surpassed by the tribes of West-Central Africa. Although their sculptors occasionally used bronze or ivory, the abundance of wood and the comparative ease with which it could be carved led them naturally to its use. It is interesting to see how they imagined their gods. They gave the carved images of these gods some human characteristics, yet the masks do not seem human. Even the animal that they deify, while recognizable as possibly a deer, an antelope, or an elephant, is endowed with an unworldly quality. How do you suppose they did this? It must be that the native talents of these sculptors prompted them to redesign natural forms rather than to copy them faithfully, and so represent their god's qualities rather than the god himself. While all the things they saw about them were undoubtedly the source of their inspiration, the African sculptors used nature as a springboard to project them into deep-flowing and mysterious channels of personal and intuitive expression. Superb in craftsmanship and vital in strength, the work of the African sculptor has greatly influenced twentieth-century painting and sculpture. Turn back to page 11 and study the *Head* that you see there. Does it not have some of the qualities of the African mask shown in Illustration 35?

The Sculptor as Stone-Carver

Stone, like wood, by its very nature affects the form of objects carved from it. This fact is clearly revealed when we study Egyptian sculpture, for we see that the carvers of those early days were strongly influenced by the twofold character of the stone cut block: its hardness and its four-sidedness. Egyptian figures have a great simplicity of form that is the natural result of having been carved from a very hard stone. In addition, they immediately impress us with their four-sided and block-like character. If you take a mental walk around the highly simplified, granite statue of *Queen Hatshepsut,* shown in Illustration 37, you are conscious of a squared-off front, side, and back view. You may also notice that the Egyptian carver's figures are remarkably lifelike in proportion.

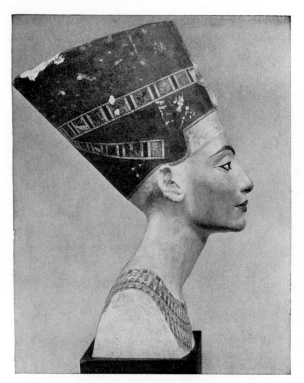

Color plays an effective part in this sculptured head, for the limestone is painted and rock crystal has been inserted to form the eyes. This proud queen was the wife of Pharaoh Akhnaton who tried to make the Egyptian people abandon their many gods for one, Aton, the sun god. Even though she lived thousands of years ago, do you not find her modern looking? Which of her features make her appear so?

39. QUEEN NOFRETETE *Egypt*

Among the many statues of the Pharaoh which adorned the rock-cut temple of Ramses II (page 30) was the one seen here. Refinement of modeling and the way in which the mass of the helmet is balanced upon the head contribute to its distinction.

40. RAMSES II *Egypt*

The impressive calm of this statue and its suggestion of immortality come both from the character of its design and the simplicity of its sculptural treatment. The planes of the figure, verticals and horizontals, follow the original planes of the rough block. The figure, which is reduced to its basic forms, is rigidly symmetrical. Its great dignity not only suggests that its subject was a queen, but it also shows how greatly impressed the sculptor was with the power and majesty of his ruler.

Egyptian sculpture became less formalized and generalized, and more personal in expression as time elapsed. If you compare the three portrait heads seen in Illustrations 38, 39, and 40, you will notice this development. The first, a superbly designed head of the same *Queen Hatshepsut,* has an aloof, formal quality typical of the sculpture of her time. We think of the head as a statue rather than that of a real person who once lived a life of ambition and intrigue.

The second illustration, the head of *Queen Nofretete,* comes from a later period. Its delicately balanced angles and sensitive modeling show us how searching the artist's eye was, and how well he chose those elements of the head, the thin neck and the angular jaw, that would best reveal the queenly and charming character of his model. In carving this head, the sculptor avoided the previous traditions of sculptured portraits. It is built upon an angular rather than on a vertical plan so that, although the head is solid, it has neither the conventional, block-like character of the earlier portraits, nor their impersonal quality.

The third and later head, that of *Ramses II,* whose rock-cut tomb you have seen on page 30, has more detailed modeling of the features and even the subtle suggestion of a smile. This treatment of a head shows us that the artist at this time felt free to search for the individuality and the human qualities of his subject and to allow them to find their way through the hard confines of stone.

Each of these portraits has its own particular qualities. Which one do you prefer? Can you give some reasons for your choice?

Mesopotamian Art

East of Egypt and less than a thousand miles away, in an Asian country now known as Iraq, there flourished a civilization contem-

A godlike creature is shown performing an Assyrian ritual. The pose of the muscular figure is very similar to that shown in the Egyptian paintings you have seen. Notice the interesting contrasts between plain and patterned surfaces, such as the smooth helmet and the elaborately treated hair.

42. **WINGED BEING**
Mesopotamia

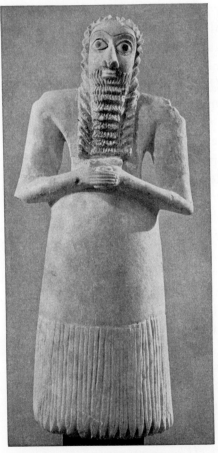

41. **SUMERIAN PRIEST**
Mesopotamia

This limestone statue represents a Sumerian priest in an attitude of prayer. A number of similar statues have been found, all of which emphasize a large, beaked nose, staring eyes formed of shell and lapis lazuli, and a heavy sheepskin garment. In spite of its stiffness, this statue has an intensity gained through a simplified treatment of the body and an elaborate treatment of the head.

porary with that of Egypt and in many ways equally important. The richly fertile valley of Mesopotamia, formed by twin rivers, the Tigris and the Euphrates, produced a succession of hardy and militant men who fought long and savagely for possession of their rivals' wealth, land, and empire. It is, in fact, strange that this country, constantly concerned with warfare for so many years and possessed by so many different races, could produce, as it did, art work of enduring quality.

Since it was the custom in those days first to sack, and then to destroy the cities of the conquered, few traces of Mesopotamian architecture remain. Within the last hundred years, however, a start has been made in excavating the sites of the ancient palaces and temples, so that in time more facts will be known about Mesopotamian civilization. These findings will create a better understanding of how it influenced contemporary art and that of succeeding periods.

How long ago did this early, Near-Eastern, civilization exist? During the long period from 4000 B.C. to 1925 B.C., Mesopotamia was possessed by the Sumerians and the Semites, the first groups to have it and the longest to hold it. These people were, like the races that followed them, hardy and practical; they were the true originators of the culture that their successors both imitated and built upon. History tells us that both the Sumerians and the Semites were resourceful agriculturists and builders of palaces and ziggurats, or stepped pyramids crowned with a small temple. Not only were these peoples accomplished carvers of stone as well as being skilled craftsmen, but they were also the inventors of a cuneiform system of writing that is the predecessor of our present-day alphabet. The figure of a *Sumerian Priest,* shown in Illustration 41 in an attitude of prayer, wears the heavy sheepskin garment of his time.

The fiercely militant Assyrians who overcame the Sumerians and the Semites were next in power and retained it until 612 B.C.

The Assyrians were efficient governors, but as artists they were somewhat limited. Their militant spirit is shown in the sculptured reliefs that adorned the palaces of their kings. In order to ensure records of their triumphs, it was customary for the Assyrian kings to take along both writers and sculptors when they went to battle. The reliefs depict the history of bloody battles, of cruel and triumphant kings, of arrogant master and abject enemies.

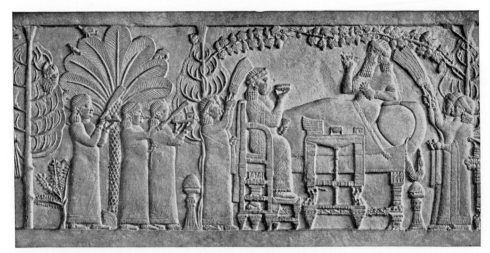

43. KING ASHURBANIPAL AND HIS QUEEN *Mesopotamia*

This Assyrian low-relief has a patterned and textured surface which adds variety to its smoothly flowing rhythms. While our eye is led inevitably to the main figure of the banqueting king, there are many details that engage our attention. Notice, for example, the design of the furniture, such as the couch and serving table of the king, and the tall chair of the queen, who sits so contentedly at the feet of her lord.

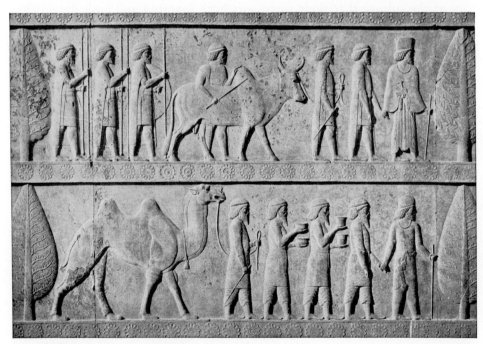

44. TRIBUTE BEARERS *Mesopotamia*

While many of the figures of this Persian low-relief mural are in a profile view, the leaders are shown in a pose common in contemporary Egyptian art.

See how well the Assyrian sculptor reflected the spirit of his times in Illustration 43, which shows Ashurbanipal dining with his wife, attended by palm-waving and food-bearing servants. The scene is regal and impressive. It includes, however, the severed head of an enemy hanging downward from a tree at the left, at which the king seems to be gazing with pleasure. A comparison of this relief with the Egyptian *Stele* on page 165 shows that the work of the two sculptors, though separated only by a comparatively brief span of time, was motivated by quite different ideals. While the Assyrian sculptor glorified physical strength and the power of the individual over his world, the Egyptian sculptor acknowledged a power mightier than that of man. The Assyrian sculptor was keenly observant and aware of physical life; the Egyptian was moved both by his imagination and by his inward and spiritual vision.

The Chaldeans, who overthrew the Assyrians in 612 B.C. and ruled until 539 B.C., are remembered in the history of art chiefly for their capital city of Babylon, the largest city of the ancient world. Under Nebuchadnezzar, a Chaldean king, the famous tower of Babel, which was a seven-storied ziggurat, or Holy Mountain, was built, a mighty mass within the walled city. In Babylon the Hanging Gardens, one of the legendary Seven Wonders of the World, were to be seen. Unfortunately, little remains of Chaldean architecture today, because sun-baked brick, of which Mesopotamian architecture was chiefly composed, had not the enduring quality of Egyptian stone. Chaldean temples and palaces have yielded to the ravages of both war and time.

Invading Persians subdued the Chaldeans; from then on Persian kings reigned from 539 B.C. to 333 B.C. Even Egypt was added to the mighty Persian Empire. Persian builders and sculptors were both ambitious and sensitive, as the few remains of their elaborate palaces testify. A relief from the Royal Palace of King Darius at Persepolis (Illustration 44) shows a procession of tribute bearers bringing gifts to the Persian Emperor. Although both the Assyrians and the Persians used relief sculpture extensively, they seldom carved figures completely free from a background. Why they did not attempt to make full-round figures is a question that has never been satisfactorily answered.

Aegean Culture

During the time that the Persians ruled Mesopotamia, both the islands in the Mediterranean Sea and the mainland of southern Europe that borders on the Aegean Sea, had been introduced to the older Egyptian and Mesopotamian culture through the enterprising Phoenicians, seafaring tradesmen of the Ancient World. Similarly, Egypt and Mesopotamia became aware of Mycenae, of the island of Cyprus, and of the island of Crete. It was in these Aegean areas that a strong art culture had long been developing, a pre-Greek culture soon to be adopted and expanded by the Greeks.

Many legends have been recounted of these pre-Greek, or as they are more often called, pre-Hellenic, days. For a long time, people believed that such well-known figures as King Minos of Crete, Theseus and the Minotaur, Odysseus, Priam, and Helen of Troy were merely romantic characters placed in mythical cities by Homer and the epic-loving Greeks. Yet the actual ruins of Troy were uncovered less than one hundred years ago on the coast of Asia Minor; the island of Crete has yielded treasures from the labyrinths of King Minos' palace at Crete. Distinctive sculpture and pottery have been unearthed on the island of Cyprus. A study of these early forms of Aegean art reveals the basis for Greek art, the first mature art of Europe.

Cypriote Sculpture

On the island of Cyprus, a notable center of art from about 1400 B.C. to 500 B.C., it was the custom for a worshiper who was busy with his worldly affairs to place at a shrine an image which presumably would act as his substitute in asking favors and offering suitable prayers to a god. The colossal limestone *Head* to be seen in Illustration 45 was probably at one time part of such a votive statue. Color, of which slight traces remain, was used to accentuate parts of the head. This color treatment was in keeping with the custom of the times, for red, black, and occasionally yellow and blue-green were used by sculptors to emphasize certain parts of their work. The most striking thing about this head is perhaps the stiff little smile, known

Do you not feel that this head has dignity in spite of its odd little smile? The four precise curls of the Santa Claus-like beard and the looped fringe of hair under the helmet furnish interesting and well-chosen contrasts to the smoothly modeled head.

45. **HEAD** *Island of Cyprus*

46. **PRIEST WITH A DOVE**
Island of Cyprus

Since the Assyrian and the Cypriote sculptors were familiar with each other's work, it is natural that each, to a certain extent, influenced the other. Compare this *Priest with a Dove* with the Assyrian *Winged Being* on page 46. What sculptural treatments have they in common?

in our times as the archaic smile. Many reasons have been advanced to explain this expression. Can you, yourself, account for it in any way?

The dignified statue of the *Priest with a Dove* (Illustration 46) is distinguished by many of the qualities we have found in sculpture shown earlier in this chapter. Do you remember seeing a cylindrical, rather than a four-sided, treatment before? Would you be inclined to agree that this treatment was a natural one for this sculptor to use since he carved the statue from a very soft limestone?

Notice that the pose of the figure, with the left foot slightly forward and the weight of the body resting equally on each foot, gives a feeling of movement without breaking up the cylindrical form. Only the arms, extending beyond the body, show that the sculptor was working toward greater freedom of action for his figures.

Other Early Sculptors

Let us leave, for the time being, the distant countries of the Near East and of Europe, and return to our own continent. Many thousand years ago the first settlers of America, who were Asiatic in origin, were believed to have crossed the frozen Bering Strait that separates North America from Asia. Most of these people, slowly pushing southward, settled in sections of their choice, while others who continued to wander eventually reached Mexico, Central and South America, and settled there. Had we, with our present-day appreciation of early forms of art, arrived at these shores with the Spanish and the Portuguese explorers in the sixteenth century, we would have marveled at the rich, thousand-year-old culture these peoples had established. Imposing, brilliantly colored and sculptured temples, as well as many forms of Minor Arts, unsurpassed even today, would have met and have delighted our eyes.

The Maya Sculptor

Of the various Indian groups, so named, according to legend, by Columbus because he thought he had discovered India, the Mayas are the most distinguished for their cultural accomplishments. They settled in Yucatan and in Central America on the narrow ribbon of land

52

Aloof, impersonal, and with a glance of compelling power, this sensitively carved head is one of the most impressive examples of sixteenth-century Maya sculpture.

This circular observatory and temple, built during the thirteenth century, may help you to realize that the Maya Indian was distinguished for his early knowledge of astronomy. Even though in partial ruins, the tower is still noted for the sculptural treatment that added to the effectiveness of its architectural plan.

47. **HEAD OF A MAIZE GOD**

Central America

48. **CARACOL TOWER** *Central America*

we know as Guatemala and Honduras. The imposing *El Castillo* on page 34, as well as the dramatic *Caracol Tower* (Illustration 48), shows that the Mayas were a religious people whose builders labored mightily for the glory of their gods. The mural seen on page 34, from a wall of their *Temple of Warriors,* describes their interests and occupations in a charming and childlike way. They are known, however, even more vividly through the work of their sculptors. The *Head of a Maize God* (Illustration 47) that adorned one of their temples is a powerfully conceived and brilliantly carved representation of one of their deities. Look at it intently for a few moments. Does his expression appear to change? Certainly his eyes seem to pierce, even to transfix with their power.

A further proof of the sculptural genius of the Maya is to be found in a *Portrait of a Maya Astronomer,* seen in Illustration 49. If you will turn back for a moment to *Queen Hatshepsut* on page 42 and compare the Egyptian and the Maya statues, the outstanding qualities of the latter will be apparent to you. Notice the movement of the body, the freedom of its pose, the vitality of its action. The Maya sculptor, unlike the Egyptian, did not hesitate to free the arms from the body, to turn the head, or to cross the legs. In simplicity of detail he conformed to the character of the hard stone, yet he conquered its four sided and rigid nature. As far as the proportions of the body are concerned, they are far from lifelike. Do you think that this detracts in any way from the quality of the figure?

Although many precious evidences of Maya civilization have been destroyed, the rapidly increasing number of records that are being uncovered tell a more and more vivid story of the accomplishments of a proud and highly civilized race.

Accomplishments of Early Sculptors

How is the work of the primitive and early sculptors best described? Do you not agree that it shows both a pioneer courage in trying out so many different ideas and a rugged power in executing them? Through their work that we have inherited, these sculptors tell us that art was a means by which they could realize their aspirations and give form to their dreams.

49. PORTRAIT OF A MAYA ASTRONOMER *Central America*

The strongly featured and oversized head, accentuated by an elaborate headdress, shows how impressed the sculptor was with the mental powers of his subject. This astronomer may well have been one who observed and charted the course of the heavenly bodies from the *Caracol Tower*.

The high quality of craftsmanship in this Yurok Indian
basket seems all the more
amazing when you learn that
it was made of white grass,
black maidenhair fern, yellow
porcupine quills, and brown
spruce roots, all collected and
prepared by the basket-maker.
The geometric pattern, which
naturally grows from the
weaving process, stands out
boldly on its glossy ground.

50. **TWINED BASKET** *North America*

Dat-so-la-lee, a Washo Indian, is one of the few basket-
makers whose names are
known. Although the exact
meaning of the symbolic pattern she wove so beautifully
into this basket is uncertain,
you may think of many ideas it
might interpret, even though
you are not well acquainted
with Indian folklore.

51. **COILED BASKET** *North America*

4.

Early Minor Arts

WE LIVE in a machine age. The hundreds of things needed for a comfortable, practical existence—automobiles, airplanes, radios, furniture, clothing, utensils, and books, to mention only a few—are all machine-made products. Today the energies of many designers and skilled workers are being devoted to making these mechanically constructed products not only efficient to use, but highly pleasing both to the eye and to the touch. It is interesting to discover that the energies of the people of the past, from early ages onward, in all lands and in all degrees of civilization, were devoted to the creation of countless handmade objects that were practical as well as esthetic in appeal.

It may be said in general that the early craftsmen were less serious-minded than the early sculptors, possibly because their responsibilities were of a more worldly nature. The images and idols carved by primitive and early man were certainly useful to him, but their services were not immediate ones. When entreated, a god might promise man fertility to his fields, might grant him success in battle, or might reward his piety with material or spiritual gifts. It would seem that the early sculptor, wanting to establish a close and comforting relationship with his gods, thought of his sculpture as a means of achieving this aim.

The early craftsman, on the other hand, directed his efforts toward a more immediate purpose. His task was to make the things needed for both practical and ceremonial use: perhaps he needed a mask for a dance, a bowl to eat from, a toy for his child to play with, or a mat for his house.

This perhaps accounts for the note of humor found in many craft products. There is often a joyousness, a gay light-heartedness about the early crafts, that is delightful. You cannot but admire their charm and the fresh, ingenious use of materials.

However, the craftsman was as important a figure in early life as the sculptor was. Each tribe, race, or group had many craftsmen; each one was a respected worker in his own field and an important member of his particular society.

The Minor Arts—basketry, pottery, textiles, metal, wood, ivory and stone work—were rich and fertile fields in which man's creative urge, his imagination, his love of color, of form, of pattern, and of texture, had free play. To realize this more fully, think of yourself as living in a primitive society, far from the state of civilization that you know today. Your practical needs would be many. Probably the first would be connected with food and with water and their storage: you would also need something to cook in, to eat and drink from, something in which to preserve, to store, and to carry things. Baskets, boxes, bowls, jars, and other utensils would have to be made from materials at hand, such as reeds, twigs, grasses, clay, stone, bone, and wood.

Then, too, you would need to make clothing and coverings to keep you warm or to make you stylish; tools to help you accomplish your daily tasks; and ornaments to make yourself attractive; as well as many other things not so practical, but certainly as necessary to a happy existence.

Making all of these things would call for resourcefulness, inventiveness, and especially for the kind of mind, hand, and eye that would find delight in them. Although necessity was the mother of the Minor Arts, the pride and pleasure that the early artists took in their work, and their ever-expanding inventiveness and craftsmanship in their use of materials, brought a unique distinction to these arts.

First Women Artists

The art of basketry is the oldest of the arts and the first human industry. Almost all of the basket makers have been women. They

58

have proved themselves to be adept, skillful craftsmen and sensitive designers. While some of our present-day artists have worked in this field and have made many fine things, they have never equaled the accomplishments of the early basket makers, nor have they improved upon the early techniques of basketry. Imagine that you were to make a basket in which to store some prized possession. You would do just what people did long ago, select a material, such as reed, bamboo, willow, or spruce, for a foundation. Several lengths of one of these materials, soaked for a time in water, crossed so that they resembled the spokes of a wheel, and fastened together at a central point, would form a flexible framework. To cover this framework you would probably take lengths of moist, tough grasses, rushes, palm or banana leaves, and weave them under and over alternate spokes, gradually shaping your basket by tightening or loosening the woven strands as you progressed upward. You could make the basket attractive by the fine quality of its form alone, or by the use of variously colored materials woven to make a patterned surface, or by the expert way in which you fashioned it.

This weaving, or twining, process, to be seen in Illustration 50, has also provided primitive man with other objects besides containers: shelters, such as interlaced frame huts; articles of clothing, such as hats and sandals; household objects, including mats and furniture; and even a method of transportation, for in some tropical areas native canoes are formed by basketwork. Although the machine has almost entirely superseded hand work, the use of the weaving process has continued to the present day.

The coiling method, with which you are probably familiar, is another way of making baskets. The basket is formed by binding or stitching together horizontal, circular coils of reed or rush with pliant grasses, as you may observe in Illustration 51. Colorful names, such as *bee skip* and *lazy squaw,* are used to describe stitches that form the coils. Here, too, pattern and color are used to add to the attractiveness of the basket. Some expert basket makers, such as the Yurok Indians of California, whose work you have seen, made such finely constructed baskets that they not only held water, but also could be used for cooking. Because such basketwork, however, was most exceptional, necessity demanded other kinds of containers.

59

52. POTTERY JUGS *Island of Cyprus*

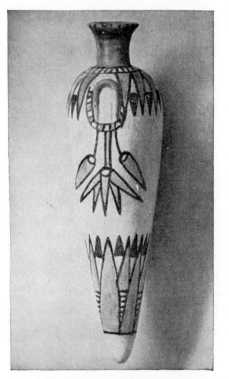

53. CERAMIC JAR *Egypt*

It is interesting to see how the Cypriote potter varied the decoration on these two pitchers. Notice the way in which the lines on the neck of each affect the appearance of its proportions.

You have probably noticed that this vessel, which was possibly used to hold a cosmetic oil, has no base. It is likely that a bracket held it upright when not in use.

Art of Pottery

Resourceful women scraped clay from the banks of streams or from almost dried-up river beds, carefully removed from it rocky or foreign substances, and moistened and kneaded it by hand into a smooth mass, as an old-fashioned baker kneaded dough.

Thus, they had a material that could be shaped into a hollow form and, after drying and baking, could receive, hold, and keep water cool. These vessels, which were strong enough to survive many uses and treatments, were built up by a laborious process similar to that used for coiled basketry.

Since most art students are familiar with coiled pottery, you probably know that the form is built up by overlapping successive coils of clay, and by expanding or contracting their circumferences in accordance with the desired form of the vessel. Each coil is attached to the previous one by pressing and smoothing it with the fingers. Both fingers and little tools are used to give the form symmetry, uniform thickness, and polish.

A clay vessel, so made and dried in the sun, and baked in a crude oven, became an object of the utmost usefulness, not only in the household of early man, but in his religious ceremonies as well.

Among early potters were the artists of the island of Cyprus, renowned in pre-Greek days, and those of Egypt. Cypriote pottery, both in form and in decoration, has a rugged, free, and direct quality that has inspired many modern designers. Compare Illustrations 52 and 53. The latter, although made in about the tenth century B.C., is far more sophisticated. Probably designed to hold a cosmetic oil, it is characteristic of the elegance of the court ladies of those times. The borders of leaves seem to spring naturally from the compact handle. Although these pieces of pottery were made centuries before the Christian era, the simplicity of design and skillful craftsmanship in them are as fine as in any piece of modern pottery.

The Zuñi Indian who made the bold and handsome piece of pottery shown in Illustration 54 was as much an artist as her sister, the Indian basket maker, and an equally fine craftsman. As you probably know, the art of pottery is still practiced among Indian tribes today.

54. POTTERY DRUM JAR   *North America*

This large Zuñi jar originally had skin tightly stretched over the opening and served as a drum. Notice that the decorative animal is in profile but both horns are shown. Does the figure remind you of some of the cave paintings you have seen?

The potters of this Mochian Indian tribe were often called upon to portray a deceased person. In spite of the oddity of the idea, the compact and curious little figure has a certain dignity.

55. EFFIGY VASE
South America

From the countless pieces of pottery made by early man and found the world over, we cannot but realize how carefully, even how lovingly pottery was fashioned, and how well it served its purpose, both practically and esthetically.

Art of Weaving

Hand weaving is another form of art that goes back to prehistoric times and that has been practiced constantly up to the last 150 years. Again, the reason for its development is an obvious one: sheer necessity prompted primitive man to make fabrics to protect him from bad weather, and inspired him, in turn, to invent a variety of weaving processes. You are all familiar with the fundamentals of simple weaving: the warp, or longitudinal threads, fastened to a frame, or loom; and the weft (sometimes called the woof), or transverse threads, that are woven under and over the warp and so interlace it to form a fabric. Through the elaboration of the simple loom, varieties in weaves, in colors, in patterns, and in materials furnish many opportunities for individual and personal work. Many types of weaves, such as the satin weave, the tapestry weave, and the twill weave, lend endless fascination and challenge to weaving.

Almost all the early weavers were women. They took great pride in their work and made it as beautiful and as perfect as was humanly possible. Nature provided them with an abundance of raw materials: wool, cotton, flax, and hemp, as well as reeds, barks, and grasses. These materials, gathered, cleaned, spun or rolled into threads, and dyed with animal, vegetable, or mineral dyes, were the media of the early craftsman, who used them as freely as the painter used his colors, and the sculptor his clay, stone, or wood.

Coptic and Indian Textiles

Among the early weavers there were some whose work was so outstanding that they are considered, even today, preëminent in their field. The textiles of the Coptic women, early Christians of Egypt, have always been greatly admired both for the vitality of their design and for the skill of their weaving. These designers used plant, animal,

56. TEXTILE *South America*

Do the little figures, half-human and half-animal or bird, that compose this Peruvian design remind you of some you have seen in the movies? It would seem that Walt Disney, the famous cartoonist, shares with the Peruvian Indians the gift of bringing to life engaging and fantastic figures such as these.

and geometric motifs beautifully simplified and adapted to the spaces they filled. Their rich patterns, woven of linen and wool, were used to decorate their costumes.

The Coptic weavers worked in the first centuries of the Christian era. Is it not strange that, about fifteen centuries later, the Indians who had long ago established themselves in Peru wove from the wool of the alpaca, textiles that were similar to the Coptic textiles in technique and equally fine in design quality? The Peruvians, however, did not use the beautiful tropical foliage with which they were undoubtedly surrounded, as the Coptic weavers did, but instead, used human figures, birds, and animals as motifs in their designs. Scarfs, belts, caps, pouches, and borders on costumes were woven in rich, glowing colors. The imaginative quality of the Peruvian designer is well displayed in Illustration 56. Although the largest section of the weaving is made up of only two alternating motifs, you will notice that the dark and light pattern of each has been varied so that the rhythmic movements have a spontaneous character.

Among the North American Indians, two groups, the Navaho of the Southwest and the Tlingit of the Northwest, are famous for their weaving. Using the wool of the sheep, an animal brought to the New World in the sixteenth century, the Navaho women soon became skillful weavers of rugs and blankets. Even today they continue this art. Their designs are mainly geometric and have great variety since each weaver is her own designer. The lines, shapes, and colors all have a symbolic meaning connected with nature. Can you find, for example, in Illustration 58, some lines that suggest lightning?

The Tlingit Indian women specialized in making a type of blanket, known as a Chilkat blanket, which was woven of mountain-goat wool in natural white, black, yellow, and pale blue-green. Since the conventions of their tribe allowed women to design only abstract or geometric forms, the designs for these blankets, based on human and animal forms, were made by the masculine artists of the tribe. Although there is a marked similarity in the design of these Chilkat blankets, close inspection shows considerable variety within conventional limitations. One of these blankets, which the owner prized as highly as a woman of today would prize her expensive fur coat, is shown in Illustration 59. The bear, a motif that constantly appears in Tlingit de-

57. WOVEN BAG *South America*

It would be interesting to know how the Cora Indian weaver intended to finish her design for this bag. The finished side shows a light and dark pattern on a dark background, while the unfinished section reverses this scheme. Turned upside down, the two lower corner shapes suggest two little flying angels.

A careful look at this Navaho Indian blanket will show you that the weaver felt free to make many little variations within the large, planned pattern of her design. Notice, for example, that the small motifs in the four corners of the rug are not similar in size and in shape. Although weaving is a mechanical process, and one that restricts the type of design that may be used, there are still many opportunities for the weaver to indulge in pleasing variations within the main scheme of the design.

To know more about the meaning of a design is to enjoy it more thoroughly. Notice, for example, the little oval shapes at the elbow joints of this bear. This symbol is the Tlingit Indian's way of expressing the crushing power of a bear's arms.

58. **WOVEN BLANKET**
North America

59. **WOVEN SHOULDER BLANKET** *North America*

You have seen that Indian designs are symbolic of nature. We, too, use design symbols in our daily lives. While an arrow might have been a symbol of war to an Indian, to us it simply points out a way of walking or driving, yet it is still a potent symbol. Just as the Yakima Indian wore a garment with wings beautifully embroidered in beads because he felt that they gave him the tireless strength of a bird, so our aviators wear wings, the symbol of fleetness, on their uniforms.

60. **BUCKSKIN DRESS** *North America*

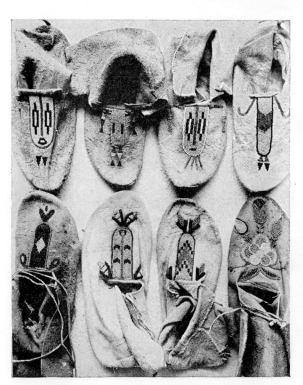

Although all but one of these moccasins, embroidered in beads by a Crow Indian, has a similar type of tongue-shaped decoration, there is, nevertheless, considerable variety to be found in their decoration. The richness of coloring which is characteristic of beadwork is also an attractive feature. Which design do you like best?

61. **BEADED MOCCASINS**

North America

sign, looks like a veritable strong man, for so he must have seemed to his Indian hunter. The fact that the bear seems almost as much a human as he does an animal is characteristic of the art of the Northwest Coast, for the Indians, as well as almost all other primitive men, thought of the creatures of the animal world as their equals, and as possessors of all the qualities of human nature.

Indian women were blessed both with leisure time and the instinct to put this time to good use. Basketry, pottery, weaving, and embroidery were all time-consuming arts in which they excelled. The ceremonial buckskin dress, shown in Illustration 60, is an interesting example of a design that has sprung from the artist's feeling for the space she decided to decorate. The winglike design, with its wavy lines that suggest flight, was thoughtfully placed across the shoulders of the garment where it could be easily seen and admired. When you observe some of the beaded moccasins (Illustration 61) that might have been worn with this garment, you can realize that the love of getting "dressed-up" is universal.

Egyptian Woodcarving

While women were the ones to make baskets, pottery, and textiles in primitive and early times, men seemed to be naturally the ones who undertook carving in wood and in stone, possibly because they liked to work with hard, resistant materials. Some of the finest early wood carvings have come from Egypt. At times Egyptian wood carving, although primarily practical, reaches sculptural levels. The carved *Offering Bearer* (Illustration 63) has many of the qualities of fine stone sculpture. However, the Egyptian woodcarver was concerned mainly with model-making, as many of the sea captains of our past have been. Illustration 64 shows how he carved and assembled a little model of an Egyptian boat to place in the tomb of a noble to accompany him on his long, after-life existence. So faithful was the craftsman in representing detail that he has devised, in this little relic, a realistic and interesting picture of an important phase of Egyptian life.

Just as the Egyptian craftsman served his rulers, so did his Asiatic contemporary, the Sumerian craftsman. In the previous chapter you became acquainted with the part this hardy race played in Mesopo-

This little painted woodcarving has an air of alertness and movement. The white lines painted on the docile, engaging horse seem to have been designed to emphasize both his trappings and the muscular structure of his body. These lines together with the position of the ears heighten the effect of movement.

62. HORSE AND RIDER
Egypt

This painted woodcarving, discovered in a Theban tomb, is typical of early Egyptian art. The girl is painted in a costume that emphasizes her slenderness. In her hand she holds a wild duck, while in the heavy box she so proudly carries on her head are pieces of meat for her master.

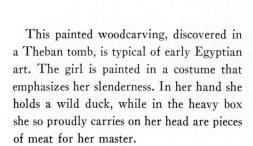

63. OFFERING BEARER
Egypt

64. BOAT MODEL *Egypt*

This is a luxurious craft of Egyptian times. The cabin sheltered the owner and his wife, both of whom seem to be gazing at the child in a nurse's arms. Twelve oarsmen speedily propel the craft down the Nile.

This elegant harp, adorned by a golden bull's head bearded in lapis lazuli, a rich blue semi-precious stone, was made for the queen's pleasure about 3000 B.C. and discovered by excavators of the royal tomb at Ur. Notice how skillfully the other surfaces have been decorated.

65. HARP OF QUEEN SHUB-AD
Mesopotamia

Among the Indian tribes on the Northwest Coast, carving a totem pole was a community project. A huge cedar log was marked off into various sections and an artist allotted to each section. The animals and birds that represented a family coat of arms were represented symbolically; that is, the artist selected certain features characteristic of the species. The bear, for example, which you have also seen used in the Chilkat blanket, is shown here at the base of the pole, and is distinguished by his many teeth.

67. HOME POST
North America

How vividly this carving reveals the Northwest Coast Kwakiotl Indian's faith in his gods! The totemlike figure symbolizes a powerful ancestral spirit protecting his living descendant. Notice that the strongly marked eyes and the elongated, beaklike nose are quite similar to those on page 40. Though primitive artists may be separated by vast oceans, their concepts and their sculptural expressions are often strikingly similar.

66. **TOTEM POLE**
North America

tamian culture. The statue of a Sumerian priest, tightly confined within a limestone block, that you saw on page 46, hardly prepares you for the elegance of one of several articles found within the tomb of Queen Shub-ad, wife of a Sumerian king, at Ur, a capital city. Her harp (Illustration 65) superbly combines the skill of the wood carver, the craftsmanship of the metal worker, and the expertness of the worker in precious stones.

Carvers of the Northwest Coast of America

Centuries later, on the other side of the world, the Indians of the Northwest, who lived along the Pacific seacoast from Alaska to Puget Sound, used their ample supply of giant cedar and other woods for many purposes. They built their several-family houses of huge planks, and carved and decorated great totem poles, boxes, masks, furniture, and utensils. From a single cedar log they constructed a seagoing canoe large enough to hold fifty men. You are probably all familiar with the Indian custom of placing a totem pole (Illustration 66) in front of a house to identify the family that lived there.

You can better appreciate the significance of the totem pole when you learn a little of the life and the beliefs of its carver. For one thing, he lived in a society that was very much aware of rank and its corresponding privileges. Several related families composed his clan, and each clan had certain acknowledged rights. These rights not only included property rights on land and sea, but in addition gave him the ownership of certain legends, songs, dances, and various concrete forms of art. If, for example, the chief of a clan claimed the raven as the founder or protector of his family, the raven became his totem, or friendly spirit, belonged exclusively to his family, as did all songs, legends, and dances about it.

Since the Northwest Coast Indian was very fond of display, his favorite form of entertainment was a prolonged party known as a potlatch. Sometimes guests were invited to such an affair a year in advance. Each guest wore his most impressive costume and brought presents to exchange or to give away, in order to "show off." The host, by lavish amounts of food, and by songs and dances that recounted the wonderful exploits of his ancestors, sought to prove how wealthy and important a person he was.

73

68. POTLATCH DISH   *North America*

Totemic designs in black, red, green, white, and yellow ornament this fantastic figure. The flattened knees hold serving bowls. Notice that the design symbols for elbow, hip, knee, and ankle joints are similar to those you have seen on the Chilkat blanket.

69. ARTICULATED DANCE MASK   *North America*

A simple arrangement of strings, manipulated by the wearer, makes the lower mask appear or disappear, and its lower jaw move. The lower beak of the raven also has a moveable joint. The mask was worn at the time of a potlatch when stories were being enacted around the fire in the house of a Northwest Coast Indian.

Illustration 68 shows a potlatch dish which was used to serve the guests hunks of fish dripping with oil. Notice that the entire piece was carved from one section of a tree trunk and that the head is covered by a mask that could be removed to place food within.

Masks played an important part in these and other affairs, and represented, in most cases, the bird or animal head of totem ancestors. A particularly interesting form of mask is the double mask, an example of which is to be seen in Illustration 69. This mask typifies a firm belief of the Northwest Coast Indians. They are confident that a bird or animal has the power to become human at will. Below the raven's head may be seen the representation of a human head that can be concealed behind another mask formed by the movable flaps on either side of the head. This is displayed at the climax of the dance.

Eskimo Art

Some of the humor and the fantastic quality of the Northwest Coast Indian is echoed in that of the Eskimo, whose Alaskan home is far to the north. The *Fish Effigy Mask* (Illustration 70), which was probably held before the face, has a quality that today is popularly called surrealistic. Perhaps this double mask with its combined fish and human elements has a meaning similar to the other double mask. The fantastic hands and feet, together with other strange shapes which encircle the frame, have a meaning which, although unknown to us, is nevertheless fascinating.

Although the Northwestern craftsman was busy making all the things needed in both his ceremonial and his practical life, he found the time to observe, to laugh at, and to record the cigar-smoking white man who occasionally penetrated his domain. The slyly humorous portrait carved by a Tlingit Indian (Illustration 71) seems to ridicule a smug and pompous visitor.

Pueblo Maskmakers

Today little remains of the old culture of the Northwest. Some of the Pueblo tribes of the Southwest, however, are now living as they lived hundreds of years ago. The Zuñi Indians, for example, still prac-

75

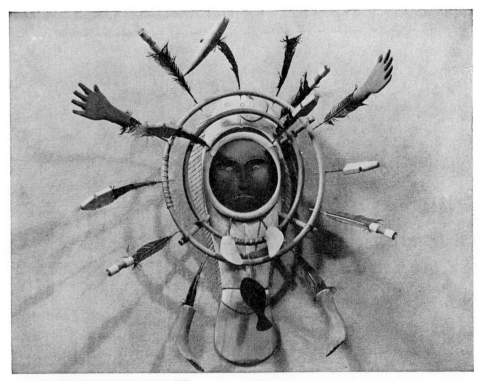

70. **FISH EFFIGY MASK** *North America*

The red-brown face that peers intently at us is framed by two wooden rings from which project strange feathered shapes painted in white, pale blue, and brown. For the Eskimo fisherman, this mask had a great significance, which unfortunately we cannot fathom.

71. **SEATED WHITE MAN**
North America

The Tlingit Indian carver combined wood and ivory in this simply carved, yet ironic portrait of a white man visiting in Alaska. In its directness of expression, it has a truly primitive quality.

72. MASK OF SAIYATSHA *North America*

A number of interesting materials have been combined to make this Zuñi Indian mask. They include elk skin, black goat's hair, cotton, and the feathers of birds. The face is painted turquoise.

73. KATCHINA DOLLS *North America*

These little wooden figures, gaily painted and ornamented, are replicas of the masked male dancers who impersonate the Hopi Katchinas. Lively and expressive, they show the Indian craftsman's delight in color, in pattern, and in texture.

tice a complex ceremonial life in which the ancient cults of the *Masked Gods* are scrupulously observed.

One of the most important of such ceremonies, the *Shalako,* is devoted to the arrival of the Zuñi gods to bless new houses. *Saiyatsha,* an important character in the *Shalako* ceremony, wears the interesting mask shown in Illustration 72. It has been described by Dr. Ruth Bunzel in the *Forty-third Annual Report of the Bureau of American Ethnology* as follows:

"He has one long horn on the right side, 'because he brings long life to all his people.' His eyes are long, too. But on the right side his eye is small. That is for the witch people, so that they may not live long, but on the left side his eye is long for the people of one heart, 'so that they may have long life.'"

Another type of *Masked God* dance may be seen in the Hopi pueblo when a number of masked dancers impersonate their *Katchinas,* or dancing gods. According to Hopi legend, these happy, companionable gods, of which there are over one hundred, dwell at the bottom of a distant lake. Through impersonation, however, they love to return to their people. Each god is represented by an individual mask and a traditional costume. Each man of importance in the tribe counts one of these masks among his choice possessions.

Little carved figures, known as *Katchinas* (Illustration 73), are to be found in each household. They are the friendly guardians of the hearth and are the favorite toys of the children there. Katchinas are close to man in spirit, for they are friendly and gay rather than godlike.

The Spirit of Early Craftsmen

The countless objects made by the early craftsmen were their valued possessions. The long hours spent making basketry, pottery, textiles, or carvings were richly repaid by the great satisfaction the primitive and early craftsmen found in their accomplishments. Their innate feeling for meaningful design and for design that was a logical outcome of the material in which it was made, was truly remarkable. Most fascinating of all their accomplishments in the field of crafts, however, was their imaginative and fresh approach to everything they did. Today all of us may truly envy them this gift.

5.

Birth of European Architecture

IF YOU had been a young Greek, living about 500 B.C., you would have had some of the following ideas:

"The world is a disk and Greece has the central position. The world is divided into two parts by the sparkling blue waters of the Mediterranean, the Aegean, and the Black Seas, and it is completely surrounded by the great river, Oceanus. On a distant shore lie the Elysian Fields where souls of those who have won the favor of the gods happily wander, forever in Paradise. In the exact center of the world towers its loftiest peak, Mount Olympus, the abode of our gods and goddesses. Mighty Zeus with Hera, his wife, Athena, Hermes, Aphrodite, Apollo, and countless lesser deities are there, overseeing our world and making occasional business and pleasure trips to it. When not busy with celestial affairs, they sip nectar and ambrosia, and gossip about the human beings below."

How do these ideas strike your twentieth-century mind? Absurd, you doubtless think, even though the Greeks of long ago believed them to be true. Is it possible that these people who had such strange ideas could have been the founders of our Western civilization? Why is it that the Golden Age of Greece which lasted only a short hundred years, could have produced an imperishable achievement in the field of art? See if you can find some answers to those questions.

The Greek Way of Life

The Greek citizen lived in the first democratic city-state. No despot ruled him; no priestly power bound him to ignorance and to slavery, as we know the Egyptian was ruled and bound. He was allowed to elect his rulers; he was responsible for his actions to no one but himself and his fellow men. Learning was not only his right, but also his delight. To challenge rather than to accept, to examine, to reason, to venture into new intellectual and artistic endeavors, were characteristics of the Greek, for he was endowed with that wonderful gift, intellectual curiosity.

What the Greek thought was the result of his reasoning, not of his fears or his superstitions. This alone was a remarkable thing in the days when millions of men were living in blind, unquestioning acceptance of their lot. What he did was likely to be the thing that he, alone, decided was the right thing for him to do. What he built, painted, or sculptured was in no way dictated by thousands of years of conventions, as it was in Egypt. The Greek artist was reasonably free from limitations because his work was the product of his own ideas, and his limitations were self-imposed.

The Greek who had leisure to pursue knowledge and to create things as he wished to create them, was so interested in gaining knowledge that he allowed few distractions to take him from his pursuit of it. All of this does not mean that the material world of the Greek was necessarily ideal according to our present-day standards. It was, however, a better world than had yet been known to any man, and one unsurpassed by many of the civilizations that followed.

The Greek Temple

The Greek turned naturally toward art for an expression of his ideals and beliefs. His serenity of spirit, his love of logic, and his joy in life are all clearly reflected in his art. The Greek temple, for example, is more than a planned and perfected architectural form; it is a complete realization of both the Greek mind and spirit. Because the Greek religion did not require its followers to assemble within a place of worship for prayer, the temples could be small, and generally were.

Their size pleased and satisfied the unpretentious Greeks, for they preferred quality to quantity, and demanded of a temple only that it be perfect in proportion, consistent in style, and restrained in detail.

The Greeks did not invent a new method of building; they took the traditional post-and-lintel type of construction, such as you have seen in the Egyptian *Temple of Amon* on page 31, and generally used it to form a rectangular, roofed building composed of one or two windowless rooms surrounded by a columned portico, or porch. Their temples differed from one another only in details. Conventions of building, known as orders, dictated the style, the proportions, and the construction of the columns and certain other parts of the building.

You can generally discover the order used in a Greek temple by examining the columns. The *Doric* order, the oldest of the three, has a shallow-fluted, sturdy column, a flat, square capital, and no base. It is a strong, simple type of column. The *Ionic* order has a more slender, graceful, fluted column, a scroll-like capital, and a base. The *Corinthian* order, the last to arrive and the least frequently used, is distinguished by a many-fluted column and by elaborately sculptured foliage on its capital. The Corinthian order is not considered by experts to be as fine as its less ornate predecessors, the Doric and the Ionic orders.

The Greeks used their plentiful supply of marble to build their temples. The solid blocks were joined skillfully with nothing more than iron devices. Although we think of their temples as being an austere white, actually, in those days, they were brilliantly colored in ochre, vermilion, blue, green, and gold. These temples must have been splendid testimonies to the deities in whose honor they were erected and whose statues were enshrined there. Their perfection of style and of construction and the beauty of the sculpture used to adorn them have never been surpassed.

In Greece during the fifth century B.C. there were two large rival city-states: Sparta to the south and Athens to the north. Athens, under the leadership of art-loving Pericles, became the most beautiful city in the Western world and its cultural center as well. Many notable buildings arose on the Acropolis, a rocky hill which served as a civic center for the city. The best known of the temples there is the *Parthenon* (Illustration 74) which was dedicated to Athena Parthenos,

74. PARTHENON *Athens, Greece*

After the fall of Greece, the *Parthenon* was used first as a Christian church and later as a mosque. When the Venetians captured Athens in the seventeenth century, the *Parthenon* was badly damaged. Soon afterward it came into the possession of the Turks and was further mutilated by them. In the nineteenth century, Lord Elgin of England received permission to remove much of its sculptural decoration to the British Museum.

This section of the *Erechtheum,* a temple dedicated to the Greek god Erechtheus, has four beautifully sculptured figures that serve as columns. Strong and serene, they adjust themselves flawlessly to the architectural plan.

75. PORCH OF THE MAIDENS
Athens, Greece

the goddess of wisdom, power, peace, and prosperity. The *Parthenon* is probably the most famous building in the world and the most perfectly proportioned.

Design of the Parthenon

Early in their striving for perfection, the Greeks had discovered that horizontal and vertical lines in a building did not always appear truly horizontal and vertical to the observer. They also noticed that, although certain parts of a building, such as its columns and the spaces between them, were of equal size, they did not give that impression, owing to what is called optical illusion. Possibly you have experienced an optical illusion when you have looked at a tall building and have noticed that its vertical lines appear to converge slightly toward the top. In order to overcome such optical illusions, Ictinus, the architect of the *Parthenon,* so planned the building that he actually constructed it in slight curves, all of which were carefully designed to give the impression of being horizontal and vertical throughout. The columns, which taper slightly at the top and at the bottom, are not set squarely upright, but incline, ever so slightly, toward the top of the building. Some of the columns are actually larger than others although all of them, eight on each end, and seventeen on each side, appear to be the same size; furthermore, they are not placed at regular intervals, but are closer together at the corners of the building. The steps and the base are not horizontal, but are slightly convex. Thus the Greeks showed that they were unceasing in their search for perfection in striving to erect buildings that would truly delight the eye of the beholder.

The Grandeur That Was Rome

The Romans and the Greeks, although they lived in an almost contemporary civilization, had little in common, and were, in fact, enemies. In 146 B.C. the Roman Empire brought to an end the "glory that was Greece."

The Roman was militant, egotistical, and far more concerned with material than with spiritual wealth. His love of ostentatious display, of pomp and power, his callous disregard for the life and liberty of

76. PONT DU GARD *Nîmes, France*

One of the finest features of Roman engineering was its system of aqueducts that supplied the Empire daily with millions of gallons of water from distant sources. The *Pont du Gard,* still standing today, was originally a part of a magnificent aqueduct, twenty-five miles long, that supplied Nîmes, then a Roman province.

77. PANTHEON *Rome, Italy*

Although the *Pantheon* no longer has the statuary, the richly colored marble, or the bronze and gold of its early days, it is still an impressive sight in Rome today.

his fellow men, not only marked his career as conqueror of Carthage and Gaul, of Egypt and Greece, but also was clearly stamped on all of his artistic efforts.

As the Romans admired all phases of Greek culture, they paid the people they had conquered the compliment of imitation, just as they had imitated the resourceful Etruscans whom they had previously vanquished. The treasures of Greece, the finest work of her sculptors and craftsmen, were carted off to Rome by triumphant generals, where the works were not only displayed as the spoils of the victorious, but also copied again and again by Roman artisans. Even the Greek gods, renamed, became Roman deities.

Although the Romans were not blessed with the artistic gifts of the Greeks, they did have other talents to pass on to the Western world. They were great engineers. Their huge and elaborately decorated temples, theaters, public baths, arenas, triumphal arches, and basilicas, or halls of justice, were remarkable feats of construction. Many roads, bridges, and aqueducts built by the Romans are in use today. The *Pont du Gard* in the south of France (Illustration 76), built to bring mountain water to a part of the Roman Empire, is an excellent example of a form which was derived solely from the functional purpose for which it was intended.

The inventive Roman builder found a way whereby he could erect very large edifices with considerable open space within the interior. This he accomplished in a variety of ways: by concrete-filled walls, by columns, arches, and cross vaults, and, in some cases, by using a dome which rested its weight upon cylindrical walls.

Structurally, Roman buildings had little in common with Greek buildings, but their builders made use of a superficial and decorative variation of Greek orders, especially the ornate Corinthian. Faced with multicolored marbles and handsomely decorated, these Roman buildings created a type of public building that, with certain variations, has lasted to the present day.

The Pantheon

Originally designed as a temple to seven gods, and used for civic purposes as well, the *Pantheon,* built in 120–124 B.C. by the Roman

78. COLOSSEUM *Rome, Italy*

It was within this tremendous structure that gladiatorial contests, naval displays, and the martyrdom of Christians took place to amuse vast Roman audiences.

79. BATHS OF CARACALLA
Rome, Italy

The interior of this famous Roman building must have been an impressive sight, since the walls, pavements, columns, and baths were of alabaster and other rare marbles from the Aegean Islands. Perpetual streams of water from many fountains flowed into marble basins and cooled the torrid air with refreshing moisture.

Emperor Hadrian, is the best-preserved building of Greek and Roman days. If you were to travel to Rome, you would find it still in use as a Catholic church and as a tomb for many notables, including the painter Raphael. The *Pantheon* (Illustration 77), a large, circular building, has twenty-foot thick walls pierced by only one doorway. This building is crowned by a low dome that has a circular opening in its apex. The only means of admitting light is through this opening, which produces a most impressive and mysterious effect.

Within the *Pantheon,* there is an amazing amount of open space, sufficient to accommodate three thousand people. The idea of open space within a building is typically Roman, for all temples built before Roman days either had an interior broken by a forest of columns, as did the Egyptian *Temple of Amon* (page 31) or were composed of only two small rooms, such as were originally to be found in the *Parthenon.*

Other Examples of Roman Architecture

Another famous sight in Rome today is the *Colosseum* (Illustration 78), the predecessor of such modern stadiums as the *Rose Bowl* in Pasadena and the *Yankee Stadium* in New York. Even though in partial ruin, a structure so colossal that it seated 87,000 persons has a certain impressiveness due to size alone. The three-tiered series of arches are flanked by columns that are purely decorative since they do not support any weight. The lower row of columns is Doric, the middle row, Ionic, and the top row, Corinthian. This scrambled use of the Greek orders is called "superimposed orders," a type of building that Greek architects would never have used.

Everyone has heard of the Roman baths, but few of us know how elaborate they were. How would you like to belong to an athletic club that has enough swimming pools, both hot and cold, to accommodate three thousand people, that has theaters, libraries, and all kinds of gymnasiums, steam rooms, game rooms and equipment? Such were the Roman baths, built by emperor after emperor to secure the vote and favor of his subjects. During the days when the Empire was at its height, there were over a thousand such baths in Rome alone. You can well imagine how imposing these buildings, especially the so-called

Imperial Baths, must have been. There are but few remains of these structures, but the general plan may be seen today, of all places, in a railroad station. Those of you who have been in the main room of the *Pennsylvania Station* in New York have seen an interior which is modeled after the famous Roman *Baths of Caracalla* (Illustration 79).

Although the *Baths of Caracalla* are in ruins, architectural studies have revealed their size and magnificence, as well as many of the interesting features previously described. The central section, used entirely for bathing, was 570 feet by 380 feet, or approximately as large as an area occupied by six city blocks. Steam rooms and numerous baths were heated by radiant heat which was carried by terra cotta pipes from fires built in the cellar to any part of the building where it was needed.

The Roman Basilica

Community life in Rome called for a large building that could serve both as a court house and as a trading center. A certain type of building, known as a basilica, met this need.

The interior of the basilica was a long, rectangular, and lofty hall. The far end of this hall, which was semicircular, formed what is known as an apse. It was here that the Roman judge sat on a raised platform, or dais. An altar in front of the apse was used to make sacrificial offerings before opening the court.

The hall was separated into one wide center aisle, or nave, and into either two or four side aisles by rows of columns that ran its length. Galleries, or balconies, were generally placed over the side aisles, but were not constructed above the back of the hall, as is often done in auditoriums today. The wooden roof over the main aisle was higher than it was over the galleries. Thus a section known as a clerestory, a kind of second story, was formed. Light was admitted through the side walls of the clerestory. It is important that we know some of the facts about the form of the Roman basilica since it served later on, with certain added features, as a model for early Christian churches.

Early Christian Architecture

The power of pagan Rome yielded, little by little, to the forces of Christianity. By the early part of the fourth century, Christianity had

88

become the established religion of the Roman Empire. Christians were no longer forced to hold their services in private homes or within the secret recesses of the catacombs, their underground hiding places. They converted pagan temples, such as the *Pantheon,* into churches dedicated to the glory of their Messiah, Jesus of Nazareth. Impressive and dignified new churches were constructed, modeled on the basic plan of the Roman basilica. Many of these churches, such as *St. Paul's Outside the Walls,* which was destroyed and later rebuilt, are well known and widely admired today.

Many of the early Christian churches, however, were more Oriental in appearance than Roman, for another type of art also influenced their design. You may think this odd until you recall the extent of the Roman Empire at this time. This vast Empire, which extended far to the east, included at this time all territories encircling the Mediterranean and Aegean seas.

In the fourth century, Constantine, Emperor of Rome, practically divided his unwieldly empire in two parts when he selected Byzantium, a prosperous city on the Bosporus between Europe and Asia, as a new capital. He renamed this city Constantinople; we know it today as Istanbul. Through his action, an Eastern and a Western Roman Empire were created.

Byzantine Art

In the Near East a distinctive form of Christian-Oriental art, known as Byzantine, emerged in the first centuries after the dawn of Christianity. Since the Christians in the Near East had not been suppressed as they had been in Rome, they were free to build churches and to worship as they pleased. Byzantine architecture became a rich blend of influences from Greece, Egypt, Asia Minor, Persia, Syria, and even from elements in the Orient. The influence of Byzantine art and architecture was felt throughout both the Eastern and Western Roman Empire, and by the sixth century, some notable Early Christian churches were erected.

An excellent example of this Early Christian architecture is in Ravenna, Italy, at one time the residence of a Roman emperor. There stands the church of *St. Apollinare in Classe* (Illustration 80), built by Byzantine architects during the sixth century. This church, out-

80. ST. APOLLINARE IN CLASSE *Ravenna, Italy*

A wooden roof and high windows were characteristics of the early Christian church. The decoration often had as its climax a beautiful mosaic above the altar.

81. MOSAIC, ST. APOLLINARE IN CLASSE *Ravenna, Italy*

The central figure of the mosaic above the altar represents *St. Apollinare* preaching to his flock. The twelve sheep are symbolic of the twelve apostles of Christ.

wardly rugged and unpretentious, has an interior which is unexpectedly impressive. Its length is accentuated by the double row of columns and the rhythmic repetitions of the supporting arches. Notice especially the curved apse crowned with a half-dome and the raised altar placed against a mosaic background.

As you probably know, mosaics are decorations formed by setting multicolored bits of stone and glass in cement. They were used extensively by Byzantine artists to add richness and beauty to the interior of their buildings, as well as to depict the story of Christianity to the people. Illustration 81 shows a close-up view of the mosaic you can see in the distance in the previous illustration. Well over a million tiny fragments of stone and glass have been carefully arranged to complete its design, a feat of artistry and craftsmanship unmatched in our day.

Santa Sophia: Gem of Byzantine Art

The impressiveness of the present exterior of *Santa Sophia,* built in the sixth century in Constantinople (Illustration 82), seems to our modern eyes to be marred by the surrounding buildings cluttered around its base. They and the four slender towers, or minarets, were added to the edifice by the Moslems who captured Constantinople in the fifteenth century and converted *Santa Sophia* into a Moslem mosque, just as the Christians had converted the *Pantheon* into a church of their faith.

It is easier to understand the architectural plan and to appreciate the beauty of *Santa Sophia* when you see its interior. This you may study in Illustration 83. The practical features of its construction, the columned nave and side aisles, the arches, the vast central dome, and the high-placed windows you have seen in other and earlier buildings. You can easily sense the skill needed to construct them. Yet the eye can scarcely find time to search for these practical features, for it is attracted by the amazingly rich surface quality created by the glittering gold and the precious stones which enhance the interior. Even the names of the rare marbles used on the patterned walls appeal to our sense of color: Phrygian white, Laconian green, Lybian blue, and

82. **SANTA SOPHIA** *Istanbul, Turkey*

The large central dome with a half-dome on either side is an interesting form of construction. The two vertical masses of masonry thrust against the front of the building are two of the four piers that support the arches upon which the central dome rests.

83. **INTERIOR, SANTA SOPHIA** *Istanbul, Turkey*

At the far end of this interior view, one of the half-domes may be seen and, just above it, an edge of the main dome, which rests like a canopy over the center.

Celtic black. Richly colored mosaics and a lavish use of gold add to the impression of almost unbelievable splendor.

Mohammedan Architecture

You have seen how the character of architecture was influenced by available materials, by the amount and kind of technical knowledge its builders possessed, and, especially, by the spirit and the interests of the people whose life it represented.

The particular qualities that have gone into the architecture of a certain age have often endured long after the culture that produced them has perished. One of the many interesting examples of this fact is the way in which many of the characteristics of Christian-Byzantine architecture were retained by the Arab followers of Mohammed, who in the seventh century invaded Persia, Syria, and Egypt. Finding in these countries the traditions of Byzantine architecture, they modified them to their own requirements and so developed a form of architecture that we now identify with the Mohammedan religion.

Later, about A.D. 1000, the Mohammedans established an empire, known as the Mogul Empire, in India. Here again, the ancient art of the Hindu culture was recreated in the magnificent palaces, tombs, and mosques erected by the enormously wealthy rulers. One of the most fabulous of their buildings is the *Taj Mahal* (Illustration 84), built by Shah Jehan as a tomb for his wife. Its rich and formal beauty is immeasurably enhanced by a stately, landscaped setting. This world-famous building constantly amazes the thousands of visitors who journey yearly to see it.

The Venetian Cathedral of St. Mark

Byzantine art was the most powerful cultural force in Europe from about the third to the twelfth century. Thus, even as late as the eleventh century, it continued to influence many beautiful buildings in many different parts of Europe.

Venice, the rich and romantic city of singing gondoliers, fabulous palaces, and merchant princes, was, in the eleventh century, a maritime state which traded with both eastern and western territories.

84. TAJ MAHAL *Agra, India*

Compare the minarets, or slender towers, encircled by balconies that you see here with those of *Santa Sophia* on page 92, and the domes with those of *St. Mark's* in the illustration below, and you will notice the similarity of their forms.

85. CATHEDRAL OF ST. MARK *Venice, Italy*

The sumptuous beauty of *St. Mark's* is greatly enhanced by its perfect setting in a vast open space framed by stately, arcaded buildings.

Since the Venetians were rich and were in love with all that was colorful and luxurious, it was only natural that they should turn to Byzantine architects for inspiration in erecting the famous and beautifully preserved church of *St. Mark* (Illustration 85).

In its present general ground plan, this church follows the Greek cross, which has four arms of equal length. The building is crowned by two large and three smaller domes, one over the center, and one over each arm of the cross. Notice that all the domes, which are a prevailing feature of Byzantine architecture, are more bulbous than the semi-spherical ones you have seen on the *Pantheon* (page 84), and on *Santa Sophia* (page 92).

Although it is not a large church, the proportions and the skillfully varied sizes and the grouping of its domes make *St. Mark's* appear larger than it actually is. Both the interior and the exterior are sumptuous in color and incredibly rich in rare materials and expert craftsmanship. The five entrances on the front, for example, are a gorgeous blend of translucent alabaster, a type of soft marble that permits light to filter through it, of other rare, multicolored and highly polished marbles, and of lustrous gold. Actually seeing *St. Mark's* would make you realize how much the Byzantine artists loved color and ornament, and how unhesitatingly they made them the most spectacular feature of their architecture.

The Byzantine style spread over Greece and Russia, as well as other parts of the world. Today it is the accepted style of the Greek church.

Coming of the Middle Ages to Europe

The eastern part of Europe, throughout the long span of time from the sixth to the eleventh centuries, was sufficiently at peace to produce the luxurious Byzantine art. However, the western part of Europe at this time was in a state of perpetual warfare. This, as you would expect, did not lead to much creative work in art.

For protection, people attached themselves either to a powerful noble in a rural community or to the bishop of a monastic order, and so became serfs in what was known as a feudal system. Under oath, they were pledged to fight for their protector and to repay him further with the products of their labors.

The fortresses of the Middle Ages were strongly built to resist attack. A stronghold such as *Caernarvon Castle* (Illustration 86) brings to us vivid mental images of tumult and shouting, and of swarming forces attacking under the fire of crossbow and arrow that came from the defenders on its parapets. This imposing castle is still standing though seven centuries have passed since it was built.

Mont St. Michel, to be seen in Illustration 87, like *Caernarvon Castle,* has a body of water which formed a natural defense, for it was built upon a rocky islet off the north coast of France and is now connected with the mainland only by a narrow causeway. Originally a small chapel built during the eighth century in honor of St. Michael, it became a retreat famous for the numbers of soldiers, nobles, and monarchs who came there to beseech the protection of that fiery saint. During the tenth century an elaborate fortress-abbey was erected, with its church rising high on the summit of the granite rock above numerous low buildings. During many wars, this monastery remained impregnable, sheltering its inhabitants from attack and devastation.

Gradually the barbarians ceased to war with one another. They settled down in sections where their descendants are living today. Men united again in a zeal for learning, for upholding the ideals of chivalry, and, since the Christian Church had become the strongest force in their lives, for crusading for their faith. Learning, religious fervor, and the impetus of the Crusades inspired the founding of churches, universities, and schools. Thus, just as the pagan world had yielded to Christianity, the Dark Ages of the barbarians gave way to the far more enlightened Middle Ages.

Romanesque Architecture

The first churches of this period in France and Italy were built in a style now called the Romanesque. As this term implies, the Romanesque style retained many of the Roman traditions of building. For example, it used the basilica church form together with its rounded arches and thick walls pierced by small openings for windows. Unlike the basilica church, however, the Romanesque church was richly decorated with sculpture that formed an integral part of its design. You may see how beautifully architecture and sculpture

86. CAERNARVON CASTLE *Wales*

This Norman castle has a shell-like plan. It was built upon and around primitive earthworks used in even earlier days for defense. The river and ocean made moats unnecessary; the narrow-slitted windows were manned by its defenders during an attack.

87. MONT ST. MICHEL *France*

Today all who visit *Mont St. Michel* marvel at the amazing energy of its almost untrained builders. Constructed of hard granite throughout, from its substructures to its lacy and intricate outer stonework decoration, every section shows an amazing degree of craftsmanship.

The river which flows through this old city is crossed by fourteen bridges. Of the city gates, one of the most interesting is the *Porte des Allemandes* which, as you can see, was solidly built to resist invaders.

88. **PORTE DES ALLEMANDES** *Metz, France*

The stalwart ramparts which encircled this twelfth-century town provided one of the most imposing fortifications of the Middle Ages.

89. **CARCASSONNE**
Carcassonne, France

90. **ST. TROPHIME** *Arles, France*

The beautiful portal of *St. Trophime* includes a continuous row of statues of various saints set within elaborately carved niches. The tympanum over the doorway, which is accentuated by a row of arches, contains a figure of Christ surrounded by beasts that symbolize the Apostles, St. Matthew, St. Mark, St. Luke, and St. John.

91. **CLOISTERS, ST. TROPHIME** *Arles, France*

Characteristic of the Romanesque abbey-church are its cloisters, or open court. Beneath its covered passageway, members of the monastic order attached to this abbey often walked in meditation.

have been combined if you look at Illustrations 90 and 91, which show sections of the Romanesque church of *St. Trophime,* built during the eleventh century.

Since often two or more centuries went into the building of a church, it is not surprising to find that many of them were not completed in a style originally intended by their builders. The world-famous *Cathedral of Pisa* (Illustration 92), although essentially Romanesque in structure, has certain decorative features of the Gothic style which succeeded the Romanesque. The *Baptistry,* which is the circular building in the foreground, is mainly Gothic in style although the cathedral itself is Romanesque.

Gothic Cathedrals of the Middle Ages

By the thirteenth century, the power of the feudal system of the Dark Ages was broken. People left the sheltering walls of castle and monastery, and gathered together in towns in order to find independence and a freedom that they had never known. The life of the town centered in its cathedral. The cathedral was not only the place of worship but also a civic meeting place and even, occasionally, a theater where seasonal plays, called mystery plays, were enacted by puppets. Mystery plays were based on stories from the Bible and were a means of teaching the people the doctrines of their religion.

There was keen rivalry among towns for the honor of having built the most magnificent cathedral. Nobles and churchmen contributed money. Craftsmen's organizations, known as guilds, such as the Masons' Guild, the Stoneworkers' Guild, the Stained Glass Workers' Guild, and the Gold Workers' Guild, contracted to build the cathedral and guaranteed the quality of their work. Rich and poor, young and old alike, labored mightily to build an edifice worthy of their Creator. From father to son, even through many generations, the task and the privilege were handed down.

The Gothic cathedrals of France, built in the first half of the thirteenth century, have probably been more highly praised than the buildings of any other period, including even the present. Their vertical upsweep toward the heavens, the delicate, nervous movement of their towers and spires, the rich tracery of stone, and the glowing

100

92. CATHEDRAL OF PISA *Pisa, Italy*

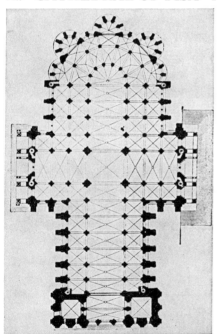

93. PLAN, CATHEDRAL OF CHARTRES *Chartres, France*

The Cathedral of Pisa, which is neither pure Romanesque nor pure Gothic in style, has another distinguishing feature, its campanile, or bell tower, more commonly known as the *Leaning Tower.* Its uniqueness of design and odd slant, due to a defect in the foundation, have attracted tourists from all over the world.

Gothic churches, in general, were designed in the shape of a Latin cross. The short arms of the cross form the north and south transepts, and the main body of the church extends from east to west. The principal entrance always faces west.

94. CATHEDRAL OF CHARTRES *Chartres, France*

Famous for the fascinating history of its building, the *Cathedral of Chartres* amazes its many visitors. One hundred and thirty magnificent stained glass windows and a rich profusion of sculptured figures bear eloquent testimony to the religious devotion of the people of the Middle Ages.

95. CATHEDRAL OF NOTRE DAME *Paris, France*

In this view of the *Cathedral of Notre Dame,* you may clearly see the use of the flying buttress in Gothic architecture. Since walls were very high and windows large and numerous, necessary reinforcement was provided by slender stone buttresses that carried the thrust of the wall's weight.

color of their stained-glass windows arouse a strong esthetic response in all who see them.

In general, French Gothic cathedrals have certain structural features in common. Although they followed the Latin cross of the early basilica (Illustration 93), they were far more lofty and elaborate. Countless vertical lines and pointed arches emphasized their vertical, upward movement. Their vast height was obtained by their architects' development and use of the pointed arch and of ribbed vaulting, a method of roofing which leaves no weight upon the walls of a structure. Supports for the walls and the roof, known as flying buttresses, were an important structural feature. Since solid walls were not needed to support the roof, stained glass was used in profusion, just as quantities of glass are used today to encase modern buildings. Other notable features of the Gothic cathedrals were their extensive sculptural decorations, their two western towers, their tapering spires, and countless repetitions of the pointed arch.

Chartres Cathedral

The *Cathedral of Chartres* (Illustration 94) has an extraordinary history. Early in the twelfth century, a little church in Chartres was destroyed by fire. United by religious fervor, rich and poor, young and old, banded together to erect a larger, loftier church, one in accordance with the new architectural ideas of the times.

It is recorded that laborer and nobleman alike dragged stones to the site of the new cathedral. About sixty years later, when the cathedral was practically completed, a second great fire almost completely destroyed it. It was again rebuilt, except for one spire which was added in the sixteenth century. The two spires of this cathedral were constructed three hundred years apart. The contrast between the first, plain and sturdy, and the loftier and more ornate later one, clearly indicates the changes that occurred in the Gothic style of architecture within that span of time.

Notre Dame de Paris

One of the oldest of the 150 French Gothic cathedrals, *Notre Dame* (Illustration 95), is more restrained and therefore less dra-

103

This famous stained-glass window over the western portal of the *Cathedral of Chartres* enriches not only the façade but also the interior because of the rich, indescribably beautiful color, which is heightened when it is pierced by light.

96. **ROSE WINDOW, CHARTRES**
Chartres, France

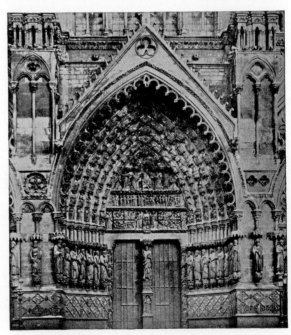

97. **DOORWAY, CATHEDRAL OF AMIENS**   *Amiens, France*

Compare the design of a doorway of the *Cathedral of Amiens* with that of St. Trophime on page 99. Notice that, fundamentally, Gothic and Romanesque façades have much in common. A strongly marked difference, however, is the Gothic stress on upward rather than on horizontal movement. This stress is easily seen when you note the difference between the pointed Gothic and the semi-circular Romanesque arch.

matic than many others built somewhat later. This effect is probably due to the fact that it is less ornate in decoration, and also because the two spires originally planned to cap its two towers have never been added.

Notre Dame, however, is truly impressive. In the illustration its unusually handsome and slender flying buttresses may be clearly seen.

Amiens and Rheims Cathedrals

Gothic cathedrals are so incredibly rich in detail that they almost dazzle our eyes. The *Cathedral of Amiens,* for example, has superbly beautiful surface carving which, although very complex, is strongly unified by its bisymmetric arrangement. We may see this clearly in Illustration 97 which shows the main portal of the cathedral. The central figure between the two doors, the *Beau Dieu d'Amiens,* is considered one of the noblest sculptured figures in the world.

The *Cathedral of Rheims,* the pride of France and a treasury of art, has an immensely beautiful façade, as you may see by referring to Illustration 98. There is a fascinating play of dark and light rippling over the surface of about 500 exquisitely carved statues set within shadowed portals. Notice how the upward movement of the elongated and pointed arches emphasizes the height of this cathedral. Over the main portal is a famous rose window, which bathes the interior with myriad, jewel-like colors.

Ste. Chapelle, a Glory of Glass

This comparatively small chapel has one of the most beautiful interiors to be found among the churches of France. We notice, in Illustration 99, that even far back in the Middle Ages men had discovered how to build walls of glass, and to turn those walls into vast windows that glowed with incomparable color. It is difficult to describe or even to reproduce satisfactorily the colors of stained-glass windows, for the light which streams through these twin triumphs of artistry and craftsmanship is truly glorious. You have all seen how light, passing through a transparent, colored material, such as gelatin or glass, intensifies and enriches its color quality. Just so, the stained

98. CATHEDRAL OF RHEIMS   *Rheims, France*

The *Cathedral of Rheims* was extensively mutilated during the First World War by repeated bombings. Skillfully repaired, it is still today the pride of France and a treasure house of art.

99. STE. CHAPELLE *Paris, France*

This small chapel, with its glorious stained-glass window-walls and star-studded ceiling, is an exquisite jewel in the crown of Gothic architecture.

glass of the Gothic churches, even this small one, *Ste. Chapelle,* bathes their interiors with brilliant colors, through which are pictured emotionally moving stories and symbols of Christianity.

Gothic Cathedrals of England

The plans for Gothic churches differed in every country in Europe. In England, for example, the cathedrals are generally longer and narrower than those in France, and they often have a high, central tower. *Salisbury Cathedral* (Illustration 100) is as characteristic of English Gothic as *Amiens Cathedral* is of French Gothic. You may notice that *Salisbury Cathedral* is not set among the houses of a town, but placed in the country on a level field near a stream which mirrors its towers. Its beautiful spire, which may be seen from many miles away, is the loftiest in England.

Many of the English cathedrals, such as *Westminster Abbey* and *Canterbury,* underwent successive periods of building and of alteration. The former, the scene of coronation ceremonies and the burial place of scores of England's famous men, is in itself a record of England's history. Architecturally, however, it lacks the appeal of the earlier, less complex cathedrals. The interior of *Wells Cathedral* (Illustration 101) although it is narrower and lower than many of the French Gothic cathedrals, is unexpectedly impressive. The rapidly moving arched lines of its ceiling are especially effective in contrast with the horizontal movements of the walls and the columned arches below.

Significance of Gothic Architecture

Gothic architecture, stately and esthetically moving, mirrors the thought and life of medieval man. It was built for the people, and by the people who gladly devoted to it their best efforts and their greatest talents. Thus it is a glorious record both of man's aspirations and of his ability to realize them in an enduring, concrete, and noble form.

108

The stately grace of the *Cathedral of Salisbury* is enhanced by the beauty of its setting. It lies close to the earth among a cluster of trees and seems to be a natural part of its surrounding landscape.

100. CATHEDRAL OF SALISBURY
Salisbury, England

The design of its arched ceiling is a notable feature of this English Gothic cathedral. Notice how the movement of the pointed arch has been repeated in both the walls and the ceiling.

101. INTERIOR, WELLS CATHEDRAL
Wells, England

Notice how the lines, so simply indicated on the marble surface, suggest the form of the upper part of the body by their flowing movements. This is an interesting contrast to the grouped vertical lines that run the length of the lower part of the figure and emphasize its height and majestic quality.

Relief sculpture has been used throughout the centuries to ornament all kinds of objects. Notice how the sculptor has kept certain parts of his design close to the surface of the stone and has emphasized other sections by modeling them more fully.

102. **HERA OF SAMOS** *Greece*

103. **BIRTH OF APHRODITE** *Greece*

6.

Development of Sculpture

TALES of the Olympic games, of their origin and later-day revival, greatly interest all of us who love sports. The Greeks, who seem to have been natural-born athletes, established the Olympic games in honor of their gods in the fifth century B.C.

At that time, Greece was composed of rival city-states, each of which was jealous of the other's accomplishments. Yet all differences were set aside for the games at Olympus. The most important event was the pentathlon. Selected athletes, boys and girls, men and women, arrived from all parts of Greece, even from its far-flung provinces, often well in advance of the event in order to go into intensive physical training. The contest, which took place before some 45,000 spectators, included running, jumping, wrestling, throwing the discus, and hurling the spear. The winners of these events, judged for their performance and for the grace and style with which it was executed, were crowned with wreaths of olive leaves. On the last day, winners were properly acclaimed at the feasts in honor of the gods.

The Greeks made a cult of physical perfection. Their heroes were those who had perfectly proportioned and magnificently developed bodies, with unusual endurance, amazing strength, or extraordinary speed. Their gods and goddesses were likewise thought of as having only the most perfect physical attributes.

The Greek sculptor left a record of this phase of Greek life and thought, for every temple and public building had sculptured decorations most of which used the human figure as a theme. Unfortunately most of the sculpture in Greece has been destroyed and even many of the remaining originals are fragmentary pieces. However, as noted in an earlier chapter, the finest pieces were brought to Rome and copied. A great deal of our knowledge of Greek sculpture derives from them even though most of the copies, together with the originals, were destroyed when pagan Rome fell.

Early Greek Sculpture

Greek sculpture, of course, did not reach the height of its development until it had gone through a number of successive stages. In what is called his archaic, or early period, the Greek sculptor was preoccupied with representing his gods and goddesses. Carving directly in stone, as countless other early sculptors did, he chiseled compact figures, one of which, the *Hera of Samos,* from the sixth century B.C., is to be seen in Illustration 102. Although the basic form of this statue is cylindrical, rather than four-sided, as in Egyptian stone carving, the early Greek sculpture had much in common with Egyptian sculpture. In both, carved figures appear, rigidly facing frontwards without any turn or twist of the body, and the tightly bound costumes suggest the bulk of the figure beneath.

It is also interesting to notice that archaic Greek sculpture has much in common both with Sumerian sculpture, carved as far back as 3000 B.C., and with Cypriote sculpture, which preceded that of Greece by a century. Turn back to pages 46 and 51 to see that a few thousand years made little difference in the viewpoint of the early sculptors.

However, after his initial attempts in the difficult art of sculpture, the Greek artist began to produce work that reflected the ruling spirit of his times. Just as the Greek philosophers, poets, and playwrights delved into the reasons for human behavior, so the sculptor explored the puzzling structure of the human body. Slowly the stiff archaic figures came to life. Although the sculptor still portrayed gods and goddesses, they appear more human, for the sculptor had learned to

104.   STATUETTE OF A HORSE   *Greece*

Beautiful pieces of bronze sculpture, such as this *Statuette of a Horse* and the *Chariot-eer of Delphi,* show that the early Greek artist was a master in the art of simplification. It is important to realize that his broad treatment was not due to his lack of knowledge of details, but rather to his understanding of the total form of his subject.

This firmly poised bronze charioteer was once part of a group which doubtless included a chariot and horses. The conventional costume of the Greek charioteer has been skillfully modeled to suggest the figure beneath, and at the same time to emphasize its columnlike character.

One of the most important parts of a Greek temple was the sculptured decoration over the pediment, or triangular space over its front columns. The *Archer's* kneeling position shows that originally he was placed at the narrow end of the pediment where his compact figure would easily fit.

105. **CHARIOTEER OF DELPHI** Greece

106. **ARCHER** *Greece*

show not only restrained body movements but also vigorous action.

The fragments of a low-relief, the *Birth of Aphrodite* (Illustration 103), was carved about 480 B.C. and shows the sculptor's facility in the use of figures in a decorative design. The supple line movement, which seems to ripple over the surface of the carving like the varied rhythms of a brook, unites the figures, even though incomplete, into a compact group. Each line movement, from the strong forces created by the action of the interlocked figures, to the subtle rhythms of their draperies, was carefully planned by the sculptor to create a harmonious whole.

The combination of sensitive realism and thoughtfully planned design to be seen in the *Birth of Aphrodite* is characteristic of the late archaic period of Greek sculpture, a period that many modern sculptors have found the most stimulating. The same assured power of the Greek sculptor is seen in the stirring bronze *Statuette of a Horse* (Illustration 104), thought to have been originally part of a large group, possibly that of a charioteer and his steeds. You can easily see that the Greek sculptor's recently acquired knowledge of anatomical structure was used with deliberate restraint. He did not show in detail the muscles, bones, and sinews of the body, but stressed instead, by smoothly flowing lines, and by the proudly poised head and legs, the nobility of a thoroughbred horse.

One of the most vigorous pieces of Greek sculpture of the late archaic period is the *Archer* (Illustration 106), which originally was one of a group of figures that decorated the pediment of the *Temple of Aphaia*. What a forceful figure he is! His erect back and powerful left arm holding his bow, and the diagonal balance of his legs establish a perfectly poised figure. You will find it interesting, at this time, to look again at the *Hera of Samos,* on page 110. She was carved only about fifty years before the *Archer*. Do you not believe that the Greek sculptor made rapid strides in reaching his goal of representing an ideally perfect figure with restraint and dignity?

Climax of Greek Sculpture

During this time, when Greece was at the height of her intellectual power, a number of sculptors produced statues that have become, for

The head of this young man has the features, deep-set eyes, straight, high-bridged nose, and full lips that we call classic. His serene beauty typifies the Greek spirit in art.

107.   **HEAD OF A YOUNG MAN**   *Greece*

Just as the *Head of a Young Man* typifies the Greek ideal of masculine beauty, so this superb *Head of Athena* portrays its feminine counterpart. Have our standards of beauty changed since those days?

108.   **HEAD OF ATHENA**   *Greece*

Although this figure is far more natural in appearance than any of the Greek sculpture you have seen thus far, you will notice that it is also restrained in action and in gesture. While rhythmic curves lend grace to the figure, their movement has been held in check by verticals and diagonals that bring your eye to and around the head of the figure.

109. **DIANA FASTENING HER CAPE** *Greece*

This statuette has a youthful and lively quality. The sculptor has subtly suggested the rhythmic movements of a gay little dance by the position of the head and leg, and by the flowing lines of the costume.

110. **DANCING GIRL** *Greece*

many people, symbols of perfection in sculpture. Myron, whose *Discus Thrower* you may have seen, specialized in figures in vigorous action. Polyclitus made extensive studies to determine the most perfect of human proportions. His intensive interest in this subject was reflected, at a later period, in the work of one of his successors, the famous and so-called perfectly proportioned *Venus de Milo.* Phidias, who was in charge of the sculpture of the *Parthenon,* may have carved some of the beautiful figures that once adorned its pediment. Only fragments of these sculptures remain, but we become aware of their serene beauty when we see the *Head of a Young Man* (Illustration 107), which might have been carved by Phidias himself. All these sculptures originally were painted, either in whole or in part, in bright colors, just as the *Parthenon* was. The color has, perhaps fortunately, disappeared, leaving only the warm, clear tone of the marble for us to enjoy.

Praxiteles, a later sculptor, became famous for the grace of his figures. *Diana Fastening Her Cape,* shown in Illustration 109, is a Roman replica of a statue of his time which definitely shows his influence. Again, we may see how the Greeks continued to idealize the human figure and to make it as beautiful a type as possible. It is as though the sculptor worked from many living models and carefully selected the best features of each one.

After the fourth century B.C., the quality of Greek sculpture gradually declined. Sculptors swung away from the restrained and noble figures carved by their predecessors and produced painfully realistic ones, often trite and in poor taste. In this period of the decline of Greek sculpture, the terra-cotta figurines from Tanagra and Tarentum are the one bright spot. Although hundreds of these beautiful little figures have been found in graves, their exact purpose there is unknown. Fresh and charming, the *Dancing Girl,* shown in Illustration 110, even though in miniature, has the fundamental qualities of fine sculpture.

Roman Sculpture

The predecessors of the Romans, the Etruscans, were artists of note. Remains of their gaily decorated homes, of their sculpture and

111. STRIDING WARRIOR *Italy*

Eight feet high and made of baked terra cotta, this Etruscan figure has added interest through the red and white design that emphasizes the eyes and certain features of the armor. The left hand at one time must have held a shield; the right is poised to hurl a spear. Balanced angular movements suggest his great strength.

Minor Arts, show that they were a creative, imaginative people, by nature akin to their Greek neighbors. Had they not been conquered and assimilated by the Romans, there is little doubt that they would have made many fine contributions to the traditions of art. The huge *Striding Warrior* (Illustration 111), with its vigorously opposed angles, is a dynamic and virile figure, and one that tells us that its creator had great powers both of invention and of execution.

The Romans, in general, were content to copy and to modify Greek sculpture in their efforts to adorn their temples and to glorify their rulers. Although Roman variations of Greek sculpture generally were far from notable, in portraiture the Roman sculptor made a distinctive contribution to sculptural art. The bronze head of *Caesar,* shown in Illustration 112, was made by an unknown artist about 50 B.C. Notice how adept the sculptor was at combining the physical characteristics of his subject with a strong suggestion of Caesar's imperious nature.

The Roman sculptor of portraits established a type of portrait bust that has been extensively copied, even to this day. You may be interested to know that the Roman was the first to work from a wax life or death mask of his subject, which helped him to obtain a striking likeness.

The Far-Eastern World

In earlier chapters, we have traced the slow course of prehistoric, primitive, and early man through his cultural infancy. We have heard of the rise and fall of Egypt, of Mesopotamia, of Greece, and of the Roman Empire; we have seen the foundations of our own cultural traditions being built upon the ruins of these ancient civilizations.

Much of this story of man's development is not new to you. Those who are especially interested in history probably know far more about it than can be told in these brief chapters. Though we are familiar with Western civilization, most of us know comparatively little of the distant civilizations of the Far East. We Westerners for a long time have either ignored the culture of the Far East or dismissed it as something foreign and unrelated to our own cultural traditions. A new and enterprising generation of art-lovers will doubtless be more in-

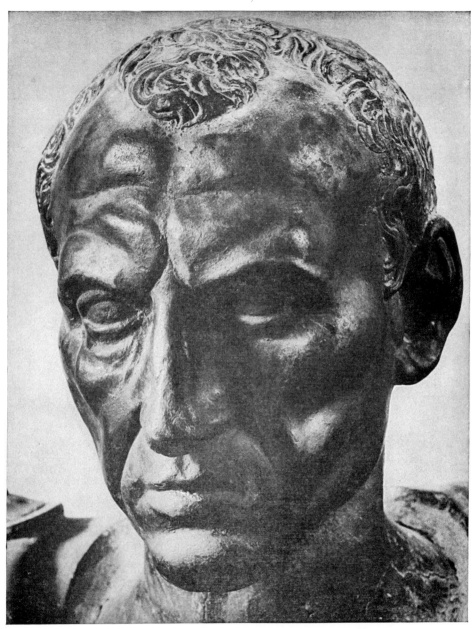

112. PORTRAIT OF CAESAR *Italy*

The play of light and shadow over the furrowed surface of this polished bronze head aids in producing an almost startling, lifelike effect. Portrait busts such as this were made to glorify the imperious Roman rulers.

Of the materials used by early man to fashion his implements and works of art, bronze is second only to stone. This beautifully designed and ornamented bronze vessel shows the mastery of its creator over the difficult process of casting in metal.

This energetic little bear has been simplified by its sculptor into a compact form. Its quietly humorous expression and agreeable alertness are appealing.

113. **WINE VESSEL** *China*

114. **STATUETTE OF A BEAR** *China*

terested in knowing something of the art of these countries with which we are becoming more and more familiar every day.

China of the Past

The vast spaces of China saw the beginnings of culture even earlier than Europe did. As you may know, archeologists determine the degree of civilization reached at various times in various parts of the world by the kind of utensil—stone, iron, pottery, or bronze—that they unearth. Thus the bronze mirrors, bells, and ceremonial vessels found in China proved that a high degree of civilization had been reached as early as 1766 B.C., for these bronzes not only are expert in craftsmanship but also show a feeling for design far beyond contemporary European metalwork. When you examine the bronze wine vessel (Illustration 113) made well over three thousand years ago, are you not amazed at the almost modern quality of its design?

China's historical and cultural development has been recorded by dynasties. A dynasty represented the span of time in which successive rulers inherited their power from some member of their family. The four dynasties notable for having produced especially fine art work are the Han (206 B.C.–A.D. 220), the T'ang (A.D. 618–906), the Sung (A.D. 960–1280), and the Ming (A.D. 1368–1644).

To Westerners the Oriental mind has often seemed difficult to understand. Yet, in many ways, the early man of China was similar both mentally and in his physical life to other early men. Like them, he was an agriculturist, and like all other men who lived close to the earth, he used the forms of nature in all of his artistic expressions. He not only delighted in making animal forms, some fanciful and others of everyday life, but also used countless motifs, such as the cloud and thunder pattern, to ornament his work.

Like other early men, he was an ancestor worshiper. He had more than pious respect for his departed ancestors, for he revered them as though they were gods and felt that by acts of reverence he could perpetuate their spirit.

It is not strange, therefore, to find that the Chinese sculptor followed the world-wide custom of making comforting effigies of humans and animals to place within the graves of the deceased. From the

123

115. LAO TSE ON A WATER BUFFALO *China*

Placidly seated on a dangerous and almost untamable beast, Lao Tse preaches his doctrine of the power of spiritual accomplishment. This small piece of sculpture in bronze is both subtle and sympathetic.

In this fragment of a stone relief several repetitions of the curve are to be seen around the top of the headdress. A second, flatter type of curve is also to be seen along the edge of the broken background. In what way do these curves express the spirit of the subject?

116. BODHISATTVA *China*

tombs of the Han dynasty many favorite pets, some of bronze and others of terra cotta and stone, have been recovered. One of these is the gilded bronze *Statuette of a Bear,* shown in Illustration 114. This is a beautifully simplified piece of sculpture, compact and highly expressive of a playful bear cub.

Religions of China

Most of us have heard of Confucius, a religious leader in China in the fifth century B.C. A great scholar, he combined the wisdom of past Chinese scholars and gave to his followers detailed formulas which told them exactly what to think, to say, and to do. Confucianism, which regulated the lives of its followers according to the precepts of the highly respected past, could not and did not produce much creative art, for individuality had no place within its beliefs and practices.

Fortunately, a second great leader, Lao Tse, a contemporary of Confucius, did not believe that thinking and action should be controlled by rules and regulations. He counseled his followers, known as Taoists, to think for themselves and to seek spiritual rather than physical satisfaction. To accomplish this, he advised them to leave crowded cities and go out into the country, there to spend hours in contemplating nature and identifying themselves with it. Belief in Taoism inspired some supremely beautiful landscape painting, an example of which may be seen on page 160.

The spirit of the leader of this movement has been most sympathetically portrayed in *Lao Tse on a Water Buffalo* (Illustration 115), a small bronze statue of the Sung dynasty. A kindly, serene, and happy figure, it is expressive of his belief in an unseen force whose energies are used for the spiritual well-being of humanity.

A third religion, Buddhism, came from India to China during the first century of this era. Buddha had taught the individual to think and act for himself, to rid himself of all earthy desires, to immerse himself in nature and to seek salvation through endless meditation. Since the Buddhists considered the human body the "temple of the spirit," Chinese sculptors, for the first time, represented the human body. Cave temples dedicated to the worship of Buddha were elaborately decorated with many figures. Some of these were cut directly into the

117.   BODHISATTVA ON A DOUBLE LOTUS LEAF
China

The serenity of Buddhist sculpture is beautifully expressed by the
flowing movements of this rhythmic figure.

rocky walls and represented Buddha and the Bodhisattvas, the half-divine beings who might one day become Buddhas.

A fragment of one of these decorations (Illustration 116) shows a figure that is expressive of the serenity and the compassion of the Buddhist spirit. The beads are praying beads, the hand is uplifted in a gesture symbolic of teaching.

The lovely *Bodhisattva on a Double Lotus Leaf* (Illustration 117) seems to breathe a message of spiritual harmony. The figure is beautifully restrained, as are the rhythmic line movements of the costume. It is interesting to note that this figure was carved during the T'ang period when China had reached its first Golden Age. At this time, Europe was yet in the dark Ages, and only one other country, India, had reached a cultural level comparable with that of China.

Early Indian Art

Hindu art had a long period of early development, for Indian civilization, like that of China, goes far back into the past, starting about 3300 B.C. To understand this art, we must have some knowledge of the principal Indian philosophies.

Either of the two most widespread religions of India, Brahmanism and Buddhism, may be said to be as much a way of life as a religion. Each completely controlled the lives of its followers. Each led to the giving up of the pleasures of the physical world and the seeking of of a spiritual world.

It is difficult for the Occidental to grasp the Oriental philosophy that denies the practical world. We accept our everyday, material world. In fact, most of us find pleasure in adjusting ourselves to take advantage of all that it offers. In contrast, the Hindu is taught that through meditation and the denial of worldly pleasures, he must elevate his spirit, or soul, into a pure state and thus ensure its immortality, or attainment of Nirvana.

The Hindu Sculptor

The Hindu sculptor approached his sculptural problem in a way that would seem very strange to you. Suppose, for example, that you

Indian civilization and religious beliefs spread to Java and Ceylon. Among the many shrines to be found in Java is the *Bawon Temple,* a small structure enlivened by the play of light and shadow that enriches its sculptured and faceted surfaces.

118. **BAWON TEMPLE** *Java*

This sculptured relief on the wall of a temple in Ceylon shows a rhythmic design which encircles a serene and beautifully poised figure of *Buddha.* This panel is typical of the hundreds of thousands that appeared on and within Buddhist temples and again reminds us how closely sculpture and architecture were connected during this time.

119. **BUDDHA** *Ceylon*

wanted to model some kind of religious figure. You might have a certain pose or a particular emotion in mind. Possibly you would get someone to pose for you. As you worked, your ideas about your subject would grow, and your final figure might be quite different from the one you first thought of.

Your way of working, in any event, would be a very different one from the way in which the Hindu sculptor worked. Do you know what he would do first? He would practice yoga, which means that he would sit silently for hours, forgetting all the world around him. Through meditation he would seek to identify himself with the religious figure he wished to portray. Only when every detail of it was clear in his mind and he felt that he himself had become that figure, would he be ready to work.

In his meditations the Hindu sculptor did not try to visualize a new interpretation of his theme, for that to him was unthinkable. Very definite and detailed rules dictated the appearance, the pose, the proportions, and all other details of the figure, even down to such minute details as the length and width of its nostrils.

These rules were accepted without question for, according to the Hindu theory, no statue could be beautiful unless it conformed to the rules. However, even within these limitations, or possibly because of them, the Hindu produced some of the most beautiful figures in all the history of religious sculpture.

Hindu Sculpture

Sculpture was the leading servant of the Hindu way of life. Profusely ornamented temples and shrines housed hundreds of sacred figures. These temples and shrines changed in character from the first century through medieval times, but all of them had sculpture as an integral rather than as an added part of the form. Although at first glance a Hindu temple may seem amazingly complex, as you can see by looking at Illustration 118, basically it echoes other early forms of architecture. Compare *Bawon Temple* with the *Caracol Tower* on page 53 and you will find that this is so.

The god Brahma, "the Creator," was the central figure of the Brahman religion. He is shown in Illustration 120, seated in a tradi-

120. **BRAHMA** *India*

The four faces of *Brahma* are symbolic of the four quarters of the earth. The monumental quality of the large stone statue is relieved by a surface decoration which, like the four faces, has symbolic meaning.

Once you accustom yourself to the idea of a four-armed body, you can find many things to interest you in this vivid bronze statue. Although you have seen strange bird, animal, and human figures that represent the gods of their creators, not one of them has shown this highly inventive conception of a deity. Notice how the multiple and significantly placed hands give a feeling of endless movement.

121. **DANCING SIVA** *India*

The excessively thin figure, almost stripped of flesh, is in striking contrast with the solidly rounded head of this bronze statue of *Kali*. The forceful quality of this piece of Brahman sculpture is also in marked contrast with the passive serenity of the Buddhist figures you have seen on pages 128 and 130.

122. **KALI WITH CYMBALS** *India*

tional attitude of worship. His figure has the calm and reposeful qualities designed to assist a worshiper in his meditations.

Another of the Brahman gods is Siva, "the Destroyer," and "Lord of the Dance." His energetically dancing figure is to be seen in Illustration 121. The Hindu describes him in these words: "Our Lord is the dancer who, like the heat latent in firewood, diffuses his power in mind and matter, and makes them dance in their turn. The drum in his upper right hand stands for creative sound; the flame in his upper left, the fire of destruction."

Kali, "Dark Mother," and wife of Siva, is the goddess of death and destruction. She is invariably represented as seen in Illustration 122, with elongated ear lobes and fanged teeth, and with her body encircled by a snake. Although her figure here is dynamic, it has a certain repose characteristic of Hindu religious figures.

Oriental sculpture, upon first acquaintance, often seems strange and even baffling. Its fantastic figures for which no model ever posed, its amazing technical skill, and its unfamiliar meanings seem far removed from our Western idea of religious sculpture. It will be especially interesting, therefore, to contrast Oriental sculpture with some work done at approximately the same time by the sculptors of the Middle Ages in Europe.

Gothic Sculpture

In the illustrations in previous chapters you have seen a few of the many famous Gothic cathedrals erected by medieval Christian builders, and you have found that sculpture was an integral part of these cathedrals. Builder, sculptor, and craftsman worked as one man, who, although forever anonymous, brought all of the rich resources of art to add to the glory of his God.

A glance back to the Gothic cathedrals you have seen on pages 102 and 106, will remind you that sculpture was always used traditionally above and around their portals. Illustration 123 shows sculpture from the north entrance of *Chartres Cathedral*. Notice that the upward movement of Gothic cathedrals is repeated in these narrow, elongated figures, each so clearly stamped with a particular individuality, and yet each an integral part of an almost endlessly rhythmical

123. NORTHERN PORTAL, CHARTRES *France*

Here you see how the Gothic sculptor taught the lessons of the Bible before the days of the printed book. Three figures from the Old Testament, *Melchisedek,* "a priest of the Most High God"; *Abraham* offering the bound figure of his young son, *Isaac,* for sacrifice; and *Moses,* holding a tablet inscribed with the Ten Commandments, all tell their stories vividly.

surface pattern in stone. The play of light and shadow upon these beautifully sculptured figures adds both to their vital, personal qualities and to the beauty of the cathedral as well.

The sculptor of the Middle Ages, whether portraying divine or human beings, seemed to infuse them with the spirit of his own warm and personal devotion. The *Shepherds of the Nativity* (Illustration 124) is, again, a story in stone told not with words but with a chisel and hammer directed by the sculptor's unfailing instinct for an unpretentious yet masterly presentation of a theme. The sculptor carved this story of the Nativity, together with a host of other subjects on the walls, not only of Chartres, but of every other Gothic cathedral in order that they might be readily seen and convey their message. The Gothic sculptor also placed his sculpture on dramatic heights. Thus the *Angel of Notre Dame, Chartres* (Illustration 125), from the towering heights of her pinnacle, stands as a guardian over the houses clustered about the cathedral to protect their inhabitants.

Sculpture and the Spiritual Life

You have seen how, for centuries, in clay and stone, in bronze and wood, man was primarily concerned with fashioning images representing his deities or honoring them. Sculpture was more than an incidental pleasure in his life; it was an expression of the strongest force within him, his belief in the existence of his gods and his need to embody them in concrete form. Thus the art of sculpture became a great and noble art, and one perhaps that speaks to us more clearly than any other form of art.

Students of art will find that these two quaint figures are not only a lively expression of a religious subject, but also interesting in appearance. The Gothic sculptor garbed his subjects in the costume of his day. The tunic, robe, and cape, the stiff, pointed hat of the shepherd on the left, as well as the stockings of the one on the right, have been faithfully reproduced in stone.

124. **SHEPHERDS OF THE NATIVITY, CHARTRES**
France

Man's eternal belief in a protecting spirit above him is typified by this sculptured angel, forever watchful and omnipotent.

125. **ANGEL OF NOTRE DAME, CHARTRES** *France*

126. THE THREE KINGS

Here you can see how bits of glass and stone were used to form a flat mosaic decoration. Close inspection makes you realize also how rigid and difficult a medium mosaic must have been.

127. MADONNA AND CHILD

At this time formulas controlled the way in which the artist was allowed to represent his subjects, just as they controlled Egyptian mural painting. The gestures of the Holy Family, for example, as well as the colors of their costumes, were strictly prescribed. In spite of such rules, the message of both this mosaic and the one above was forcefully expressed.

7.

Early Painters

MANY of you love to draw and paint, and have done so since your childhood days. Suppose that an artist saw your work one day and was so impressed with it that he took you to his studio and gave you lessons in drawing and painting. This happened to many a youthful artist in the past and, in some cases, he became more famous than his teacher.

At the close of the thirteenth century in Italy, a Florentine painter, Cimabue (1240–1301), took into his studio a young boy named Giotto. The legend is that Cimabue discovered the youthful artist drawing pictures of the sheep he was tending. At twelve years of age, Giotto (1266–1337) was a pupil; when only twenty-four, he was a recognized master of painting. Today he is considered one of the greatest painters of all time.

To understand Giotto's unique accomplishments, you should first review your knowledge of the age in which he lived. It was an age of great religious fervor, and building and ornamenting Christian churches was the concern of every man. One of the most important features of the churches in Italy at that time was the interior wall decoration. The churches, Italian Gothic in style, were so constructed that they provided ample wall space on which to portray, and so to teach to the illiterate worshipers, all the important concepts of the Christian religion.

137

128. THE VIRGIN ENTHRONED *Giotto*

In an almost childlike way, Giotto made the Mother and Child larger than the attending saints and angels in order to emphasize Their importance. The way in which he placed the lesser figures, one behind the other, adds to the compactness of the group and detaches it from the flat gold background.

Before Cimabue and Giotto started to paint religious themes, mosaics were the accepted form of church decoration in Italy, and had been for about eight centuries. On page 90 you have seen the mosaic decorations over the altar of the early Christian church of *St. Apollinare in Classe.* Another equally famous church, *St. Apollinare Nuevo,* also built during the sixth century in Ravenna, was similarly decorated with rich and colorful mosaics. Illustration 126, a section of a continuous mural that decorates its upper walls, shows *The Three Kings* bringing gifts to the Christ Child. He appears with His Mother and attendant saints in the next panel, to be seen in Illustration 127. As with all Byzantine mosaics, rich colors and beautifully patterned surfaces gleam against a resplendent gold background. The vigorous pose and lively movements of the kings are a contrast to the almost motionless figures of the Mother and Child. Incomparable dignity and a restraint imposed both by the spirit of the times and by the nature of mosaic itself, combine to give us a memorable example of early Christian art.

The Painter Offers His Services to the Church

As the fame of Giotto's painting spread, he was called upon to decorate church after church. He chose to execute his religious themes in paint rather than in mosaics. It is fascinating to see how Giotto, a highly creative painter, departed little by little from the traditional and prescribed Byzantine way of presenting the story of Christianity. Compare Illustrations 127 and 128, and you will see that although at first he retained the flat gold background used by the Byzantine artists, he gradually introduced a feeling of roundness in his figures and of depth in his scene. Figures no longer were placed in a straight line across the front of a picture; they move back into it as well as across it. Even the throne of the Virgin has a three-dimensional quality.

In his early twenties, Giotto painted his famous murals in the *Church of St. Francis* at Assisi. When you look at his *Adoration of the Magi,* shown in Illustration 129, you will see how he expanded the realm of painting, for more and more of his compositions became definitely three-dimensional. They included a landscape background,

139

129. ADORATION OF THE MAGI *Giotto*

Eleven people and three camels appear in this tenderly emotional scene, yet it does not seem crowded because of Giotto's mastery of compositional arrangement. Which figure do you feel is most important?

130. THE ANNUNCIATION *Simone Martini*

The line movements of the pointed Gothic arches that frame this altar piece are the key to its line scheme. Search carefully for these movements throughout the painting and you will see how they unify the figure of the Virgin and the lightly poised angel.

131. **JOURNEY OF THE MAGI** *Sassetta*

even though it was a limited one somewhat like the backdrop on the stage of a theater. Notice how his figures, by their gestures as well as by their grouping, move through a definite space, even though a narrow one. They are so convincing as figures that we feel we could easily walk around them. The little architectural structures that Giotto devised, which are reminiscent of stage sets, are an important part of his compositional arrangement.

Giotto's supreme triumph was his capacity for making his holy subjects appear both ideal and human. Again compare his figures with the aloof and formal Byzantine figures and you will see how different they are in spirit. His simple, warm, and intimate approach to his subjects is felt. In these qualities he reflects the teaching of St. Francis of Assisi who, discarding all worldly goods and assuming the humble garb of a beggar, taught by word and by deed both the dignity of the human soul and the beauty of the world his Maker had created.

Many contemporaries and followers of Giotto were impressed with the spirit of St. Francis, and were equally inspired to place their art at the service of Christianity. One of these, Simone Martini (1285–1344), a Sienese artist, painted with the great delicacy and individual style that we notice in his *Annunciation* (Illustration 130). The gold background, together with the poetic, rather than human qualities of the figures, are typical of the painters of Siena, who retained many of the decorative features of the Byzantine artists.

While many of the paintings of this time were murals painted with fresco paint directly on the walls of the churches, many others were executed on elaborately framed wooden panels and were used as altar pieces. Tempera was used by the artists, for the use of oil as a painting medium had not been discovered.

The *Journey of the Magi* (Illustration 131) by Sassetta (1392–1450), who, like Simone Martini, was a Sienese painter, has an irresistible, naïve charm. Bright reds, pinks, and blues contrasted with subtle background colors help to suggest lively movement.

Fra Angelico's Paintings

Almost one hundred years from the time that Giotto became famous, another remarkable Florentine painter, Fra Angelico (1387–

1455), made a supremely beautiful contribution to religious painting. Already highly trained as an artist at the age of twenty, he entered the Dominican order and became famed for his piety and humility. His *Paradise* (Illustration 132), a section of his *Last Judgment,* is radiant with love for his Lord and His Heavenly Kingdom. Much of the beauty of Fra Angelico's painting comes from the care with which he painted the details of nature. This precise and naïve way of working is called "primitive" today, although there was nothing primitive about the way in which Fra Angelico thoughtfully organized and skillfully executed his paintings.

When you look at his *Flight into Egypt* (Illustration 133), as well as at other paintings you have previously seen in this chapter, you will notice that some of the figures are dressed in the costumes of the painter's own time, although they represent in many cases people who lived in another country over a thousand years before the artist himself lived. You may wonder whether these Italian artists worked from posed models. There is little evidence to show that they did. It is believed that instead of using models, they constantly observed the people around them and painted from a memory sharpened by habitual use.

Although Giotto, Fra Angelico, Simone Martini, and Sassetta lived in the first part of the age called the Renaissance, their paintings were medieval, rather than Renaissance in character. Let us consider briefly the spirit of that period, often called the Golden Age of painting.

Italian Renaissance

The Renaissance may be considered, above all, an age of intellectual curiosity. Its scholars, seeking for learning in fields beyond religion, delved into the art, literature, and philosophy of the forgotten Greek and Roman classics. Interest in learning flourished even in the home of the common man, for the invention of the printing press had placed books at his disposal.

The Crusades had long ago opened up the Orient to Europeans and had revealed to them cultures other than their own. The resulting world trade had enlarged the mental and physical horizons of man.

132. PARADISE, DETAIL *Fra Angelico*

The tranquillity of this scene of dazzling heavenly glory and the tenderness with which the figures were painted reflect the gentleness and sweetness of Fra Angelico.

133. FLIGHT INTO EGYPT *Fra Angelico*

The color quality of a painting is generally one of the greatest sources of the pleasure that it gives. It is unfortunate, therefore, that you must often imagine the color when you are unable to see the original. Fra Angelico used clear, jewel-like colors in this small painting. Notice how the repetitions of various line movements add to the impression of weary flight.

134. THE TRIBUTE MONEY, DETAIL *Masaccio*

The figures encircling Christ are organized into a compact group which is set in a deep, open space. Notice the atmospheric quality which pervades the painting.

A continuous flow of line rhythms unites this group and also relates it to the background. Notice the particular quality of the curve to be seen, for example, in the light robe of the nearest figure. You will find that this curve, which effectively contrasts slow with rapid movement, is to be seen again and again throughout the painting.

135. VISIT OF THE QUEEN OF SHEBA
Piero della Francesca

Then, at the end of the fifteenth century, Columbus and other daring explorers discovered the rich and dazzling New World for the men of the Renaissance to explore, to settle, or to dream about.

The Renaissance is said to have produced more geniuses than any other age: supremely gifted scholars; literary men of the stature of Dante, Petrarch, and Boccaccio; scientists as great as Copernicus and Galileo; such remarkable painters as Leonardo da Vinci, Michelangelo, and Titian.

In your study of painting, it is profitable to see the work of some of the artists who came before these three great masters. One of these is Masaccio, who most perfectly typifies the adventurous spirit of the Renaissance.

Paintings of Masaccio

Masaccio (1401–1428), a young and highly gifted painter, made more use in his paintings of his keen observation of the visible world than any of his predecessors. His painting, *The Tribute Money,* shown in Illustration 134, is our first glimpse of what is now customarily called realistic painting. Notice that Masaccio defined his figures by broad planes of light and shadow, in contrast with Giotto and his contemporaries, who painted solid forms without using natural light and shadow. Parts of the bodies of Masaccio's figures are foreshortened; that is, they move away from or toward the spectators. Masaccio was the first both to pose and to paint figures in a way that made them appear more realistic.

Another interesting thing that Masaccio did was to create distance in his paintings, in contrast, again, with previous painters, who worked either within a flat and often gold background, or a restricted, boxlike setting. Masaccio did not clearly define his middle and distant areas, for he noticed that atmosphere makes these areas somewhat blurred and softened. Thus, the landscape areas of *The Tribute Money* are more realistic than any of those previously seen in the illustrations.

Although Masaccio died at the early age of twenty-seven, his few brilliant paintings pointed the way to a new approach in painting, a stress on realism. The science of light and shadow, of anatomy, and of

136. MADONNA ADORING THE CHILD *Fra Filippo Lippi*

This painter was more interested in realistic painting than his predecessors were. He shows the Mother and Child as people of his own, everyday world. Notice how compactly he has grouped the four figures in his composition.

perspective were to become the new goals toward which many of the Renaissance artists strove.

Other Early Renaissance Painters

This new approach to painting is very much in evidence in the work of Piero della Francesca (1416–1492), who shared with Masaccio the ability to plan and to execute his paintings with scientific detachment. Illustration 135 shows a detail of his famous *Visit of the Queen of Sheba.* Although Piero did not use light and shadow to model his figures, they are so convincingly drawn that they appear quite real. Notice that the figures toward the front of the painting are large, while those in the immediate background are proportionately smaller. The contrasted sizes of the figures help to suggest space and movement in the painting. The sky has been painted so that it suggests limitless distance.

In contrast to Masaccio and Piero, several artists at this time were not in the least interested in the newly discovered scientific rules of painting. Each was moved, instead, to paint in his own particular and independent way.

One of these painters was a Florentine, Fra Filippo Lippi (1416–1469). His robust vitality, his warm and essentially human rather than spiritual approach to his subjects, produced paintings that communicate their message in a most sympathetic way. His *Madonna Adoring the Child,* seen in Illustration 136, shows real people of the Florentine world. The Madonna is no longer traditionally gowned in a heavy, enshrouding cloak and veil; she is wearing a headdress that actually might have been worn in Fra Filippo's time. Her Child, a chunky, very human infant, is clearly a baby who is held up from time to time to pose for the painter. Of His two youthful angel-bearers, the one in the foreground searches for our approval of his good deed. It is evident that Fra Filippo Lippi was sufficiently interested in realism to use models for his paintings and to paint them as he saw them, with but little idealization.

Sandro Botticelli (1444–1510), a pupil of Fra Filippo Lippi, was another Florentine painter who was not primarily concerned with scientific painting but who centered his interpretations on his emotional

147

137.   THE VIRGIN, INFANT JESUS, AND ST. JOHN

Botticelli

Few observers fail to notice the spiritually moving appeal of this painting. Notice how beautifully hands describe the character of each figure: the humility of St. John, the tender protectiveness of the Virgin, and the trusting love of the Child for His Mother.

reactions to his themes. Like his teacher, he was a realist but unlike him, Botticelli saw the world through idealistic eyes. We have but to compare his *The Virgin, Infant Jesus, and St. John* (Illustration 137) with the *Madonna Adoring the Child* of Fra Filippo Lippi to see that his figures have a delicate and spiritual, rather than an earthy, quality.

Botticelli brought his figures to life through the vitality of their line movements rather than by showing their three-dimensional qualities. Notice how lines spring upward to unite the two figures, those of the seemingly weightless Child and His Mother.

Pageant Painters

Life in Italy during the Renaissance was a curious blend of the spiritual and the worldly. Painters were still preoccupied with religious themes, but many of them began to paint the actual people in the life about them. The first painter to combine a religious with a nonreligious theme in a vast panorama was Gentile da Fabriano (1360–1427). Illustration 138 is his *Adoration of the Magi.* You will notice that although the painter was interested in realism as so many of the painters of his time were, he still retained the richly decorative quality seen in earlier works, such as Fra Angelico's. Countless figures weave their way to the manger where the three kings present their traditional gifts to the Christ Child. Some of the vast amount of fascinating detail in the painting is symbolic. For example, the doves and certain of the animals are Christian symbols. Other little details, such as the servant removing the spur from the foot of the standing king, capture interest, for they are intimate bits of the life of the times.

Still another pageant painter, Benozzo Gozzoli (1420–1497) later chose the identical theme (Illustration 139) for his decoration of the Medici palace. The Medici, the ruling family of Florence at that time, gave him this commission and, possibly as a return of courtesy, he included four of their portraits in his scene. The *Journey of the Three Kings* is a vast panorama of figures and animals weaving their way along a rocky mountain pass. Again, the endless detail is fascinating. Notice, for example, the small figure in the background that is doing a little energetic hunting along the way.

138. ADORATION OF THE MAGI *Da Fabriano*

It is interesting to see how this painter has combined piety with
worldliness, and humbly garbed with sumptuously dressed people.
These contrasts make an unusually effective painting.

139. JOURNEY OF THE THREE KINGS *Gozzoli*

As with all pageant paintings, a rich, tapestry-like design of color in-
terwoven with gold creates a sparkling pattern. The procession weaves
its way through a landscape which combines fantasy with the spirit of
the local Italian countryside.

Da Vinci, Genius of the Renaissance

A famous biographer, Vasari, who lived in the days of the Renaissance, described Leonardo da Vinci (1452–1519) in the following way:

"The Heavens often rain down rich gifts on human beings. Sometimes, with lavish abundance, they bestow upon a single individual such beauty, grace, and ability that he outdistances all other men, and clearly displays how his genius is the gift of God and not an acquirement of human art. Men saw this in Leonardo da Vinci, whose personal beauty was remarkable, whose every movement was grace itself, and whose abilities were so extraordinary that he could readily solve every difficulty. He possessed great personal strength and courage, and a spirit invariably kind and generous. His fame so spread abroad that, not only was he valued and honored in his own day, but his renown has greatly increased since his death."

Leonardo da Vinci is probably one of the best-known artists of the world. His amazingly varied activities, his accomplishments as mathematician, scientist, engineer, poet, musician, and painter; his highly inventive mind; and the breadth and quality of his intellectual curiosity, together with his remarkable paintings, have marked Leonardo as the greatest figure in an age of greatness.

With our present-day interest in science and in engineering, every student knows that Leonardo was the first to foresee the submarine and the airplane, and that he actually constructed models of a "flying machine." Even designing many weapons of warfare, such as tanks, cannon, and other projectile-hurling instruments, was a part of his many and varied activities. Lovers of art, however, are particularly concerned with his accomplishments as a painter.

Because of his interests in so many other fields, Leonardo left only a few superb paintings for us to see and to admire. His *Virgin and Child with St. Anne* (Illustration 140) is a beautifully organized group of figures which, by the directions of line and form movements, creates what is called a pyramidal composition. One of the chief distinctions of Leonardo's painting is his subtle use of gradations, or tones shading from light to dark. Light bathes his subjects, shading

140. THE VIRGIN AND CHILD WITH ST. ANNE *Da Vinci*

Between Giotto and Leonardo there was a span of two hundred and fifty years. Ideas about painting naturally changed during that time. From Giotto's measured formality we come to Leonardo's masterful informality. His genius was such that he could combine both the human and the spiritual aspects of his subjects in a way that immeasurably increased their emotional appeal.

141.   MONA LISA, DETAIL   *Da Vinci*

The subtle quality that distinguishes Leonardo's painting is clearly seen here. Study the modeling of the head to see how deftly its solidity is suggested, as is the fleeting suggestion of the famous Mona Lisa smile.

imperceptibly into deep, mysterious shadows. Notice this quality here in his atmospheric landscape as well as in his figures.

The *Virgin and Child with St. Anne* was painted with oil paints, a new medium which had been perfected by contemporary Flemish painters. The use of an oil base produced a technique that allowed more fluidity than did the earlier tempera painting, for oil paint, as you probably know, is a very flexible medium.

The best-known of da Vinci's paintings is his *Mona Lisa,* a section of which is shown in Illustration 141. Again you see Leonardo's mastery in handling the most subtle gradations of light and shadow, and in interpreting his subjects with both grace and dignity.

The *Mona Lisa* is probably the most extensively discussed painting in history, both because many writers have been intrigued by the elusive and haunting personality of the sitter, La Gioconda, the wife of a Florentine merchant, and because of its spectacular theft from the Louvre Museum in Paris and its subsequent recovery.

Michelangelo, the Titan

You have seen *Moses,* one of the sculptures of Michelangelo, on page 3. It should not be a surprise to you to find power and virility in his paintings. Michelangelo was commissioned by Pope Julius II to decorate the ceiling of the *Sistine Chapel* of the Vatican at Rome. He complained bitterly before undertaking the momentous task because he considered himself primarily a sculptor.

It was, indeed, an ordeal which few painters could have survived. Michelangelo spent four and one-half years lying on his back on a scaffold in the Sistine Chapel painting the grandiose decorations which included three hundred and forty-three figures. A study of one of the figures, the *Delphic Sybil* (Illustration 142), shows that Michelangelo, the painter, was greatly influenced by Michelangelo, the sculptor. The powerfully painted figure has the same monumental quality found in his *Moses.* The vigor of its movements, accentuated by the forceful lines of drapery, reveal his tremendous power as a painter. The *Delphic Sybil* appears so solid that one might almost feel that it is a piece of sculpture rather than a painting.

Michelangelo's mastery of figure drawing has never been surpassed. He was not only a magnificent draughtsman but also a painter who used his understanding of the human figure to express in a powerful and individual way the complex ideas of his times.

142. **DELPHIC SYBIL** *Michelangelo*

Raphael's religious figures are far more human and less spiritual than Leonardo's, as you may see by comparing this painting with *The Virgin and Child with St. Anne* on page 152. Which interpretation do you prefer?

143. **MADONNA** *Raphael*

Raphael, the Beloved Painter

Raphael (1483–1520), like Giotto, was already famous at twenty-five, and until his death at the age of thirty-seven, was a favorite of fortune. The two great painters, Leonardo and Michelangelo, were his contemporaries and, in many cases, his rivals for fame and patronage. His accomplishments, seen through twentieth-century eyes, were not so great as theirs, because his paintings lacked Leonardo's subtlety and Michelangelo's force. Yet his popularity probably will always remain because of the refinement and charm of his religious paintings. The Madonna, Holy Child, saints, and cherubs who were depicted in his paintings have an immense appeal to many people because of their naturalness, their grace, and sweetness.

The *Madonna of the Goldfinch,* shown in Illustration 143, shows three figures set in a beautifully simplified but convincing landscape. They form the pyramidal composition used by Leonardo in his *Virgin and Child with St. Anne* (page 152), and they are firmly united both by gestures and by the way they look toward each other. Raphael's characteristic sweetness is evident.

Renaissance painting in Florence and in Rome, two of the important cultural centers in Italy at this time, was primarily intellectual. It was a magnificent product of sane, rational, and scientific thinking that appealed to the mind before it appealed to the senses. On the other hand, in Venice, the celebrated trade center of Europe, another phase of Renaissance art of quite a different nature may be seen.

Renaissance Painting in Venice

You have already seen the sumptuous *St. Mark's* in Venice on page 94, and have noted its Oriental features, so typical of the luxury-loving and emotional Venetian character. Venetian painting also appeals first to the emotions, then to the mind. Venetian painters thought naturally in terms of rich and sumptuous color, of jeweled and brocaded patterns and textures, of all the Oriental trappings that played such a part in their lives. Merchant princes and doges, or chief magistrates, demanded paintings that had a spirit of luxury

144. MIRACLE OF THE HOLY CROSS *Bellini*

Presenting memorable occasions in a pageant is a tradition with which we are all familiar. In Venice during the fifteenth century this colorful scene inspired Gentile Bellini to record his impressions of a moving and complex drama.

Historians generally describe famous men in a clear, concise way. Painters, too, are equally skilled in interpreting the personalities of the notables of their day. You may find it interesting to describe in your own words the qualities you think Giovanni Bellini brought out in his portrait of this magistrate.

145. DOGE LEONARDO LOREDANO
Bellini

or of pageantry, and often asked for paintings in which they themselves would be shown to great advantage. The Venetian painters gladly executed numerous oil paintings, in which they used color as it had never been used before.

The Bellini Brothers

A painting by Gentile Bellini (1429–1507), the *Miracle of the Holy Cross* (Illustration 144) records a pageant scene in Venice in which many figures, kneeling, sitting, and standing, encircle a central group. This group, in turn, rotates about a dramatic figure emerging from the waters of the canal. The organization of the numerous subordinate figures is masterly; the careful rendition of detail is charming.

A younger brother, Giovanni Bellini (1453–1516), gave the world, among his numerous paintings, a striking record of a famous personality of his time, the *Doge Leonardo Loredano*, chief magistrate of Venice, shown in Illustration 145. This direct and forceful portrait combines astute characterization with superbly rendered texture and pattern. Notice how the roundness and the solidity of the head have been suggested by the way in which the oddly shaped cap has been both drawn and painted.

Titian, Master of Venetian Painting

Venetian painting reached its climax in the work of Titian (1477–1576). This great master of painting had a long and spectacular career as a painter. Living to the ripe old age of ninety-nine, he did some of his best work when he was eighty. Titian's talent, like that of Giorgione and Tintoretto, his distinguished contemporaries, combined an intellectual vision with a remarkable and sure feeling for color. At times it was glowing, at other times subdued, but always color was used as a structural part of his painting.

One of his many highly admired works is *The Strozzi Child* to be seen in Illustration 146. The little light figure so effectively brought out by the dark, rich background seems to be in suspended motion. Some of this effect is due to the way in which her head is turned to face the artist. Titian's rich, glowing harmonies of color afford the

158

146. **THE STROZZI CHILD** *Titian*

eye great pleasure. You may want to compare this painting with Illustration 1 and search for similarities and contrasts in the work of Titian and Picasso.

The close of the Renaissance period in Italy was marked by a decline in painting. The great qualities of Michelangelo, Leonardo, and Titian were not matched by the painters who followed them. Fortunately, however, the rich benefits of this period were handed on to other countries. The great traditions of the Renaissance traveled abroad to the nations of the Old World and the New. Renaissance art, which was born in Italy, took on a different aspect in each country, according to the economic and social conditions, and to the temperament of its people. Before considering this development and continuity of a great tradition in painting, it would be of value to look at another, very different but equally brilliant kind of painting in the age-old country of China.

Chinese Painting

Just as in Italy the Renaissance produced poets and philosophers, scholars, and painters of great renown, so in China the Sung Dynasty (960–1280), known as the Second Golden Age of China, was distinguished by a fine flowering of creative thought and expression. An age of glorious painting, it was one that produced some of the most exquisite landscape painting of all time.

To grasp the full meaning of Chinese painting, you must know something about the philosophy of the Chinese painter which is, on the whole, quite different from that of the European painter, whose ideas are more familiar to you.

Chinese painters had an immense love of nature. They felt very close to it, for they identified themselves with each of its many and varied forms. The Chinese religion founded by Buddha urged each painter to observe and to meditate, long and thoughtfully; to seek the "essence" of a cloud, mountain, stream, tree, or blade of grass rather than only to observe its external, or outward, appearance. Suppose that you are a landscape painter. You might see a certain mountain and want to paint it because it looks unusually light and far away, or because it appears exceptionally colorful in the bright sun-

159

147. LANDSCAPE *Tung Yüan*

The vast mountains of China, rocky and topped with trees, rise above mist-filled valleys. Far below and to the left of the painting, are a temple and two minute figures overshadowed by the immensity of the surrounding landscape. What difference do you notice between the Eastern and the Western way of landscape painting?

This painting is a powerful illustration of what is meant by "painting the essence of a subject." Its emotional quality is inescapable.

148. TIGER *My Ch'i*

light, or because you observe some other unusual change in its general appearance. The Chinese painter, on the other hand, would never have been interested in painting such a temporary aspect of his subject. He trained his eye and his mind to search for and to record only its eternal qualities, such as its massiveness, its calmness, its delicacy, or its vitality. To him, only the "feeling" of his subject was important.

After a long, serene contemplation of nature, the painter retired to his studio and there painted the scene "he found in his heart." The quality and precision of each brush stroke placed on the paper or silk was of great importance for, since he used indelible ink, he could not go over his work. The freshness and vitality that came from this direct way of working are apparent in all Chinese painting.

In addition to paintings to be hung on a wall, Chinese painters often made continuous landscapes on long strips of paper or silk which unrolled from left to right and could be leisurely contemplated. The *Landscape* by Tung Yüan (Illustration 147), painted in the tenth century during the Sung Dynasty, is a section of a scroll painting. Notice that the feeling of depth has been achieved by the movement of the dark foreground tones to those of the lighter central section which move again to deeper tones. The painter made no use of shadows, such as those that might be cast by the trees or seen on the sides of the mountains. Shadowless painting is characteristic of all Chinese painting.

In contrast to the serene landscape by Tung Yüan, *Tiger by Waterfall* (Illustration 148) is arrestingly dynamic. Deep tones create a mood in keeping with the sinister beast that dominates the subtly suggested background.

The art of painting in China was early established and remained fixed by unchanging ideals for almost ten centuries, a remarkable span of time in the history of painting. In addition to the esthetic pleasure that it gives, it is worth while learning more about this art for it has greatly influenced many of the painters of our own generation, as is pointed out in a later chapter.

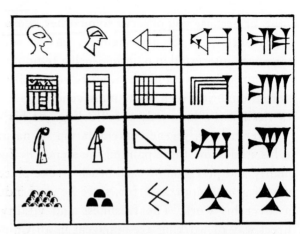

Writing made up of wedge-shaped letters was called cuneiform writing from the Latin word *cuneus*, which means wedge.

149. **WRITING: PICTOGRAPH TO CUNEIFORM**   *Mesopotamia*

The precision and detail seen in these tiny clay reliefs is truly amazing since the seals are only the size of a small spool. The owner of the upper seal, who was in the employ of the king, is shown standing before him. The lower relief seems to have an unmistakably humorous appeal.

150. **INSCRIPTIONS, CYLINDER SEALS**   *Mesopotamia*

8.

Enrichment of the
Minor Arts

YOU have been familiar with the alphabet for such a long time that you scarcely remember how you learned the A B C's. Your mastery of these letters has opened many new fields for your exploration. Writers of the past communicate with you directly through letters placed together to form words. These letters which represent sounds in words comprise an alphabet whose history has a direct contact with art, for the earliest form of letter or symbol was the pictograph. In other words, the earliest form of writing was picture writing.

Primitive man felt a need for communication that could not always be attained by voice or gesture. If for example, he wanted to warn his friends about a dangerous lion that frequented their hunting ground, he drew or scratched a picture of a lion on the ground or on a rock. He did not always draw the entire animal; sometimes he drew merely its sharp teeth or fierce claws, knowing that this communication would mean much to his companions who would arrive a little later on the scene. This use of symbols to convey ideas is picture writing, or a pictographic form of writing, and has been used the world over by primitive man.

Pictographs were used also to inform future generations of important historical events. Some of the earliest pictographs, which date as far back as 3200 B.C., were made by the Sumerians, early settlers of Mesopotamia, who scratched their symbols on moist tablets of clay with a triangular reed called a stylus.

The pictographs were greatly simplified into wedge-shaped symbols, as you may see by referring to Illustration 149, but they still represented ideas rather than sounds. Column 1 shows four drawings: a head, a temple, the Mother-Goddess, and a mountain, all taken from Sumerian cylinder seals, such as those you see in the following illustration. Column 2 shows the pictographic symbols for these same four drawings. Column 3 describes how these pictographs were gradually simplified, probably because it was easier to draw straight lines in sticky clay than it was to make them curved. During this same period in the development of writing, signs were turned at a right angle, as you notice, and were read from left to right instead of from top to bottom, as they had previously been read. In column 5 the symbols are further simplified. While the changes pictured here seem very logical, they developed over a long span of years, between 3200 B.C. and 400 B.C.

Cuneiform writing was used for thirty centuries by the Sumerians, the Assyrians, the Babylonians, and the Persians. Western scholars, after about fifty years of investigation, can now decipher this baffling alphabet.

Another interesting use of cuneiform writing is seen in Illustration 150. The Sumerians used small, beautifully engraved cylinders of stone to place their private inscriptions on records and on personal property. The little cylinder which was rolled over clay made a design such as you see here. When not in use, the cylinder seal was worn around the neck or the wrist of the owner as a lucky stone. The cuneiform inscription which was, of course, engraved in reverse on the seal, recorded the owner's name and business.

Egyptian Writing

The Egyptian form of writing, too, has its direct contact with art. This writing, known as hieroglyphics, literally means "sacred carving." Its beautifully designed symbols of people, animals, insects, and plant

151. STELE OF SENU *Egypt*

Hieroglyphics have been beautifully used as a meaningful part of the design of this finely carved limestone relief.

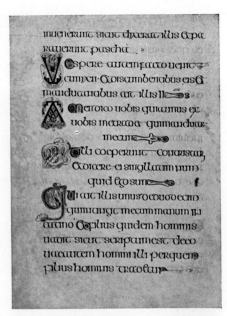

152. PAGE, BOOK OF KELLS
Ireland

You may see here not only the superb lettering but also the beautifully ornamented initial letters for which the *Book of Kells* is famous. Celtic craftsmanship in this art reached a degree of perfection that has never since been excelled.

**153. INITIAL LETTER,
BOOK OF KELLS** *Ireland*

life originally characterized ideas only, but later on the alphabet represented sounds in words as well. For example, the outline of an eye could stand for an eye, for the word "I," or for a vowel sound. Thus one letter had a three-fold message: first, it was the picture of an object; second, it represented a word by association, that is by what we call a pictograph; and third, it represented a sound.

The writer or artist, for he was both, inscribed his message with brush and ink on paper made from papyrus reed, or with chisel and paint on the surfaces of tombs, temples, and statues.

Illustration 151 shows an inscription carved in hieroglyphics on the face of a limestone stele, or memorial stone. Although some of us may be able to recognize a few of the individual pictorial symbols, on the whole we have no idea of the message they conveyed to the Egyptian reader. Fortunately, just as scholars persevered for years until they discovered the clue to cuneiform writing, so they labored until they finally deciphered the famous *Rosetta Stone,* which gave them the key to the Egyptian hieroglyphic alphabet. Thus a four-thousand-year record of Egyptian history and culture was made available to us.

Phoenician Alphabet

These two alphabets were so complicated and so difficult to read and to write that the services of a trained person, known as a scribe, were required both to read and to record a message, a business transaction, or a significant event. The Phoenicians, however, being both enterprising and practical, used a system of writing that represented sounds rather than pictures of ideas. Although this important step from recording pictures or symbols to writing sounds in words is somewhat shrouded in mystery, scholars agree that the Phoenicians adapted an archaic form of a Semitic alphabet to their needs. In any event, we know that our present alphabet descends from one used by the Phoenicians.

Phoenician navigators brought their alphabet to Greece where it was adapted to the language there. Next the Romans took it over for Latin, but their alphabet differs from the Greek because they took the Western form rather than the Athenian letters.

154. COVER, MANUSCRIPT OF THE GOSPELS *France*

This ninth-century cover for a precious manuscript, made of beaten gold and inlaid with elaborately set jewels, is considered one of the most beautiful pieces of craftsmanship of that period.

Our alphabet as we know it for English came to us by way of Ire-land. When St. Patrick was sent as a missionary from Rome to Ireland in the fifth century, he brought with him not only the teachings of the Christian religion, but the Roman alphabet as well. The Celts of Ireland, who were followers of the Druids at the time, and who were soon converted to Christianity, used the alphabet St. Patrick taught them for the writing of Old Irish. By the eighth century, Celtic monks had become renowned for their learning in the classics and in religion.

To further this new teaching, books were needed. The Celtic *Book of Kells,* two pages of which are shown in Illustrations 152 and 153, is considered one of the most beautifully hand-lettered books of all times. Not only the calligraphy, or beautiful hand-lettering, but also the intricate and handsomely decorated, or illuminated, capital letters show a high degree of artistry.

Medieval Manuscripts

During the Middle Ages, in many of the European countries, il-luminated manuscripts reached a peak of craftsmanship and of design never to be equaled in the next centuries. Almost entirely religious in character, for they were usually copies of the Bible in whole or in part, they were the prized possessions of churches, monasteries, and kings. These manuscripts reveal an amazing patience and disregard for the passage of time on the part of the scholar and artist. Their bindings, including covers (Illustration 154) and even containers in which to place them were richly decorated, often with enamels and jewels.

From England, for example, comes the fourteenth century *Wind-mill Psalter* (Illustration 155) and from Italy, the fifteenth century *Choir Book* (Illustration 156), both of which are magnificently de-signed and executed.

During Gothic and early Renaissance times, the craft of book-making no longer was centered in the monastery, but made its way into the universities that were slowly developing. It was customary for the rich men of those days to have made for themselves a *Book of Hours,* or a collection of prayers, psalms, and calendars to guide them in their religious devotions. See how beautifully the miniature painter

155. PAGE, WINDMILL PSALTER *England*

The lifelike figures that illuminate the capital letters of this famous fourteenth-century Latin manuscript reflect the contemporary painter's interest in realism. The calligraphy, written with a hand-shaped reed pen, is admirable for its perfection.

The illumination of manuscripts reached a high peak with medieval Italian choir books. Miniature paintings, brilliant in color and finely executed, were combined with lettering and musical notes.

156. PAGE, CHOIR BOOK
Italy

157. PAGE, HOURS OF THE VIRGIN *Portugal*

You may see here how beautifully the devotional books of this period were illustrated.

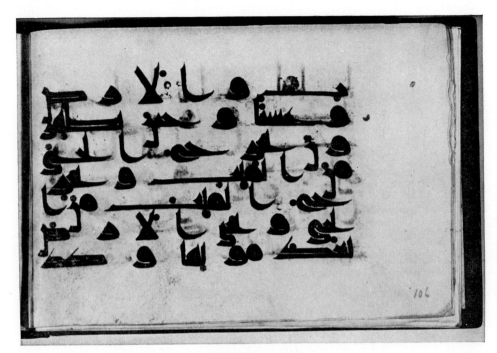

158. PAGE, THE KORAN *Persia*

Arabic script, with its interesting and varied symbols, creates a vigorous pattern of dark and light, well set off by the generous surrounding margins.

This *Description of Animals,* or *Bestiary,* describes their structure and habits, and gives almost 1000 prescriptions for medicines that can be made from various parts of their bodies.

159. MANUSCRIPT *Persia*

illustrated these books by examining a page from the *Hours of the Virgin,* shown in Illustration 157. Exquisite coloring, perfection in design and in craftsmanship, and a fine feeling for the design of the whole page made his work unique in the annals of art.

Contemporary with the spread of Christian learning and books of devotion, Jewish scholars and rabbis were inscribing beautifully illustrated little manuscripts that told stories from the Old Testament. These books, which were designed to make the stories more attractive to the readers or hearers, performed much the same function as the illustrated manuscripts of the lives of saints in the early medieval Christian church.

Oriental Calligraphy

The art of calligraphy was also considered one of the highest forms of art in the Near and the Far East. In luxury-loving Persia, for example, during the sixteenth century, the Shahs, or rulers, who were great admirers of beautiful books, kept at their courts the best artists of the times to produce them. In Illustration 158 is shown a page from the Koran, the sacred book of the Islamic religion, which is comparable to the Christian Bible. It is beautifully lettered in Arabic script, an alphabet that might have been the one adopted by Europeans if the Roman alphabet had not developed as it did.

The traditions of the Koran did not permit illustrated texts, but countless nonreligious books gave the Persian illustrator, or miniature painter, a wonderful opportunity to display his feeling for beautiful design and rich color. Illustration 159 shows a page from a thirteenth century Persian manuscript which is decorated with ninety-four miniature paintings. An inscription at the end of the book states that "it was finished with fortune and happiness." Notice how the rich surface pattern of the illustration and the Arabic script combine to form a unified and harmonious page.

In China, the vast and mysterious country of the Far East, the calligrapher is considered as important an artist as the painter. There the two arts have much in common. So many of us who scrawl, scribble, and in general take no pride in our handwriting, find this idea very "foreign." Chinese writing, based on what are called ideographs, is composed of highly abstract and beautifully designed symbols which

160. **BAMBOO IN THE WIND** *Wei Chû*

You may see here how Chinese calligraphy is treated as an important part of a painting. Infinitely subtle variations of brush strokes create significant shapes.

can be placed in endless combinations. Not only do the various combinations of their extensive alphabet give infinite variety to the idea expressed, but also the way in which the ink-laden brush of the writer touches the paper or silk is significant. For example, the Chinese symbol for "man" may be written so that it shows by the quality of the brush strokes whether the writer is referring to a strong man, a weak man, a scholar, or a lazy man. Illustration 160 shows a beautiful piece of Chinese calligraphy with its fascinatingly designed letters. If you could read Chinese, you would start at the right and read down each column. This is, of course, a complete change from the way of reading to which you are accustomed.

Block Books

In the fifteenth century, European artists discovered a way of reproducing drawings quickly and cheaply. This was by a block print. You are all familiar with the process of cutting a wood or linoleum block; so you know that you simply cut away all the parts that you do not want to show and you leave standing all those that constitute your design. You then ink the surface of the block and stamp it on paper and so produce a block print.

By this process cards showing pictures of saints or of religious scenes, with bits of lettering as part of the design, were made and sold to people for their private devotions. When a number of these block prints were bound together, they formed a picture prayer book which often included quite a little lettering, cut in reverse on the block. Bright color was generally added to the pages by hand. This art of printing religious pictures was a popular one. Equally popular was that of designing and printing playing cards that were similarly hand colored.

Art of Printing

About 1450, Johann Gutenberg (about 1398–1468), a German printer who had had considerable experience in printing block books, produced a printing press, one of the most important inventions of all time. The use of movable letters, or type, held together in a frame and printed mechanically on a printing press, made possible the rapid

161. PAGE, BLOCK BOOK *Netherlands*

This fifteenth-century block book, which illustrates the *Song of Songs of Solomon,* shows an early and interesting stage in the development of the art of woodcutting. Notice that various figures and architectural units are in different scales, for the artist was interested in creating a symbolic rather than an actual scene.

162. PLAYING CARDS *France*

The evolution of the playing card and the widely varied forms it has taken throughout the centuries would make a fascinating study for students of art. Here are some block-printed playing cards. Their vigorous patterns were generally enhanced by brilliant spots of color applied by hand.

duplication of books, made them substantially cheaper, and thus available to everyone. You must realize, in order to fully appreciate this invention, that up to this time only scholars could read and write. Now, through the medium of books, all could become literate and all could thus possess the key to learning.

The famous *Gutenberg Bible,* a page of which is shown in Illustration 163, is the first Latin Bible as well as the first large book to be printed in Europe. For its type, Gutenberg copied hand-lettering from a manuscript similar to that shown in *The Windmill Psalter,* page 170. The letters were first engraved in a block of metal, then cast in quantity in lead.

Even with the help of the press, printing the two-volume *Gutenberg Bible* must have been a laborious process, for only one page could be printed at a time. Certain letters of the text were subsequently colored in by hand, and the illuminated capital letters, such as the one you have doubtless noticed, were drawn and similarly colored by hand. A lavish use of color and of pure gold enriched the illumination. The general effect of this book and others that followed was naturally similar to that of a hand-lettered manuscript.

Subsequent improvements in the construction of the printing press, and the development of printing by folios, that is, printing two, four, or eight pages at a time, speeded up actual production. Although quantities of religious books were still produced, the works of classical writers, such as Cicero and Homer, together with treatises on science, astronomy, and poetry were popular. Eventually the works of contemporary writers, such as Chaucer in England and Villon in France, found their way into print, thus giving great impetus to popular and contemporary writing. Illustration 165 shows a page from the *Canterbury Tales,* by Chaucer. This book was the second edition of that now famous work to be printed, and the first edition to be illustrated with block prints.

Each country in Europe produced outstanding printers who were very much concerned with making their books works of art. Many of these early master printers designed type faces which bear their names today. This book, for example, is printed in Caslon type, a modern version of a type face designed by William Caslon (1692–1766), a famous English designer and printer.

Naturally, the early printed books were illustrated with woodcuts,

163. **PAGE, GUTENBERG BIBLE** *Germany*

This handsome page contains a part of the preface written by St. Jerome, who made the Latin translation of the Bible. Of the three hundred copies printed of this famous Bible, only forty-five are known to be in existence.

164. PRINT SHOP *Germany*

A sixteenth-century engraver left us this interesting record of an early stage in the printing industry. At the left, a worker is pulling the press; in the background, type is being set.

165. PAGE, CANTERBURY TALES *England*

William Caxton, a famous English printer of the fifteenth century, designed this edition of Chaucer's *Canterbury Tales*. Although few can read the English text of that period, the direct and almost childlike quality of the illustrations has a universal appeal.

166. TEMPTATION OF ST. ANTHONY *Schöngauer*

What fascinating creatures of evil the medieval mind of this artist has depicted! You may well marvel at the crisp clarity of line and the varied patterns and textures so typical of this master of the art of engraving.

167. ST. EUSTACE *Dürer*

When you see this print, you can well understand why Dürer is considered the supreme master of engraving. His complex subject is held together by a masterly triangular scheme. The richness of the medieval landscape and the detailed rendition of its
textures are all a part of its fascinating quality.

for their making was a well-known art. Gradually artists found a new medium, a metal plate, on which they could engrave their illustrations with great precision and infinite detail. Some of you may know that the hand engraving process is the reverse of the woodcutting, or relief, process. These engravings are made by cutting into the surface of the plate with a special tool called a burin. Ink is forced into these cuts, the surface of the plate is wiped clean, and the paper-covered plate is passed through a press which squeezes the ink from the engraved lines onto the paper.

Early Engravers

Of the early engravers, Martin Schöngauer (1450–1491) of the German school was the accepted master. Under his sensitive hands, the art of engraving developed, revealing unexpected qualities and possibilities. The *Temptation of St. Anthony* (Illustration 166) shows us that Schöngauer was an imaginative artist, an excellent draughtsman, and an accomplished engraver.

Albrecht Dürer, whose self-portrait may be seen on page 189, was a youthful artist at the time when books were first being printed and when people were clamoring for illustrated religious texts. Highly inventive and versatile, he used both wood blocks and metals, such as copper, zinc, and iron, to make the engravings for which he is justly famous. Enriching the technique developed by his German predecessors, he made many notable engravings of which *St. Eustace* (Illustration 167) is an excellent example.

Importance of the Minor Arts

As you have seen in this chapter, the art of bookmaking required the services of many artists and craftsmen. During these times handmade objects reached incredible heights of perfection. Tapestries, embroideries, and laces; carvings in stone, wood, and ivory; work in gold, silver, and other metals, all show a wonderful feeling for originality of design and superb technical skill. Master craftsmen taught apprentices, and thus, for centuries, until the arrival of machines, the handicrafts played an important part in the life of every man.

9.

Development of Painting

ONE of the outcomes of the Renaissance in Italy was a direct and vital interest on the part of the artist both in the individual and in the particular world that surrounded him. During the fifteenth century this lively interest in ordinary folk greatly influenced the painters of Flanders, a country now known as Belgium.

These Flemish painters differed significantly from their Italian contemporaries. For the first time in the history of European painting, the artist was concerned not only with religious themes, but also with ordinary people and everyday scenes. He painted what we now call *genre* paintings, that is, scenes that showed the everyday activities of the plain people, both at home and out-of-doors.

The Flemish painter, in contrast with the Italian Renaissance artist who received his commissions from the Church and from the nobility, was employed by the Church and by the prosperous middle classes rather than the nobility. The rich merchants and traders of Bruges, Antwerp, and Brussels who could afford to pay a painter well, loved to have portraits of themselves and their families. Often when one of these prosperous men ordered a religious painting to be presented to the Church, the donor had his own likeness included among the various secular, or worldly, figures.

A typical family group portrait of this time is *Giovanni Arnolfini and His Wife* to be seen in Illustration 168. The painter, Jan van

168. GIOVANNI ARNOLFINI AND HIS WIFE *Van Eyck*

The fine organization of this painting is achieved mainly by the use of light. Sunlight, streaming through the window, fills the room and dramatizes its occupants. A path of light, encircling the heads and hands of the couple, unites them, both pictorially and emotionally.

Eyck (c.1390–1441), skillfully combined impressive portraiture with the compositional elements needed to join the two figures in a unified group. Notice that, in addition, many details of pattern and of texture attracted his observant eye, and he recorded them faithfully. This painting, and many others that are also typically Flemish, is highly descriptive of the people of that era. While it has none of the inspired greatness of a painting by da Vinci or Michelangelo, it is a type of painting that has great appeal because of its association with ordinary human relationships.

Another Flemish painter of this time, Rogier van der Weyden (about 1400–1464), had great ability to observe honestly, as well as to compose simply and effectively. His *Portrait* (Illustration 169) shows us how carefully he selected only the essential features of his model and how he painted them with a restraint in keeping with her character. Notice how the light flesh tones hold their own against the equally light headdress.

Of the Flemish painters of the following sixteenth century, the best-known is Pieter Breughel the Elder (1528–1569). Many of us have seen reproductions of his lusty, vigorously colored paintings of the peasant life of his time. Breughel specialized in large compositions that included crowds of people eating, drinking, sleeping, dancing, or making love. Each scene was painted with an equal degree of sympathy and of Flemish heartiness. Illustration 170 shows Breughel's popular *Peasant Dance*. Burly farmers and their wives, a robust musician, and reveling onlookers are combined with great skill into a lively composition.

The last of the important Flemish painters, Peter Paul Rubens (1577–1640), also had a typically Flemish enjoyment of life. His work was distinguished by immense vitality and diversity of theme, by fluid movements of line, of pattern, of color, and, especially, by great technical skill. Rubens lived for a time in Italy and had seen and been influenced by the work of Michelangelo and Titian. He had also visited Velázquez in Spain, and so was familiar with the highly polished technique of that master.

The portrait of *Suzanne Fourmont* (Illustration 171) has a remarkable all-over movement and surface richness. Compare it with van der Weyden's placid *Portrait* (page 186) and you will become

The beauty of this lifelike portrait lies in its careful draughtsmanship, its flat patterning, and the delicacy of its restrained modeling.

Breughel here reveals both his keen power of observation and his remarkable ability to organize details into a compact whole.

169. **PORTRAIT**   *Van der Weyden*

170. **PEASANT DANCE** *Breughel the Elder*

171. **SUZANNE FOURMONT** *Rubens*

Rubens painted many masterly and appealing portraits such as this one. Notice how the sweeping curves of the hat lead the eye to the head of the subject.

even more aware of Rubens' vitality as a painter. The bold pattern of lights and darks centers in the brilliant eyes of the solid figure.

Painting in Germany

The sixteenth century in Germany was distinguished by the work of two well-known painters, Dürer and Holbein. The first, Albrecht Dürer (1472–1528), is by common consent Germany's greatest artist. Just as Leonardo da Vinci's name is closely associated with the Renaissance, so Dürer, too, typifies the striking imagination, the inventiveness, and the intellectual curiosity of the period.

Dürer, again like Leonardo, was a master of many mediums: pen, watercolor, oil, chalk, engraving, etching, and woodcut. Illustration 172 shows us a self-portrait of the artist. The painstaking care with which he painted his flowing hair reveals the fact that Dürer was an artist who observed keenly, and that he loved to paint with sensitive fidelity.

Hans Holbein the Younger (1497–1543), the second outstanding painter of Germany, specialized in portrait painting. He had great ability to show his subjects to best advantage through his own good taste and superb draughtsmanship. Summoned to the English court of Henry VIII, he painted countless royal portraits in a style characteristically his own.

His portrait of *Catherine Howard* (Illustration 173), one of the six wives of the king, shows how he made use of flat pattern, strong line movements, and a restrained, almost shadowless modeling, to produce a stately yet sympathetic interpretation of his subject.

Like his contemporary, Dürer, Holbein, who was a master in the art of wood engraving, illustrated many books of his period.

Painting in Spain

The background of countless Renaissance painters in Europe followed a general pattern. They received their training at an early age in the studio of a recognized master, starting with such practical things as learning how to clean brushes, to grind colors and to prepare canvases. Many of these young artists had no further training beyond

Artists throughout the centuries have gazed into a mirror and painted the image reflected there. Dürer's portrait of himself is interesting not only for its description of the appearance of a man of medieval times but also because it is searching, honest, and effectively composed.

172. **SELF-PORTRAIT** *Dürer*

Holbein, who was essentially a fine draughtsman, also had a rare feeling for flat pattern and strong linear movements. His ability to portray his subjects in all their royal dignity made him an appreciated court painter.

173. **CATHERINE HOWARD**
Holbein the Younger

174. THE HOLY FAMILY *El Greco*

The deep, penetrating darks and vibrant lights that characterize all of El Greco's paintings convey his mystical temperament. Through his deliberate elongation of forms he accentuates the spirituality of his subjects.

their work with one master, and few traveled in countries other than that of their birth to see what other painters were doing. Often, therefore, their work did not break sharply from existing traditions but, rather, added to and enriched them.

The general pattern of this type of training, however, was spectacularly broken by El Greco, "The Greek." This genius (1541–1614) was born on the Greek island of Crete. In his youth he went to Italy and became a pupil of Titian, the great Venetian master. From Italy he went to Spain, where he became the most Spanish and the most brilliant of all Spanish painters.

By analyzing the work of a great painter, it is possible to discover certain qualities that mark him as a genius. In El Greco's paintings there are two qualities which are outstanding.

First, there is his intensely personal way of working. Once you have seen some of El Greco's paintings you will be able to identify others of his quickly, even though you are seeing them for the first time.

Secondly, no other painter has used darks and lights in such a variety of ways as El Greco. With light and dark he models figures, suggests backgrounds, creates great swirling patterns, and heightens the drama of his themes.

Look at *The Holy Family,* shown in Illustration 174. Do you not feel the painter's intense religious emotion dramatically conveyed directly to the canvas? El Greco's devotion seems to be a blend of tenderness and of awe in the face of majesty. The strikingly composed group brings out the Child in countless ways. His light body is clarified against a dark background. The lights in His Mother's dress lead your eye to Him. The brilliant play of light and dark carries you past the Child, back to and around the supporting figures of St. Anne, the Virgin, and St. Joseph. Notice that the forward thrust of the bodies and the heads of St. Joseph and St. Anne establishes a dynamic movement toward the figure of the Child.

Almost all of El Greco's paintings were religious in theme. An exception, however, is his *View of Toledo* (Illustration 175), one of the first outstanding landscapes in the history of European painting. This landscape is presented on a grand scale, with a weaving pattern of light and dark that bursts dramatically over the cathedral on the high hill. Notice the spot of light directly over the spire.

175. VIEW OF TOLEDO *El Greco*

The artist's deep love of his adopted city of Toledo is revealed by the way in which he painted this moving landscape. His intense spirituality is here, as always, the keynote of El Greco's painting.

The city of Toledo, which El Greco painted, was the religious center of Spain. The city of Madrid, on the other hand, was the center of fashionable court life. There Philip IV of Spain ruled in opulent splendor. To his court he summoned Spanish-born Diego Velázquez (1599–1660) to be his court painter. Velázquez spent the remainder of his life there, where among many other portraits he painted forty of the king alone.

Velázquez's paintings are far removed in spirit from those of El Greco. Calm, impersonal, completely detached, or objective, he put none of his own emotions into his work. In essence, he may be compared with a highly skilled reporter who selects and molds his theme so that it may appear to best advantage.

Look at Illustration 176, *Infanta Margarita,* painted by Velázquez. His exceptional ability to bring his subjects to life on canvas and his great command over the technique of painting are immediately apparent. The gleaming brocades, precious jewels, and frothy laces worn by the little princess have been painted with a seemingly effortless ease.

After the notable accomplishments of Velázquez in the seventeenth century, Spanish painting declined, only to re-emerge brilliantly a century and a half later when Goya appeared on the scene.

Francisco Goya (1746–1829) was both a painter of his times and a painter far in advance of his times. What does this double statement really mean?

On one hand, like Velázquez, he was a court painter, the favorite of Charles IV of Spain. His portraits of the Spanish aristocracy were penetrating and masterly. Goya not only observed the visible charac teristics of his subjects but also analyzed their characters. Later, in a subtle way, he combined in his paintings both his visual image of his models and his personal reaction to them.

In addition to his portraits, Goya painted many themes which showed how much his emotions were affected by what went on outside the protecting walls of the Spanish court. At this time the Spanish Empire was crumbling from within and was suffering outside attacks from the armies of Napoleon. Many a lesser court painter might have stayed withdrawn in comfortable security, but Goya did not choose to do this. His reactions to the brutality of war were too vividly im-

The background space in this painting is admirably well handled as a means of bringing out the figure, which has been placed low on the canvas in order to emphasize its small stature.

It has been recorded that Goya, having been informed secretly of the impending execution of his Spanish compatriots, secretly witnessed the cruel nocturnal scene and later painted his impression of it.

176. INFANTA MARGARITA *Velázquez*

177. EXECUTION OF THE MADRILEÑOS *Goya*

printed on his mind. An artist, he chose his most powerful weapons, paint and brush, to portray the evil consequences of war.

How effective may the painter's medium be as a plea for peace? The *Execution of the Madrileños,* shown in Illustration 177, was painted with inescapable vividness. Notice how Goya dramatized the scene by focusing our attention on a single defiant victim. A painting as powerful as this makes an immediate and deep impression on all who see it.

Painting in Holland

In the seventeenth century Holland won her hard-earned political freedom from Spain and became a rich, independent nation, very conscious of her heroism. She also, in an equally great struggle, established Protestantism as her national religion.

Both events deeply affected the Dutch painter. Since there was no longer contact with a royal court that had long been accustomed to patronize and to support artists, he lost all chance for commissions from the aristocracy. Protestantism did not permit religious paintings; so the Dutch artist, and there were many Dutch artists, lost the age-old patronage of the Church as well.

Fortunately for the artist, the people of Holland were not only extremely proud of their newly won independence, but also of their civic, scientific, and social accomplishments. The middle class burghers who now in effect ruled Holland wished everyone to know of their wealth and importance. To the Dutch as to the Flemish mind, the answer to that desire was a portrait. Individual or family portraits or group portraits showing several men engaged in their civic affairs, their scientific interests, or their social affairs provided many a painter's commission.

Of course, as you probably can guess, the lot of a portrait painter is not always a happy one. First and foremost, the artist's task is to please not only his customer, but also the latter's friends and relatives. Almost always the customer wants to look more impressive or more more glamourous than he actually is. Think of your own experiences with a photographer.

Among the Dutch painters who complied with this desire of their

178. YOUNG GIRL AT A HALF-OPEN DOOR *Rembrandt*

Among Rembrandt's many portraits is this memorable one of a young girl. His mastery of the painting of a figure alternately revealed by brilliant light and obscured by deep shadow can never be challenged.

patrons was Frans Hals (1580–1666). He enjoyed prosperity and success, for a time at least. However, the one great painter of Holland, Rembrandt, refused to make only flattering portraits, for he was too much of an artist to do that.

Rembrandt van Rijn (1606–1669) was a giant who towered over all of his contemporaries. His first group commission, *The Anatomy Lesson,* pleased his patrons highly, for at the beginning of his career he was conscious of the need to make an individual and distinctive portrait of each man who contributed to his fee.

The Anatomy Lesson, however interesting in detail, was not completely successful as a unified painting, as Rembrandt well knew. Therefore, when he executed another group portrait, his famous *Night Watch,* he deliberately obscured many figures and faces in order to add to the effectiveness of his painting as a whole. This did not please many customers who had hoped to be unmistakably recognized in the painting. From that time on, he was not in demand as a group portrait painter.

Although Rembrandt's life was by no means an easy one, either practically or emotionally, his strength of purpose and his unswerving character led him to create many memorable paintings. Among these, his portraits will always be considered masterpieces both of composition and of psychological insight. The *Young Girl at a Half-Open Door* (Illustration 178) shows us how interested he was in creating an expressive figure. The high-placed source of light is so typical of the artist that painters and photographers today call it Rembrandt lighting. It concentrates on the upper part of the head and touches the background and the body just enough to suggest the young girl's figure.

While Rembrandt concentrated on portraits and religious themes and, in addition, made the etchings and drypoints that established him as one of the greatest graphic artists of the world, contemporary Dutch painters were turning their efforts to other fields, those of genre and landscape painting.

Of this group of so-called "Little Dutchmen" which included Pieter de Hooch (1629–1677), Gerard ter Borch (1618–1681), Jacob van Ruisdael (1628–1682), and Jan Vermeer (1632–1675), the last was by far the most talented. His interiors, which generally included

197

179. **WOMAN WEIGHING GOLD** *Vermeer*

Vermeer loved to paint figures standing in a softly lighted room. Notice how the light is concentrated on the head of the woman.

one or two figures in the corner of a room, were not only recorded with unerring truth, but also with an innate feeling for organization. Vermeer's use of light was masterly. He never chose a strong light; rather he used a half-light which, as it streamed in through a casement window, intensified certain important parts of his painting.

Woman Weighing Gold (Illustration 179) is a serene, impersonal painting, without a trace of sentimentality. Notice that Vermeer includes some furnishings of the room as a part of his composition, and that he relates them to it through a perfect merging of line, of tone, and of light.

English Painting

Many reasons have been advanced for England's lack of accomplishment in the field of painting in the past. Whatever the reasons may be, it is an undeniable fact that not one of her painters reached the stature of Giotto, Leonardo, Michelangelo, Titian, El Greco, or Rembrandt.

England, like Holland, became a Protestant country, and her painters inevitably turned to portraiture, for in that field there was a great demand for the artist's services. Since our early childhood, we have all been familiar with the charming, lively, or impressive portraits of Sir Joshua Reynolds (1723–1792), Sir Thomas Lawrence (1796–1830), and Thomas Gainsborough (1725–1788). Of these popular painters, the last was the most preoccupied with the painter's structural problems. As noted during the discussion of Dutch portrait painting, an artist working in this field may be tempted to lose the significant aspects of his model in his efforts to render a flattering likeness. Gainsborough, although he was a painter of the fashionable world, and one that always saw his subjects in a favorable light, maintained a certain dignity and solidity in his work. The *Blue Boy,* seen in Illustration 180, is probably one of the most widely known portraits of the English school. The grave dignity of the subject and the spontaneous rendering of the painting have endeared it to many people.

In the field of landscape painting, John Constable (1776–1837) pursued what was then a revolutionary idea. He actually painted landscapes out of doors. Accustomed as is the passerby to see a painter

It is said that Gainsborough painted the *Blue Boy* in response to a challenge wherein a contemporary painter flatly stated that it was not possible to make a successful painting of a subject clad all in blue.

Constable shows his great love of nature in this spirited landscape. It conveys a strong feeling for the swiftly moving pattern created by alternating bright and obscured light.

180. **BLUE BOY** *Gainsborough*

181. **HAMPSTEAD HEATH WITH A RAINBOW** *Constable*

working at an easel in a park or in a field, he does not find the practice at all unusual today. Yet it was in Constable's day. Landscapes, like other paintings, were done in the studio. Constable's interest in the actual effects of light and of air on a landscape is reflected in his paintings. He influenced other painters to experiment with this new way of working and, in effect, revolutionized landscape painting.

Hampstead Heath with a Rainbow (Illustration 181) shows how alive Constable was to the quality of his surroundings at the particular time he was painting them. The drama of an after-the-storm light and the vigorous breezes that bend the trees, stir the windmill, and send clouds scudding across the sky have been captured in paint by a fresh and broad treatment. Because of his emotionally felt landscapes, Constable is often called the first modern landscape painter.

French Painting

The close of the eighteenth century in France brought an extravagant and corrupt court, that of Louis XVI and his queen, Marie Antoinette. Its frivolities were mirrored by elegant painters, such as Antoine Watteau (1684–1721), François Boucher (1703–1770), and many others who assumed the mantle of the fashionable painter with great lightheartedness.

At this time there was but one painter, Jean-Baptiste Chardin (1699–1779), who unassuming and steadfast, ignored the artificial and sought the commonplace. In his paintings again are found the unaffected subject, the quiet grace, and the simple virtues of genre painting at its best. When you look at Chardin's *Saying Grace* (Illustration 182), you see an everyday scene made memorable through the organization of compositional elements. Notice that Chardin, like Vermeer, whose *Woman Weighing Gold* you have seen on page 198, loved to paint a dimly lit room into which a softly streaming light brought the figures to life.

Chardin's interest in painting simple, unspectacular subjects even included painting still life alone, jugs, bottles, pipes, loaves of bread, and odds and ends of things he saw on his kitchen table. In his day still life was an entirely new subject for a painter, and later-day painters profited by his discovery of it.

This intimate and tender scene of everyday life was sympathetically rendered by a skillful master at a time when few artists were interested in their own particular environment.

182. **SAYING GRACE**

Chardin

183. **THE UPRISING** *Daumier*

Through the use of strong value contrasts, the artist dramatically projects an exciting subject. The main figure is emphasized by its foremost position and by its contrast with the darker figures in the background.

Just as the end of the eighteenth century in France saw a revolution which led to the downfall of the aristocracy and the establishment of "Liberty, Equality, and Fraternity," so it saw a sharp conflict in the ideals of its painters. One group was known as the Classicists. As the name implies, its leaders, Jacques David (1748–1825) and Jean Ingres (1780–1867) were influenced by certain features of classic art, such as its formality and precision.

On the other hand, another group of painters, the Romanticists, saw their subjects with greater warmth and interpreted them in a much more dramatic way. Théodore Géricault (1791–1824) and Eugène Delacroix (1798–1863) were both vigorous examples of the romantic style.

A direct outcome of Romantic painting was the Barbizon school. Led by Camille Corot (1796–1875), the group which included Théodore Rousseau (1812–1867) and Jean-François Millet (1814–1874) congregated in and around the town of Barbizon to paint their impressions of the forest of Fontainebleau. Landscape scenes were the favorite interest of almost all painters at this time.

Daumier, the Crusader

As in every era, however, there were rugged individuals in the nineteenth century in France who did not belong to any one school of painting. Honoré Daumier (1808–1879), who made his living as a cartoonist, but who had the artistic reputation of being both an excellent painter and graphic artist, was a vigorous crusader for human rights. Like Francisco Goya of Spain, he undertook to depict the political and social injustices of the times, as well as man's emotional foibles and weaknesses.

His subjects were everyday people caught in a dramatic moment. Had he been concerned only with realistic representation, we would probably know little of his work today. Since, however, he was a painter who instinctively used all the elements of art to project his message, he is considered one of the most outstanding painters of his time.

See how he has presented *The Uprising* (Illustration 183). Actually few figures are shown, yet we feel the presence there of a turbulent

203

184. REHEARSAL OF BALLET ON STAGE *Degas*

Light and dark shapes, carefully designed and effectively contrasted, show the artist's interest in tone and pattern relationships. Paintings of the ballet by Degas have an irresistible, flowerlike charm.

Beautifully designed, flat areas of dark and light, as well as lively line rhythms, distinguish the highly stylized Japanese print. Notice how the heads are emphasized by the exaggerated shapes of their headdresses.

185. THREE GEISHA

Utamaro

mob. The dramatic and forceful central figure sets the mood of the painting both by pose and gesture. Strong diagonal lines and a vigorous dark and light pattern add to the strength of the message.

Degas, the Innovator

Edgar Degas (1834–1917), well known for his paintings of the ballet, the race track, and the labors of working women, was, like Daumier, a highly independent painter. Certain of his characteristics are now an accepted part of our modern painting, but in his day they were radical departures from tradition. For example, his partial figures cut by the edge of the frame were innovations. His fondness for unusual angles from which to view his subjects, and what might be described as a balcony view of them were also new to painting.

Both of these characteristics of Degas' painting are displayed in his *Rehearsal of Ballet on Stage* (Illustration 184). As you will quickly notice, the grouped figures on the left, none of which are shown completely, all lead our eye to the central group. The two smaller figures in the background are placed higher in the painting, showing that the artist viewed the scene from above.

Degas was greatly impressed, as were a number of his contemporaries, with the beautiful and decorative Japanese wood-block prints that had just become generally known to the Western world. Their rhythmic line movements, their organization into superbly designed shapes, and their flat, carefully modulated tones are reflected in his work. You may see this by comparing the *Three Geisha* (Illustration 185) by Kitagawa Utamaro (1753–1806), a famous Japanese printmaker, with *Rehearsal of Ballet on Stage*.

The Impressionists

The people of France have always taken the work of their painters very seriously. Paris, where artists seemed to congregate naturally, was, at the close of the nineteenth century, the scene of many a heated argument. Conservative painters refused to allow experimental artists to display their work in their important exhibitions, or salons. Independent painters retaliated by showing their paintings in an exhibition

186. BAR AT THE FOLIES BERGÈRE *Manet*

A mirrored wall reflects the barmaid and a customer, as well as the large and brilliantly lighted café.

187. BOULEVARD DES ITALIENS *Pissarro*

Notice how distinct is the sensation of movement conveyed by this lively and free painting.

of their own, the celebrated "Salon des Refusés." There, their work was either unsparingly ridiculed or highly praised depending, of course, on the convictions of the beholder. Then, as today, there were more people who liked familiar types of painting than there were those who could accept the challenge of new ideas concerning it.

At this time a group considered wildly radical by the conservatives evolved an almost entirely new theory about painting and its techniques. The Impressionists, as they came to be called, painted both in and out of doors. They were interested primarily in the effects of light and of atmosphere on a landscape, on figures, and on objects. You may see in Illustration 186, the *Bar at the Folies Bergère* by Edouard Manet (1832–1883), how much the artist was interested in painting light. Although using real people in an actual scene as his subject, he concentrated on capturing the elusive and multiple lights that danced over surfaces and through spaces, casting sparkling and brilliant reflections everywhere.

Many artists of the Impressionist group, including Claude Monet (1840–1926), Alfred Sisley (1840–1899), and Camille Pissarro (1830–1903) confined themselves almost exclusively to landscape. They became so fascinated with recording the changing effects of light on color that they often recorded the same scene many times under varying atmospheric conditions. Monet, for example, painted countless pictures of the same haystack seen at dawn, midday, and dusk. Pissarro's *Boulevard des Italiens,* shown in Illustration 187, is a brilliant example of the technique used by the Impressionists to show moving figures and landscape in full sunlight.

Renoir, the Colorist

Pierre Renoir (1841–1919) used a method of painting similar to that of the Impressionists, but he was not content merely to record his subjects as they often were. Greatly interested in composition, he organized its elements, lines, values, colors, forms, and spaces to create richly colored and lively paintings. The artist conveys his love of the attractive, pleasant, and even sentimental things of life in *Luncheon of the Boating Party* (Illustration 188). Each one of the fourteen figures there has been caught by the painter in a characteristic atti-

207

188. LUNCHEON OF THE BOATING PARTY *Renoir*

The Impressionist technique was to place strips or daubs of pure color directly on the canvas. Seen from a distance, they produce an effect of brilliant, direct, and vibrating light.

189. SUNDAY ON GRANDE JATTE ISLAND *Seurat*

Painting with tiny dots of color, Seurat not only created solid forms, but also arranged them in a vast area of space. The composition is unified through its light and color movement.

tude, yet in spite of its apparent casualness, the grouping of the figures is highly organized. Notice how your eye is carried effortlessly and smoothly from one figure to another.

The Neo-Impressionists

Just as Renoir was influenced by the theories of the Impressionists, so a small group of painters, who became known as Neo-Impressionists, became interested in the breaking up and scientific placing of pigment on canvas. Using a method known as pointillism, the Neo-Impressionists built their paintings with tiny spots of color. Their slow, precise way of working gave them ample opportunity to study in a highly scientific way the effects of colors placed either near or next to one another.

Of this group of painters, Georges Seurat (1859–1891) is the best known. His paintings have a monumental quality, that is, they seem to have been built with an architectural precision. His *Sunday on Grande Jatte Island* (Illustration 189), a very large painting that took him several years to complete, reveals a vivid pattern of sunlight and shadow falling on figures that start near us in the foreground and move into a distant plane. This distant plane, in terms of painting, is known as deep space.

Although both Renoir and Seurat used many figures in *Luncheon of the Boating Party* and *Sunday on Grande Jatte Island,* you will notice that each interpreted his theme in quite a different way. While Renoir's background space is limited, Seurat's is deep. Renoir's figures give the impression of being casually arranged; those of Seurat are as tightly locked into place as the pieces of a completed jig-saw puzzle.

Renoir and Seurat trod separate paths, but each of their ways led into a new field of painting, known today as Post-Impressionism, from which, as we shall see in a later chapter, our modern concepts of painting were derived.

190. **CATHEDRAL OF FLORENCE** *Florence, Italy*

The exterior of this cathedral is surfaced with colored marbles. Its horizontal lines, small windows, and high, pointed dome are characteristically Renaissance.

The simplicity of the carefully balanced verticals and horizontals that compose this small chapel, together with a sparing use of curves, gives it a restrained dignity.

191. **PAZZI CHAPEL** *Florence, Italy*

10.

Development of Architecture

DURING the Renaissance, man's mental horizon was enlarged to include a keen interest in the accomplishments of the past. The invention of the printing press at this time gave scholars greater opportunity to study the treasures of Greek and Roman literature that had long been hidden in monasteries. Just as the men of letters delved into books, so the artists of the Renaissance came to search for the secrets of beauty to be found in the long-buried statues and monuments of ancient Rome.

Inevitably, first in certain sections of Italy and finally in other parts of Europe, Renaissance architecture took on a classic character. In the beginning, the classic influence was most apparent in architectural details, such as the Corinthian column, the pediment, and other traditional forms of ornamentation. As time went on, however, Renaissance buildings assumed more and more the outward forms of Roman building. The aspiring verticals of Gothic building were discarded, and the stable horizontals of classic building reappeared to characterize again man's rational and serene outlook, rather than his emotional and yearning view of life.

The *Cathedral of Florence* (Illustration 190) is an interesting example of this new spirit in building which sought new forms based

The entrance to Renaissance palaces generally led into an open colonnaded court from which a stairway ascended to the living quarters above. Notice the characteristically rough stone below and the smooth stone above.

The openwork of the three-tiered arches flanked by balconies is interestingly contrasted with the plainly surfaced right side of the façade of this famous building.

192. **MEDICI-RICCARDI PALACE**

Florence, Italy

193. **CA D'ORO** *Venice, Italy*

upon the past. Since it was started at the beginning of the thirteenth century, this cathedral was first planned in the Italian Gothic style. Giotto himself at one time was in charge of its construction, and it was he who designed its beautiful campanile, or bell tower. The huge, fifteenth-century dome, however, is a new feature in building, quite unlike other domes we have seen previously. The *Pantheon* (page 84) and *Santa Sophia* (page 92) are both domed buildings, yet their domes are not a major feature of the exterior of the building. The dome of the *Cathedral of Florence,* however, dominates not only the church, but also its surroundings. Designed by Filippo Brunelleschi (1397–1446), who previously spent many years studying the construction of the *Pantheon* and other Roman buildings, it pointed the way to a long series of churches impressively domed in the new classically influenced style of the Renaissance.

The Renaissance architect was greatly interested in formal and carefully balanced design. The irregularity of medieval building, such as its dissimilar spires on a cathedral, did not appeal to him. Brunelleschi's *Pazzi Chapel* (Illustration 191) was built completely in the Renaissance manner. Restrained and delicate classic motifs, such as the Corinthian columns and the decorated bands which appear over them, are evident.

It was during this time that a manuscript copy of a book on Roman architecture, written in the first century by a Roman, Vitruvius, came to light in a Swiss monastery and was eagerly studied. Roman architectural theories now came to have an even more concrete part in the viewpoint of the Renaissance architect, especially in Italy where the still impressive ruins of Roman buildings could so easily be examined.

Civic Building

During these times when civil architecture was becoming more important than religious architecture, countless elaborate structures were built to house the wealthy rulers of the land. In Florence, for example, the palaces of the Medici, one of which is seen in Illustration 192, were important buildings in the history of architecture. While they were essentially fortresses, since these rulers maintained their power through force of arms, they were also the first town houses of

194. ST. PETER'S CATHEDRAL *Rome, Italy*

The *piazza* in front of *St. Peter's Cathedral* was the first large open space to be laid out within a city. It contributes immeasurably to the effectiveness of this world-famous structure.

The main altar of *St. Peter's* is unusually lofty, as is its elaborately decorated interior. The latter is as high as one of our early skyscrapers.

195. INTERIOR, ST. PETER'S

Rome, Italy

the Renaissance era. During the same period, however, the Venetians continued to build their particular version of Gothic architecture, first because they liked it better than the new Renaissance style, and second because their more stable government made strongholds unnecessary. Thus we find that, in contrast to the rather forbidding-looking Florentine palaces, the Venetian palaces are open, airy, basically Gothic structures with all of the rich ornamentation so dear to the Venetian heart and eye. The *Ca d'Oro,* or *House of Gold* (Illustration 193), the palatial home of a merchant prince, is a splendid reflection, as is all fine architecture, of the particular spirit of its owners.

Baroque Architecture

Essentially a form of building that relied upon size and complexity for its effects, Renaissance architecture became increasingly dramatic and ornate. The term baroque is used to describe late Renaissance architecture. It implies a serious loss of the fundamental simplicity and good taste and of the serenity and harmony which is the basis of all fine architecture.

We may see this tendency toward elaboration in the stupendous *St. Peter's Cathedral,* shown in Illustration 194. Built in Rome at a time when that city was the artistic center of Europe, it is the largest church in the world. Notice that the dome of *St. Peter's,* one of its most impressive features, is placed over the center of the church rather than over one end, as it is placed on the *Cathedral of Florence.* *St. Peter's Cathedral* was constructed under the direction of a series of artists, including Raphael and Michelangelo. It was the latter who was responsible for much of its plan, including that for the magnificent dome, which was completed from his drawings after his death. It may surprise you to learn that Michelangelo was an architect as well as a painter and a sculptor. The days of the Renaissance produced many artists, but none greater than Michelangelo and Leonardo, both of whom had the enviable capacity to apply their talents to many fields of endeavor.

We have seen in Chapter 5 how the Gothic style of building spread through Western Europe in medieval times and how it was modified

VERSAILLES   CLICHE C.A.F.

196. PALACE OF VERSAILLES *Versailles, France*

Nearly a half century passed during the construction of this famous palace. Never before had so large a community been housed under one roof in the open country.

197. GALLERY OF MIRRORS, PALACE OF VERSAILLES
Versailles, France

Mirrored walls reflect hangings of silk, velvet, and tapestries; brilliantly painted ceilings add to the colorfulness of this stately Renaissance interior.

in each country in accordance with the ideals of native builders. Similarly, the Renaissance style became the heart of architectural planning in many countries outside of Italy, the home of its birth.

French Renaissance Architecture

The kings and princes of Europe in the seventeenth century discovered, as had the Roman Catholic church, that Renaissance architecture greatly impressed its beholders. Absolute rulers, such as Louis XIV of France who said, "*I* am the state," deliberately built elaborate palaces to display their royal power and to better impress it on the minds of their subjects. Among these grandiose structures is the vast and superbly planned *Palace of Versailles,* which was large enough to accommodate the social and residential needs of Louis XIV's entire court as well as to house all of the chief administrators of France.

The air view of the *Palace of Versailles,* seen in Illustration 196, shows the façade, which is a half-mile long. The two main gardens, so formally and beautifully landscaped, include elaborate fountain displays. Their planning is considered one of the greatest accomplishments of Renaissance times. Surrounding parks extend for several miles and a broad highway links Versailles to Paris. The interior decorations are breathtaking in the luxury of their architectural settings. A sequence of halls across the front has as a climax the *Gallery of Mirrors* (Illustration 197), which has a magnificent dignity.

A vast expenditure of money and labor, coupled with masterly planning, made the *Palace of Versailles* a landmark in the history of architecture. At this time, the same expansive type of plan was applied to redesigning crowded cities. Avenues, squares, public gardens, following boldly conceived schemes, were cut into and through the heart of important French cities. Thus we find today that many of them, Paris, for example, present beautiful vistas and impressively grouped public buildings and grounds.

English Renaissance Architecture

The ideas of the Renaissance builders were slow to affect English achitecture. Isolated from other countries in Europe, and devoted to

198. **ST. PAUL'S CATHEDRAL** *London, England*

St. Paul's Cathedral is distinguished by the careful proportioning of its various parts and by the concentration of ornament on its upper section. Two beautifully tapered steeples frame the impressive dome, which is considered the finest in England.

her own strong variations of the Gothic style, as you have seen when looking at the *Cathedral of Salisbury* and *Wells Cathedral* on page 109, conservative England did not welcome innovations.

Finally, however, a famous English architect, Inigo Jones (1572–1662), accomplished what was practically an architectural revolution. He had traveled in Italy and had become familiar with the buildings of classical antiquity, as well as those designed by Italian Renaissance architects. Of the latter, one especially, Palladio, became his idol. It was Palladio's ideas that, through the efforts of Jones, brought Renaissance building to England.

Since the way still had not been paved for new ideas in architecture, it was only natural that a second famous English architect, Sir Christopher Wren (1632–1723), who also greatly admired Italian architecture, should be allowed to design in the new Renaissance style the churches needed in London after its disastrous fire in 1666.

The best-known of Wren's churches is *St. Paul's Cathedral,* to be seen in Illustration 198. Notice that, although by no means a simple structure, it has a dignity and restraint often missing in late Renaissance design. The high dome, which of course suggests the one that crowns *St. Peter's* in Rome, makes *St. Paul's* a conspicuous sight amidst the host of buildings that surround it.

We have seen how architecture in the Old World became, by the seventeenth century, a highly intricate art, one that required of its designers not only knowledge and skill, but also a vast amount of cultural background. Classical and Renaissance traditions bound architecture firmly in their grip and linked it to the past, so firmly indeed that their force eventually was felt in other countries far removed from the source.

Building in Colonial America

When the early colonists landed on the shores of North America, they carried few possessions, yet among these were family heirlooms, such as a coverlet, a bit of silverware, or even something as practical as a farming implement. For their possessors these treasured mementos were a link between their distant native land and their newly adopted one. The colonists must have thought of their homeland often and have loved it even though they had left it forever. When they grew in numbers and prospered, and could build more than crude dwellings and stockades, their thoughts naturally recalled their homes in the distant countries they and their forefathers had left.

That is the reason why, scattered over the face of our country, we may still see replicas of the homes of England, of France, of Holland, of Germany, of Sweden, and of Spain. Often the early colonists from these distant countries found themselves in a region where the available building materials were quite different from those found in the Old Country. In many of the northern sections of America to which the early settlers came, there was an abundance of wood and a scarcity of stone, while in the south the reverse was true. Building in Colonial America was naturally influenced by this factor. Then, too, the climate in the various parts of America necessarily influenced the ideas of the early Colonial builders. In New England the severity of the winter and the heat of the summer as well as rain and snow had to be considered. In the South, on the other hand, the semitropical warmth was an important factor in the local architectural plan.

As we know, too, the colonist's way of life was conditioned by his environment. He might be living near the sea and be wresting his living from it, as he did in New England. He needed little land there, but his house had to be a compact, sturdy one that would withstand the ravages of winter storms. If he were in an agricultural section, such as Pennsylvania or Delaware, sturdy barns for his cattle and produce might be far more important than the actual house where he and his family lived. If he were a wealthy plantation owner in the South, he needed not only extensive quarters for himself and his family but also for his servants.

The actual character of the early settlers of America varied widely. You may remember, for example, that New England was first settled by Puritans who came here in search of religious freedom. Their austere attitude toward life strongly affected both their mode of living and their architecture. The South, on the other hand, was colonized by the far more well-to-do Cavaliers, who also came from England but who, unlike the Puritans, loved luxury, leisure, and an expansive way of life.

199. JOHN WHIPPLE HOUSE *Ipswich, Massachusetts*

The glass for these small casement windows was, of necessity, imported from England, since the Colonists had at that time no means of producing such a luxury.

200. MOUNT VERNON *Mount Vernon, Virginia*

The horizontal lines of *Mount Vernon*, agreeably balanced by its vertical columns, seem to make it a natural part of the gently rolling landscape.

Thus we may see that many factors influenced early Colonial architecture: a natural desire to repeat the architectural forms of the homeland; the available building materials; the climate; the way of living; and the natural temperament of the people of the locality.

For an example of one of the early Colonial houses, look at Illustration 199, which shows the *John Whipple House* at Ipswich, Massachusetts. Built some time before 1669, it is in both plan and construction similar to English medieval half-timbered houses and differs from them only in a few details. Its frame structure, for example, is surfaced with clapboards. These, as you may see in the photograph, are overlapped boards which were used to give its inhabitants greater protection against the severe New England winters.

Spanish-American Architecture

In the Spanish colonies the architecture closely followed that of Spain, the mother country. Designs for important structures were often prepared in Spain, and skilled monks were sent to this country to supervise their execution. The Indians of Mexico and Peru, who were extraordinarily accomplished stone and woodcutters, made their own unique contribution to the beauty of churches; their love of intricate ornament, of pattern, and of color can be seen in most Spanish colonial architecture.

The church and monastery of *San Francisco* in Quito, Peru (Illustration 201), shows the typical Inca contribution of plain stone surfaces broken occasionally by carved wooden balconies and windows. The almost unadorned exterior of this building gives no hint of its highly ornate interior where carvers and painters contributed their skills to create an elaborate baroque altar.

Although almost all Spanish-American culture is a fusion of Spanish and Indian elements, in Cuba, where the native Indian, the Siboney, was not so civilized as the Aztec, the Maya, or the Inca, this Indian influence is not felt. Spanish colonial architecture in Havana is, therefore, purely Spanish in design. Notice in Illustration 202, the *Cathedral of Havana,* the curved lines and broken surfaces which are typical of Spanish baroque architecture.

In North America, in Texas and Arizona, for example, which were

222

201. **SAN FRANCISCO** *Quito, Peru*

This low, sturdy structure is typical of ecclesiastical architecture in the high Andes. Nearly a city block long, its extended façade, which is unlike that of most churches we have seen, has its ornamentation concentrated around and over the doorway.

202. **CATHEDRAL OF HAVANA** *Havana, Cuba*

This building and countless others in Havana are examples of pure Spanish architecture in the New World. When seeing this cathedral, you might easily imagine yourself in Spain.

203. **MISSION OF SAN XAVIER** *Tucson, Arizona*

The thick adobe walls of this mission church are an interesting example of an ingenious use of native materials.

Notice the beautifully carved doorway, which is effectively contrasted with the plain, surrounding surfaces.

204. **MISSION OF SAN JOSÉ Y SAN MIGUEL DE AGUAYO**

San Antonio, Texas

once a part of the old Spanish Empire, there are some fine examples of Spanish Colonial architecture in the famous mission churches. These buildings were usually designed by the mission priest and built by the Indians. The *Mission of San Xavier* (Illustration 203) near Tucson, Arizona, is notable for its boldly designed plan which includes the generous courtyard needed to accommodate throngs of Indian converts. In contrast, the *Mission of San José y San Miguel de Aguayo* in San Antonio (Illustration 204), shows a greater richness and delicacy of design than the mission in Arizona. Notice its richly ornamented doorway where the work of skilled carvers is evident. This difference in skill is probably due to the fact that San Antonio was in much closer touch with the cultural centers of Mexico than was Tucson.

Eighteenth Century Architecture

The century following Colonial times, the eighteenth, was one of industrious building. Homes, churches, and town halls were essential to the many little communities that had grown up in the East, the Middle Colonies, and the South. The new structures again mirrored the prevailing styles in England, all of which, as was previously noted, stemmed from the Renaissance. The modifications were due chiefly to the materials then generally in use: timber in the north, stone in the Middle Colonies, and brick in the South.

Information concerning these styles came to our builders in those days from English building manuals which local carpenters used as guides. At that time there were no trained, professional architects. There were, however, skillful builders and gentlemen planners. Some knowledge of architecture was an expected part of every gentleman's education. George Washington himself planned and supervised the modeling of his home, *Mount Vernon,* shown in Illustration 200. The general classic design echoes that of an English variation of Renaissance architecture known as the Georgian style. The long house with the open portico, and with servants' quarters connected with the rear of the house, is well adapted both to the climate and to the Southern manner of life.

Shortly after the American Revolution, Thomas Jefferson (1743–

205. NATIONAL CAPITOL *Washington, D.C.*

The vast plan for the city of Washington was the work of a Frenchman, Pierre L'Enfant, and was modeled after that for Versailles. The *National Capitol* was placed in a focal point of this plan. An impressive structure, it served as a model for many state capitols throughout our country.

206. LINCOLN MEMORIAL *Washington, D.C.*

Designed by the architect Henry Bacon, this noble memorial to one of America's greatest men makes excellent use of the classic style of architecture to achieve a highly impressive dignity.

1826), the third president of our nation, and one of its most illustrious statesmen, a scholar, a musician, a lawyer, and a gentleman architect, designed the capitol of Virginia at Richmond. This capitol was one of the very first of the government buildings of the new republic. Jefferson's plan for it, as well as his plans for the University of Virginia and his own home, *Monticello,* were based on classic models. In some cases he even directly adapted the architecture of certain buildings in France and Italy.

Many people wondered why Jefferson, in his day our foremost champion of democracy, felt that the architectural styles of the past should form the basis for the architecture of a brave new country. It would seem that his travels in Europe and his conviction that the American form of government had its origin in antiquity led him to this belief. At any event, subsequent architects, for by now there were in America professionally trained architects, followed the generally imitative pattern laid down by Jefferson. These same imitative patterns were typical also of the manuals imported from England which were in those days the architects' bible. American as well as foreign-born and foreign-trained architects used classic formulas for our public buildings, such as the *National Capitol* and the *United States Treasury* in Washington, D.C. Compare, for example, the dome of the *National Capitol* (Illustration 205) with that of *St. Peter's* in Rome (page 214) and of *St. Paul's* in London (page 218) to see evidence of this fact.

Later American Architecture

In the middle years of the nineteenth century, the constant use of classic forms and ornamentation was occasionally varied, owing to the great interest certain architects had in Gothic architecture. The homes of the wealthy as well as cathedrals and churches often reflected this style although they did not actually follow its traditional methods of construction.

By the end of the nineteenth century, America, architecturally speaking, reflected almost every European country. Between the architect who was trained to copy the past, and the ordinary man who was unschooled in architecture but had his own ideas about the kind of house he wanted and who hired a carpenter to build it, America became flooded with many odd structures, most of which are still in use today. They include banks and public buildings that look like Greek or Roman temples, churches that look like Gothic or Romanesque cathedrals, movie houses with interiors that ape Moorish splendor, and private homes that look like Swiss chalets, Bavarian cottages, French farmhouses, or Spanish haciendas. Even entire buildings were transported from Europe, stone by stone, by wealthy worshipers of European culture.

The leavening agent in this deluge of transplanted forms was the persisting tradition of Colonial architecture which, though it continued to retain many traces of its European ancestry, yet assumed a great deal of the honest, sturdy, and independent quality of a people proud of their own accomplishments.

The end of the nineteenth century was the logical time for a new form of architecture. You will read the interesting story of its development in a later chapter.

207. **CARD PLAYERS** *Cézanne*

11.

Modern Painting

ONE of the fascinating things about painting is the way in which it flourishes in different countries at certain times. For two hundred years after Giotto's time, Italy fostered painting, raising it from childhood to maturity. Then for three hundred years, Spain, Flanders, and Holland gave impetus and new vision to painting; yet after this period of time, painting was a lost art in these countries.

It would almost seem that painting, facing a decline in one country, sought refuge in another. In more recent times, in the nineteenth and the first part of the twentieth centuries, France took painting to her heart. As a result, Paris became the artistic center of the Western world. Even today, probably, when you think of a typical artist, you visualize him dressed in a French beret and smock, and living in a garret in Paris.

In Chapter 9 you saw the work of a number of vigorous French painters, some of whom, like Monet and Pissarro, were Impressionists. Contemporary with the Impressionists, yet not one of them, was Paul Cézanne (1839–1906), the genius of his time and a founder of modern painting.

The Accomplishments of Cézanne

Although he lived six centuries after Giotto, Cézanne is often compared with him, for each turned the path of painting into new

229

directions. Cézanne himself said, "I am the primitive of my way." Within his mind there was a great discontent with painting only what his eye saw. He believed that he should be able to penetrate the surface of nature, to discover and then to reveal in his paintings its essential, rather than its superficial, characteristics. The Chinese painters, you remember, felt that way too about their painting. However, while the Chinese painter rarely used color, Cézanne made it his most important instrument of expression. Through color he obtained solidity and structure; through color he brought forms and planes forward or sent them back into space; through color he created glowing visual harmonies.

You may gain an understanding of Cézanne's use of color by studying the *Card Players,* shown in Illustration 207. Notice how solid the figures seem. You might imagine that you could place your hand on a shoulder and feel its muscular and bony structure. There is a feeling of space between and around the absorbed players. The suggestions of solidity and of space have been created by Cézanne's color treatment of his subject, especially his use of alternating warm and cool colors, both within single areas and within the total composition.

A study of Cézanne's paintings also reveals his frequent use of distorted shapes, for he often felt that distortions were necessary to his compositional scheme. At first the odd appearance of some of Cézanne's subjects startled people, for they had forgotten that many painters before Cézanne, notably El Greco, had also made use of distortion. Today, emotional rather than realistic drawing and painting is considered a natural thing for painters to do if they so wish. Therefore, when seeing Cézanne's *Still Life with Fruit Dish* (Illustration 208), you will probably be far more interested in the total composition than in the fact that certain objects within it, such as the dish and glass, do not conform to the rules of perspective drawing.

Another characteristic of Cézanne's painting is his simplification of nature into its basically geometric forms. *Mont Sainte-Victoire,* shown in Illustration 209, reveals how he reduced the complicated elements of a broad landscape into a few boldly defined forms.

Some of the painters working in Cézanne's time or slightly later, who were influenced by his idea of reducing objects to their basic

208. STILL LIFE WITH FRUIT DISH *Cézanne*

An apparently casual arrangement of still life is, in reality, a highly complex and carefully organized composition.

209. MONT SAINTE-VICTOIRE *Cézanne*

Notice how solid and three-dimensional the tree, hill, and mountain forms appear in this painting. What basic shapes do you recognize?

210. COUNTRY ROAD BY NIGHT *Van Gogh*

Flamelike upward and rotating movements give Van Gogh's painting a tremendous feeling of vitality.

211. **LA MOUSMÉ** *Van Gogh*

forms, used it as a starting point for their own particular type of painting, Cubism, as you will see later in this chapter.

Paintings of Van Gogh

The fame of Vincent Van Gogh (1853–1890) has spread far and wide. Although a contemporary of Cézanne's, both his actual career and his aims as a painter were unlike those of that master. Practically all Van Gogh's important paintings were done in a three-year period, at a time when he was often penniless and far from well. Cézanne, on the other hand, had sufficient money to pursue his studies in peace. Van Gogh by nature was intensely emotional; Cézanne was primarily an intellectual artist. Yet each, in his own way, lit the fuse of painting so dynamically that the effects were felt not only all over Europe, but also in the Americas as well.

In the work of Van Gogh you see the beginnings of what today is called Expressionism. Not in the least concerned with exact representation, he relied primarily on colors and forms to convey what he felt, and what he wished others to feel, about his subject. Painting for most of the time in the hot, almost tropical sunlight of southern France, he was moved to a frenzy by colors, and in his haste to get them down on canvas, he not only used broad brushes and a palette knife, but also squeezed pure pigment directly from the tube. As he himself said, "When emotions are so strong, one works without being aware of working."

When you see a landscape painting by Van Gogh, such as his *Country Road by Night,* shown in Illustration 210, even the paint itself suggests the painter's intensely nervous energy and his urgent need to capture on canvas his emotional reactions to his subject.

Van Gogh's portraits are equally vivid. Using broad areas of color without a hint of shadow, and ruthlessly simplifying his subject, he produced many bold yet sympathetic portraits, one of which, *La Mousmé,* is shown in Illustration 211. The artist, you readily see, was not interested in producing an idealized portrait of his subject. Her self-conscious expression and stiff pose, her awkward and labor-worn

212. THE WHITE HORSE *Gauguin*

Starting in the lower right-hand corner, trace with your finger the angular movements which make this painting so compact.

hands, have been deliberately emphasized. As a contrast, the brilliant color notes of her costume are particularly effective.

The Paintings of Gauguin

The end of the nineteenth century in France saw, together with Cézanne and Van Gogh, a third great painter, Paul Gauguin (1848–1903). While Cézanne sought above all for order and for control over his subject, and while Van Gogh struggled to express the emotional excitement aroused in him by his subject, Gauguin, in a quite different way, sought a freedom and an independence of personal expression.

You know, of course, that Gauguin started his career as a "Sunday painter." Finding that nothing in his life mattered more to him than the fascination of painting, he eventually went to the South Sea Islands, where he made the paintings for which he is now famous.

Perhaps many of you feel that if you could get away to some faraway, exotic land, you, too, could make exciting paintings of the people and of the scenes there. It is true that much of the appeal of Gauguin's paintings comes from the very strangeness of his subjects, from the richly tropical colors and lush foliage of those distant islands. Remember, however, that Gauguin did not paint these people as a visitor might, for he completely identified himself with them; he lived among them, led the life they led, and so, in reality, painted his own life experiences there.

Gauguin's eye and mind were attracted by the everyday life of the primitive people among whom he lived. *The White Horse* (Illustration 212) shows his mastery of a flat, decorative pattern that reveals how sensitive his eye and hand were to the commonplace scenes of his strange existence.

Cézanne, Van Gogh, and Gauguin received almost no recognition during their lifetime. Their paintings were far too revolutionary to be understood by the public. Fortunately for modern painting, their dissatisfactions, their struggles, and, especially, their accomplishments were understood by a younger generation of painters who, in turn, took up the challenge of searching for fresh visions and for independent ways of expressing them.

The Early Expressionists

Among the early Expressionists were Henri Matisse (1869–), André Derain (1880–), Maurice de Vlaminck (1876–), Georges Rouault (1871–), Raoul Dufy (1877–), and André de Segonzac (1884–). As you may well imagine, their work was often ridiculed, just as yours might be if you painted something that no one could understand. In fact, after seeing an exhibition of the work of *les fauves,* or "wild beasts," as they came to be called, one critic announced that a donkey could paint as well, and tying a paint-laden brush to that animal's tail, let him swish it across a canvas to try to prove his point.

The Paintings of Matisse

However, people have fortunately increased in understanding, so that many of the radicals of the early twentieth century are now its accepted masters. Of that particular group, Henri Matisse is perhaps the best known. Two characteristics of his work are easily apparent. One is its simplification. If you were to tell Matisse that he draws and paints like a child, he would feel complimented as he greatly admires the fresh and unsophisticated qualities of children's work.

A second and still more striking characteristic of Matisse's work is seen in his joyous use of color. Daring and richly patterned flat areas of color make up a brilliant surface, which impresses you with its vigorous and active movements. You may see this in Illustration 213 which shows his *Vase with Poppies.* The fresh pattern of color creates a strong feeling of movement throughout the entire painting. Its simplicity and directness have a great appeal for those who particularly admire these qualities in painting.

Other Expressionist Painters

Another painter, Georges Rouault, also considered an Expressionist, has interests far removed from those of Matisse. While the latter used his subjects simply as a web on which to weave his

213. **VASE WITH POPPIES** *Matisse*

214. **PIERROT** *Rouault*

215. **GIRL IN PINK** *Modigliani*

tapestry-like patterns, Rouault infuses his characters with meaning. His color is especially well suited to his generally serious treatment of his themes. Early training as a designer of stained glass seemed to have brought him naturally to use rather somber areas of color boldly outlined in black, somewhat like stained glass in which sections of color are held together by strips of lead.

Rouault's *Pierrot,* shown in Illustration 214, reveals an aloof, almost melancholy personage. Our feeling that he has withdrawn from a world of pleasure is heightened by the painted frame which narrowly confines his head and shoulders. Almost flat areas of cool, grayed color are contrasted with light flesh tones. The boldly accented features have a simplicity of modeling reminiscent of Gothic stone carving.

Just as Rouault's paintings are instantly recognizable because of his highly individual way of working, so those of another Expressionist, Amadeo Modigliani (1884–1920), have an unmistakable and particular quality. This artist, although Italian, lived and painted in Paris. Desperately poor, often unhappy and physically wretched, he left, amazingly enough, over three hundred paintings of sustained freshness, almost poetic in quality.

His *Girl in Pink* (Illustration 215) shows his characteristic way of simplifying and elongating his subject and of using almost flat areas of color, with an occasional, deft outline. A wide range of pinkish tones pervades and harmonizes the color scheme, appearing even in the greyed background.

A somewhat similar feeling for warm harmonies of color is to be seen in Illustration 218, the pastel *Vase of Flowers* by Redon. Small areas of contrasting cool color make the rich, deep scheme unusually effective. All of the work of this French artist, Odilon Redon (1840–1916) is distinguished by a mysterious, supersensitive quality which you can sense in this bouquet. Although you can recognize the various kinds of flowers, they seem dreamlike, rather than solid and earthy.

Expressionism was not a phase of painting unique to France. In fact, the very term itself came from Germany. Oscar Kokoschka (1886–   ), although an Austro-Czech, was the leading spirit of a group of painters in Germany that included, among others, Emil Nolde (1867–   ), Edvard Munch (1866–1944), Max Beckman

216. PORTRAIT OF DR. TIETZE AND HIS WIFE *Kokoschka*

The difficult problem of uniting two figures has been solved by presenting one in profile and the other facing forward, and by a thoughtful use of arm and hand movements.

217. RAIN IN THE JUNGLE *Rousseau*

Do you not find this scene both dramatic and highly original?

218. **VASE OF FLOWERS** *Redon*

(1884–1950), Wassily Kandinsky (1866–1944), and Paul Klee (1879–1940).

Kokoschka painted with an emotional power akin to that of Van Gogh. His portraits, especially, convey his sensitiveness to the character of his model. We may see this in Illustration 216, the *Portrait of Dr. Tietze and His Wife*. Notice how much use he has made of a thin, nervous line to bring out his figures. This line, and the ribbon-like brush strokes seen in the hands reveal an artist who was aroused by his subject to a high pitch of excitement.

Rousseau, the Primitive

Many of the artists who came after Gauguin admired his insistence on the primitive qualities that he felt were essential to painting. Their admiration of him and his work led them to discover a truly primitive painter, Henri Rousseau (1844–1910), who had for some time faithfully trundled his canvases in a wheelbarrow through the streets of Paris to show them in the same exhibitions where professional artists displayed their work.

Rousseau's childlike paintings truly express his native character. He was as naïve as a child and equally fearless in painting when, where, and how he wished. A self-taught amateur, he had none of the traditional knowledge that the professional painter slowly acquires. It is not surprising, therefore, that he painted unexpected subjects with a freshness and an imagination to which everyone who sees his work instantly responds.

Just what made jungle scenes one of Rousseau's favorite subjects is difficult to explain, although it is thought that he might have retained some memories of the semitropics of Mexico from his service there with the French army. At any rate, his tropical landscapes, inhabited by all kinds of beasts and birds almost concealed in luxuriant foliage, have an elemental and dramatic quality that makes them especially fascinating. Let us look at his *Rain in the Jungle* (Illustration 217). Agitated line and color movements indicate the path of a torrential rain. Even though they were whipped into violent movement, Rousseau, true to the impulse of the primitive artist, painted each tree, each plant, each leaf and blade of grass, as well as the very frightened

239

219. STILL LIFE: THE TABLE *Braque*

In this semi-abstraction, a beautiful pattern has been created through a careful selection of shapes which were suggested both by the objects themselves and by the play of light and shadow on them.

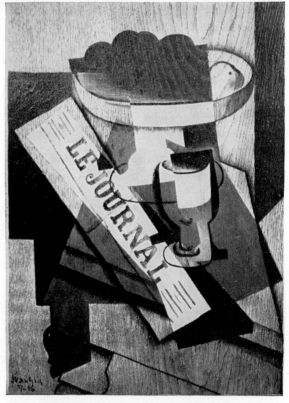

Added variety is given to the surface of this painting by the texture of the wooden panel on which it was made.

220. STILL LIFE: LE JOURNAL *Gris*

tiger, as though they had been rendered rigid by means of a photograph.

Those of you who enjoy *The Peaceable Kingdom* shown on page 268, may easily sense its kinship with the painting of Rousseau, as well as with those of present-day primitive and self-taught painters, such as Grandma Moses and Horace Pippin, both of whom have painted with a robust dignity.

Picasso and the Cubists

Cézanne once wrote: "Everything in nature takes its form from the sphere, the cone, and the cylinder." Certainly his paintings show how he searched for these elemental forms. It was this idea of his which interested a number of younger painters and led them to experiment with, and to ultimately develop, a new type of painting that came to be known as Cubism.

Of these Cubists, Pablo Picasso is probably the best known. Early in his career he showed himself to be an experimental painter, making startling shifts from one kind of painting to another. First he went through a "blue period," in which he painted sad figures in shades of blue; then there was a period in which he painted harlequins and clowns in a few subdued colors; next came his "rose period," during which he painted pinkish figures reminiscent of Greek sculpture.

From these many stages you may easily imagine how Picasso's mind would welcome a change in ideas. Other painters, too, notably Georges Braque (1881–   ), Albert Gleizes (1881–   ), Jean Metzinger (1883–   ), Marcel Duchamp (1887–   ), Francia Picabia (1879–   ), Fernand Léger (1881–   ), and Juan Gris (1887–1927), plunged into experiment. At first they generally worked from a definite subject, such as still life or figures. Since they felt that their subject matter was in itself unimportant, they often used, over and over again, certain commonplace objects, such as a guitar and a sheet of music, glasses, jars, and fruit on a table. Illustration 219 shows a still life painting by Braque. Notice the simplification of subject matter into geometric and semi-geometric shapes, all organized into bold and powerful plane movements. Each dark area of plane seems to be moving in some general direction. Some of the planes move vertically or horizontally and others at an angle to these move-

221. **THREE MUSICIANS** *Picasso*

Search carefully and you will find a number of musical instruments playing a part in this lively pattern.

ments, thus adding contrast as well as force to the composition.

In the cubist still life painting of this time, observers were often startled to find that the painter had used other media in addition to paint. Bits of textured and printed papers, cloth, playing cards, and other odds and ends were pasted onto the composition so that their varied textures became a planned part of the scheme. Paintings of this type were known as *collages.*

Another step in the development of Cubist painting was made by Picasso, who departed still farther from reality by taking his subjects apart and recombining the various parts in such a way that they are, at times, difficult to recognize. Thus you will see in his *Three Musicians* (Illustration 221) that parts of three figures were arbitarily moved around until they satisfied Picasso's idea of an organized whole. Compare this painting with Braque's *Still Life* and you will notice similarities in treatment. For example, both painters limited the depth of the background spaces and kept them close to the front of the picture. For a contrast, look at Seurat's painting on page 208 and you will notice that the latter painter was interested in deep rather than limited space.

The basic idea of Cubism spread rapidly both through European countries and America. By 1923 there were hosts of cubist painters, some of whom followed closely in the footsteps of the innovators of the movement, while others developed it still further.

The Paintings of Kandinsky

Most of the cubist painters had retained traces of subject matter; that is, if one looked hard enough, certain things might be recognizable. In other words, they were semi-abstract. Wassily Kandinsky (1866–1944), a Russian painter who worked both in Germany and in the United States, felt strongly that a painting should be entirely without recognizable subject matter. It would then appeal to the observer purely on the strength of its organization of the elements of line, dark and light, color, texture, and space. Kandinsky's experiments led to paintings we now call *non-objective.* Illustration 222 shows us *Light Form* by Kandinsky. Notice that he paints with freely-flowing lines, shapes, and colors rather than with those that are geo-

222. LIGHT FORM *Kandinsky*

Kandinsky's flowing, musical rhythms avoid any suggestion of depth, for the artist felt that since paintings are made on a flat surface, they should remain flat.

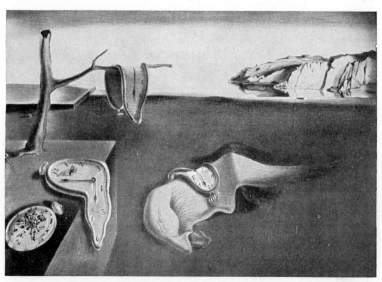

223. PERSISTENCE OF MEMORY *Dalí*

"How can the flexible quality of time be better expressed," says the artist, "than by painting watches which are soft and flaccid." His explanation of the background is that it represents eternity.

metric and tightly organized. Here, again, as with the Expressionists, we find color being used to project a mood, or what Kandinsky calls a "soul state."

The Surrealists

All of you, without doubt, have seen some surrealist paintings. You were probably intrigued, puzzled, or scornful of them, as many others have been. At any rate, the work of these painters is always challenging. Why do they paint such odd things, you may ask? There are clearly recognizable objects in these paintings, yet they do not remind us of still-life or figure paintings in general.

The surrealist painter applied himself to a task that was, on the whole, new in the annals of painting: that is the painting of the dream world and the realm of the subconscious. Most people have had dreams that have seemed more vivid than reality itself. In dreams strange fragments of life often combine themselves in utterly fantastic ways. Similarly, in daydreams, when we allow our thoughts to wander freely, we often lose, even though briefly, all contact with reality. Even when we are thoroughly awake, our thoughts are inclined to take little excursions of their own, and we are often surprised to find that we have been thinking such unexpected things.

Just as our dreams are so often fantastically woven around things that are distorted and weirdly combined, so surrealist paintings combine the seemingly unrelated fragments of dream recollections. The *Persistence of Memory* (Illustration 223) by Spanish-born Salvador Dalí (1904–   ), with its blue-faced dripping watches, challenges our imagination. The painter's explanation is that to him time is flexible, not rigid. Those who are ruled by time signals, such as alarm clocks and classroom bells, may particularly enjoy this painter's fantastic ideas concerning time.

The Surrealist group, in addition to Dalí, has included at one time or another such painters as the Spaniard Joan Miró (1893–   ), the Italian Giorgio de Chirico (1888–   ), the Russian Marc Chagall (1887–   ), the Frenchman André Masson (1896–   ), the German Max Ernst (1891–   ), and the Chilean Roberto Matta Echaurren (1911–   ).

224. PEOPLE IN THE NIGHT *Miró*

This tiny painting, so far removed from reality, has a startling, almost disturbing quality.

The horizontal lines on this face seem somewhat like venetian blinds behind which the actor peers at his audience.

225. ACTOR'S MASK *Klee*

All surrealist paintings are provocative; those of Miró seem to be especially so. Let us look at his *People in the Night,* seen in Illustration 224. There is a definite suggestion of "doodling" in the way these figures have been set down. You know that when you "doodle," your conscious mind is elsewhere, and that your hand simply follows subconscious dictation. In this way we often make drawings and designs that are strange and exciting. Miró says quite frankly that his paintings are always conceived in a state of hallucination "in which I am utterly irresponsible." From this way of working, as we can see, Miró arrives at freely improvised paintings that are very reminiscent of those of children. Certainly with an apparent minimum of effort he achieves a maximum of boldness.

Many people find themselves unable to take Miró's paintings seriously, just as they find the work of Paul Klee (1879–1940), a Swiss-born artist, far removed from their idea of what painting should convey. However, others find their spontaneity and directness very refreshing. Klee's *Actor's Mask,* shown in Illustration 225, is reminiscent of some of the masks made by primitive people. In spite of, or possibly because of its vagueness, it has the same odd power of holding us in some sort of weird spell, one of uncertain source but nevertheless compelling.

Directions of Modern Painting

As painting developed between the time of Giotto and Cézanne, its realm was greatly expanded. Not only did it become far more varied in technique but also in breadth of subject matter. Rather than dwelling on man's spiritual life, it came to be concerned primarily with man's everyday experiences in the world about him. From Cézanne's time onward, however, you have seen an even more radical break from early traditions, a departure from reality, or from what our eyes actually see to what our minds perceive. The twentieth century artist, as you have seen, came to be almost exclusively interested in expressing with a high degree of intensity his personal reactions to the inner, rather than to the surface, quality of his subject. This interest, as we shall see in a later chapter, is still the motivating force of the artists of your particular generation.

The effective silhouette of
this statue and the dramatic
energy of the tense, armored
figure reveal the creative
power of a notable sculptor.

226. COLLEONI *Verrocchio*

It is a generally accepted
fact that Michelangelo made
a self-portrait when he represented the Biblical character,
Nicodemus, as one of the figures in his last magnificent
stone carving.

227. LA PIETÀ, DETAIL *Michelangelo*

12.

Development of
Sculpture

THE present-day sculptor often makes references, half-humorous and half-serious, to his lot in life. Many people, he finds, buy paintings, but few buy sculpture. A painter, he says, can carry his supplies and his paintings around with ease, whereas a sculptor is weighed down by a mass of heavy and varied materials and equipment. Only a musician who has to transport a large instrument can appreciate the problems of a sculptor, particularly one who works in stone or solid metals, or on an unusually large scale.

It is true that the sculptor of today is not in the enviable position of the sculptor of the past. Consider briefly the Renaissance sculptor. He received commissions from the Church and State and from wealthy patrons of the arts. Sculpture was then an established part of every architectural scheme, both as exterior and as interior decoration. The sculptor was not only well paid, but also highly honored for his accomplishments.

Andrea Verrocchio (1435–1488), for example, was commissioned to do an equestrian statue of *Colleoni,* a great soldier of his age, for a public square in Venice. The dramatic strength of this larger-than-life bronze statue (Illustration 226), considered one of the noblest of its kind, has inspired many later sculptors of equestrian monuments.

228. **LORENZO DE' MEDICI, DETAIL** *Michelangelo*

Michelangelo's vitality, imagination, and keen intellect are all reflected in this world-famous figure.

Michelangelo, too, executed countless pieces of sculpture, all designed as a definite part of an architectural setting. His great accomplishment as a sculptor was the way in which he used the human figure to convey emotions. Compare his *Moses* on page 3 with *Queen Hatshepsut* on page 42. You will see that Michelangelo has gone far beyond the calm serenity of the Egyptian sculptor. Even if you were unable to see the face of *Moses* or the detailed modeling, the vigor of his pose would convey a message of prophetic power.

Michelangelo often spent months searching for just the right stone from which to carve his magnificent figures. While some are finished in careful detail, others retain a more rugged quality. Notice, for example, Illustration 227 which shows a section of a large figure group, *La Pietà,* the last piece he carved. You can almost see the motion of the sculptor's chisel as he brought out the simply suggested head from the hard stone.

Another well known statue by Michelangelo is his idealized figure of *Lorenzo de' Medici* (Illustration 228) which was commissioned by that nobleman for his own tomb. By the thoughtful pose of the head and hand we see that Michelangelo interpreted Lorenzo as a dreamer rather than a man of action.

Although sculpture was still greatly in demand, after Michelangelo its quality suffered a marked decline due to a prolonged interest in the mere imitation of the human figure. Sculpture, in fact, was not elevated until the twentieth century from its ignominious position in the arts, with the possible exception of the efforts of Auguste Rodin (1840–1917). Interestingly enough, Rodin worked in sculptural media with very much the same aim as his contemporaries, the Impressionist painters. Study Illustration 229 to verify this fact. It shows an amazingly lifelike figure that almost seems to have been painted rather than sculptured. By skillful surface treatment, the manipulation of clay and polishing of bronze, a shimmering light plays over the surface of the figure of *Balzac* and heightens its dramatic quality.

The work of Rodin brought the art of sculpture back into the public eye and again made people conscious of it as an important part of the creative arts. Shortly after this time, sculpture received renewed strength from the work of two sculptors of note: Wilhelm Lehm-

This statue seems almost more like a painting or a snapshot than like a piece of sculpture. Rodin was less interested in sculptural organization than in expressive surface modeling.

229. **BALZAC** *Rodin*

All of Maillol's sculpture, like the art of antiquity, has a timeless spirit. This young girl could easily represent one of your contemporaries or someone who lived centuries ago.

230. **HEAD OF A YOUNG GIRL**

Maillol

bruck (1881–1919), a German, and Aristide Maillol (1861–1944), a Frenchman.

Beginning of Modern Sculpture

You have seen how modern painting contains elements which originated in the past, as well as elements which are clearly the result of modern thought. Maillol's sculpture has an evident link with the Greek masterpieces of the early fifth century B.C. Like the sculptors of those days, he worked toward the goal of suggesting human beings as serene, stable, and possessed of almost godlike strength. Unlike the Greeks, however, Maillol also found delight in human qualities. Instead of perfecting and refining his figures, he made them more human and near to us, rather than godly and remote.

You may see this by contrasting his *Head of a Young Girl* (Illustration 230) with the *Head of Athena* on page 116. Both are modeled in the classic manner, but the *Head of a Young Girl* has an additional quality which suggests a real rather than an ideal person.

During Maillol's period, preceding the First World War, there were many sculptors who later became famous. This group included Henri Gaudier-Brzeska (1891–1915), a Pole, Georg Kolbe (1877–) and Ernst Barlach (1870–1938), both Germans, and Constantin Brancusi (1876–), a Rumanian.

Barlach's sculpture has enormous vitality, as you can see by looking at his *Singing Man,* shown in Illustration 231. A strong silhouette and opposed angular movements together create a dynamic figure. Just as the Expressionist painters, such as Van Gogh and Kokoschka, reached a high peak of emotional intensity in their work, so Barlach created a powerful figure through his strong feeling for his subject.

A great contrast to Barlach's work is that of Brancusi whose creations are almost completely abstract. His *Miss Expanding Universe* (Illustration 232) is a form that has been stripped of human identity. Its floating outline is strongly suggestive of a superhuman being or a force in continuous movement.

That sculptors should begin to think in terms of abstract and semi-abstract forms should not surprise you, for you have seen how modern painters at this very time were becoming equally interested in the

You will find it interesting to trace with your finger the movements which balance or stabilize this fine figure.

This streamlined form suggests an airplane in motion. It shows the artist's awareness of the new forms which have emerged from the Machine Age.

231. **SINGING MAN** *Barlach*

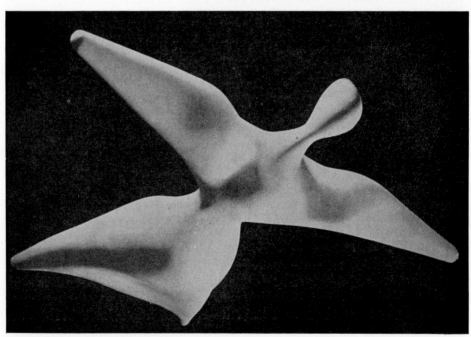

232. **MISS EXPANDING UNIVERSE** *Brancusi*

This figure was intended for an outdoor setting. It is, therefore, carried out in metal, a highly appropriate material. Light and space are planned elements in its design.

As with much of the Surrealist work, the ideas embodied in this piece of terra cotta prevail over its sculptural organization. It is, primarily, a challenge to our imagination.

233. **FIGURE** *Lipchitz*

234. **THE CITY** *Grippe*

non-objective phase of painting. From Brancusi's time on, in addition to an age-old preoccupation with the human figure as a subject, the sculptor also concerned himself with nonrepresentational themes.

The well-known French-American sculptor, Jacques Lipchitz (1891–), for example, created the geometric figure shown in Illustration 233. This idol-like form will undoubtedly remind you of some primitive and early sculpture you have seen, for the sculptor combined greatly simplified circular, oval, and rectangular forms. Notice, especially, how the interlocked spaces between these solid forms, known as open volumns, or voids, are an integral, rather than an accidental part of the strongly stressed pattern.

Since you have already discovered some of the theories of the Surrealist painters, you doubtless will be interested in seeing how they may be embodied in a sculptural medium. Look at *The City* (Illustration 234), the work of Peter Grippe (1912–), an American sculptor. There is a recognizable element in this terra cotta form similar to that seen in Lipchitz' metal *Figure,* for both pieces of sculpture suggest primitive idols. *The City,* however, instead of being built of precise, machinelike forms, is a freely composed mass with a contour reminiscent of the island of Manhattan. The surrealist element appears in the fantastic conception which mingles blocklike architectural forms with apparently disassociated symbols of heads, hands, and feet.

The Revival of Stone Carving

The traditional media of the sculptor—clay, wood, and stone—have been used since primitive man first played with a lump of clay, whittled a piece of wood, or hacked away at a stone. Since those days each era up to the present seems to have used one of these media more consistently than another. An example of this is the constant use of stone for direct carving in Egyptian, Greek, Gothic, and Renaissance times. The use of stone, of course, may be traced directly to the fact that the sculpture of those days was a distinct part of architectural construction, which also utilized stone.

As sculpture gradually became detached from its role in the architectural plan, direct stone carving both as an art and as a craft was supplanted by the use of far more malleable media, such as clay or plasticine, from which a model for a metal cast could be made. You have seen, for example, that Rodin first modeled his statue of *Balzac* in clay.

The modern sculptor, however, became greatly interested in direct stone carving and revived that almost lost art. As a result, today there are countless sculptors who work directly in this difficult medium. One of the established American stonecarvers, William Zorach (1887–   ), shows great vitality in his work. His black marble statue, *Affection* (Illustration 235), is built up of broadly simplified planes and masses which lead the eye to the climax of his piece, the head of the child. Notice how simply the gestures of the child interpret the theme of childish affection.

The endless variety of stones available to the sculptor: alabaster; porphyry; black, red, pink, and green marbles; granite; fieldstone; and limestone, to name but a few, stimulates the sculptor to take advantage of a wide range of color and texture. For example, alabaster, a soft, semi-transparent stone, can be so polished that highlights make its forms unusually dramatic. *Crying Woman* (Illustration 236) by Charles Salerno (1916–   ), an American sculptor, shows an unusually effective use of this medium. The sculptor has reached a high peak of intensity in this head in which he expressed not just the grief of one person, but that of millions when they learned of the invasion of Poland during the Second World War.

The All-Around View

When you see a fine color reproduction of a modern painting you can enjoy it almost as much as the original. A photograph of a modern building, too, can tell you a great deal about its subject, for you may see things in a photograph that escape your eyes when you view the complex original. A photograph of a piece of modern sculpture, however, fails to reveal completely one of its most important features, namely; it was designed to be seen, not from a single point of view but from many points of view, and its forms seem to move as our eye travels around it.

This modern idea of designing sculpture so that it is satisfactory

Notice how this statue retains the solid character of stone by avoiding the pierced openings which are appropriate only to clay, wood, or metal.

235. **AFFECTION** *Zorach*

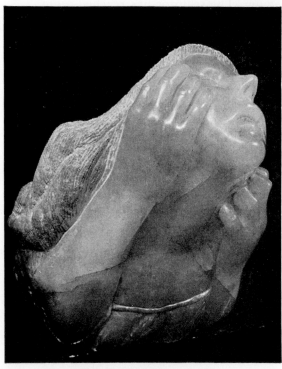

Polished, translucent alabaster gives a subtle suggestion of skin tones, and contrasts beautifully with the suggested texture of hair.

236. **CRYING WOMAN** *Salerno*

from almost every angle is a marked departure from the ideas of the past. For centuries sculpture was designed to be viewed from one angle only. Moreover, it was generally placed so that the most striking view was presented to the observer. Glance back through chapters 3 and 6 to confirm this fact.

Now contrast the equestrian statue of *Colleoni* on page 248 with the *Horse and Rider* (Illustration 237) by Marino Marini (1900–   ), a contemporary Italian sculptor. The view that you see of *Colleoni* is the one specifically designed for you to view, just as you are supposed to look at a painting, from one fixed position. A view of this statue from the front, back, or other side would be infinitely less interesting than the one presented. In contrast Marini's *Horse and Rider* was designed, as practically all modern sculpture is, both to carry the eye around it, and to make it interesting or exciting from many angles. This is the element you miss when you see this piece in a photograph. You must, therefore, walk around this statue in imagination to appreciate the continuous flow of its rhythms and the subtle balance of its masses.

Another interesting feature of this *Horse and Rider* is its bronze surface which has been treated to give it an antique look, as though it had been dug from an earthen grave that had protected it for centuries. Marini prefers to work in the crowded city of Milan, but he finds much of his inspiration in its surrounding countryside. He says, "When I visit the Roman countryside, I sit quietly and listen for the sounds of the past which sometimes rise from the ground. Then I go back to Milan and work."

In imagination, too, walk around the *Young Monk* (Illustration 238) by Henry Rox (1899–   ), an American sculptor. Although the photograph presents a single view, try to visualize the other views of this statue. You can almost feel the line and plane movements which unite the side and front of the figure and then continue to move around it. Notice, for example, the movements of the upper arm and hand which by their directions lead your eye around the head. How beautifully the sculptor has created both the character and mood of his subject! The withdrawn pose of the figure with its restrained and subtle movements and gestures are reminiscent, in their dramatic sense of fitness, of those you have seen in Giotto's paintings.

The backward glance of this horse and his rider suggest a reluctance to depart from a beloved countryside.

237. **HORSE AND RIDER** *Marini*

Contemplation, humility, and spiritual repose are expressed here in a subtle, deeply satisfying way.

238. **YOUNG MONK** *Rox*

There is a long passage of time from the days when Michelangelo, with almost superhuman strength and skill carved his great statues, to our present days and modern sculptors. Some of you may prefer contemporary sculpture when it is linked to the past and to long established sculptural traditions. Others may find a distinct challenge and excitement in contemporary work which seems to make a clean break with traditions and to establish entirely new ideals. You have seen such a break in Brancusi's *Miss Expanding Universe,* shown on page 254; you see it again in the work of Henry Moore (1898–   ), a highly creative English sculptor. Although Moore frequently uses the human figure as his starting point, as he does in his *Family Group* (Illustration 239), he freely simplifies, distorts, and recreates figures to suit his purpose. The members of the *Family Group* have a curiously elemental quality. They seem to be far removed from civilized man as we picture him today. Rather they appear to belong to an earlier age, one in which man and nature were closely identified, an age when man was an elemental part of nature.

Further Experiments in Sculpture

The urge to express themselves in a new way has stimulated the creative activities of countless modern sculptors. The terra-cotta head of *Henry* (Illustration 241) by Louis Dlugosz (1915–   ), although it is an open rather than a solid construction, attempts to suggest solidity through the use of shadows. To judge the success of this attempt, you must look at the head with half-closed eyes. Do you find that the shadows take their natural place on the surface of the head, and that it appears to be solid?

In your study of various phases of modern sculpture, you have seen many departures from traditional concepts. In the work of an artist such as Naum Gabo (1890–   ), a Russian, you find still more revolutionary ideas which embody much of contemporary thought about art. Study *Linear Construction, Variation,* shown in Illustration 243, by this artist. What are the characteristics you first notice? Of course, since it is completely abstract, it can in no way be identified with a recognizable subject. In fact, it is so far removed from what we

One of the greatest strengths of Moore's sculpture is its appeal to the sense of touch. Would you not like to run your fingers over these smoothly flowing and cool metal forms?

239. **FAMILY GROUP** *Moore*

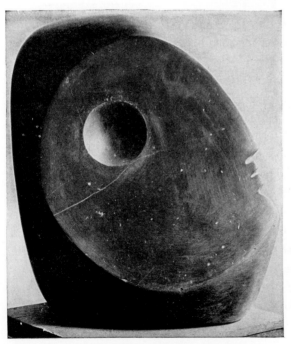

240. **THE COSDEN HEAD** *Hepworth*

What qualities do you find in this abstract head that remind you of those seen in the *Family Group?* It was carved in dark blue marble by Barbara Hepworth (1903–   ), an English sculptor.

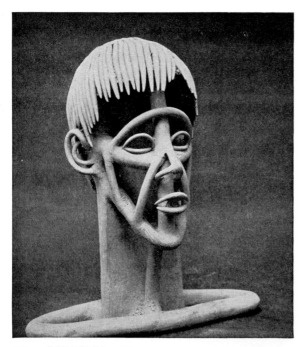

Frankly experimental, this head attempts to suggest rather than to reveal its forms. Do you think that the sculptor has succeeded in his purpose?

241. **HENRY** *Dlugosz*

A somewhat similar attempt to express form by means of open spaces is shown in this *Head* by Rudolf Belling (1886–   ), a German sculptor. The machine-like, metallic parts suggest that the sculptor was influenced by the mechanical spirit of his times.

242. **HEAD** *Belling*

243. LINEAR CONSTRUCTION, VARIATION *Gabo*

Transparent plastic, molded or shaped by hand, furnishes a medium that enriches contemporary sculpture.

generally think of as a fitting sculptural subject that it, together with other forms similarly inspired, is called a construction rather than a piece of sculpture.

Gabo has used plastic, a medium new to sculpture. Since all artists, painters, architects, sculptors, and craftsmen have become greatly interested in experimenting both with new materials and with new ways of using those that are traditional, you can easily understand how plastics, especially, challenge the imagination because of their various qualities, such as the ease with which they may be molded, their lightness, and their transparency.

Transparency, for example, brings a new feature to sculpture, that of light. While sculptors have always been aware of light and shadow as a part of their design, light now, with a plastic medium, becomes an integral part of the plan. This is clearly demonstrated in *Linear Construction, Variation,* for light pierces the transparent planes of plastic and reveals their rhythms.

When making this construction, the artist was primarily interested in developing a concept of space. By means of curved and diagonal transparent planes he has intercepted, or cut through space very much as an architect does by erecting the inner and outer structure of a building. The form of this subject is not the result of the artist's emotional reaction to his subject, as it might be if he were an Expressionist. Rather, it has been developed by means of mathematical theorems which, as you know, bring thought to a precise conclusion.

An especially noticeable quality of *Linear Construction, Variation* is its continuous, circulating movement. You have probably noticed how your eye travels endlessly around and through this construction, without being stopped by a definite center of interest.

This same quality of continuous movement began to interest other modern sculptors also. "Why only suggest movement, why not construct something that can actually move?" they thought. Marcel Duchamp (1887–   ), a French artist, then made an experimental construction which he mounted on a pedestal that could be rotated by hand. In this way, he invented the first piece of moving, or, as it is sometimes called, kinetic construction, a type of sculpture that he called a mobile.

When you see a mobile, even in its motionless, or static state, you can find esthetic pleasure in its beautifully balanced weights.

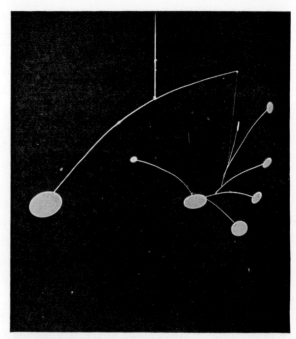

244. **HANGING MOBILE** *Calder*

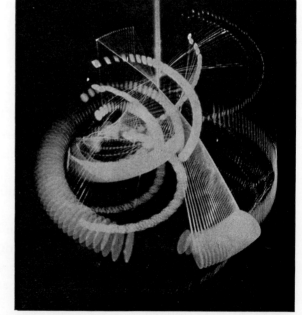

The identical mobile, however, is infinitely more interesting when in motion, as Calder intended it should be. Its lines and shapes then create rhythmically described forms which are capable of great variation.

245. **HANGING MOBILE IN MOTION**
Calder

Mobiles

Thus you see that sculpture had arrived at the point where it might give an impression of movement, since its forms were so designed that they seemed to move when the eye traveled around them. Today you may see and enjoy sculpture in which actual movement is a planned and essential part of its design. Whether this movement lasts only a second or is continuous, a design is created by motion and another element new to the art of sculpture is added, that of time.

Does this idea puzzle you? To clarify it, look at Illustration 244 which shows the *Hanging Mobile* by Alexander Calder (1898–   ), an American sculptor who is well-known for his highly inventive mobiles.

Notice that in this view its design elements are composed of a few thoughtfully balanced lines and shapes. When the *Hanging Mobile* rotates, however, its various parts, through their complex movements and counter-movements, create a far more rhythmic and exciting form, as you see in Illustration 245. Varying images of this mobile occur within certain cycles of time. Time is needed to complete the full image; thus time becomes the most important factor in its design.

Significance of Modern Sculpture

New ideas of what may be expressed in a sculptural form have brought into being a wide variety of three-dimensional works of art. Through a frankly experimental attitude, combined with a fresh and inventive use of materials, contemporary sculpture has become not only infinitely rich and varied, but also a fascinating means of individual expression.

The quaintness of this little boy is accentuated by his long, elaborate "Sunday dress" and his lace-trimmed bonnet.

The adult faces of the three children in this painting will remind you of some of the Italian primitive Holy Children you have seen.

246. **HENRY GIBBS** *Unknown Artist*

247. **THE PEACEABLE KINGDOM** *Hicks*

13.

Painting in the Americas

THE early settlers of New England, preoccupied with wresting a living from the soil or the sea, had little time to think about art. Furthermore, their Puritanical beliefs led them to frown upon any form of vanity, such as having one's "effigy," or portrait, painted. However, later in the seventeenth century, as they became more prosperous, they too, like the Flemish and Dutch people, began to enlist the services of an artist to portray themselves and their families.

These early painters, known as limners, were on the whole self-taught and highly versatile. Clock making and repairing, sign and portrait painting, and decorating carriages were all trades with which they were familiar. As might be expected of these untrained artists, their work was often childlike. That they lacked both knowledge and technical skill is easily seen. Equally apparent, however, is their sincerity and their undaunted spirit.

Typical of the work of these anonymous and primitive painters is the portrait of *Henry Gibbs* (Illustration 246). Painted by an unknown artist, it shows a sturdy little figure solemnly holding a bird. The smallness of the figure is emphasized by the amount of space around it and by the large-checked floor.

Another primitive American artist, Edward Hicks (1780–1849), painted in very much the same naïve spirit as Henri Rousseau, whose work you have seen on page 238. *The Peaceable Kingdom* (Illustra-

269

Sensitive modeling and close values subtly keyed to the tone of the child's face make this a highly appealing portrait.

248. **LITTLE ROSE OF LYME REGIS** *Whistler*

249. **THE BATH** *Cassatt*

Would you not agree that by looking down on her subjects, the artist obtained a particularly interesting view of them?

tion 247) includes a friendly collection of animals, some of which seem to be posing attentively for their portraits. Hicks found his inspiration for this painting in the Bible—sixth, seventh, and ninth verses of Chapter 11, Isaiah.

"The wolf also shall dwell with the lamb, and the leopard shall lie down with the kid; and the calf and the young lion and the fatling together: and a little child shall lead them.

"And the cow and the bear shall feed; their young ones shall lie down together; and the lion shall eat straw like the ox.

"They shall not hurt nor destroy in all my holy mountain: for the earth shall be full of the knowledge of the Lord, as the waters cover the sea."

Arrival of the Trained Artist

In the nineteenth and the early part of the twentieth centuries in America, it seemed almost imperative that painters travel or study abroad. Paris, especially, was considered the artistic center of the world. Just as her fashion designers dictated the styles in costume, so her painters were the ones to inspire most of the American painters of that time. Few as yet thought of themselves as American painters, nor did they in most cases seek to identify themselves with the life of their native country.

James McNeil Whistler (1834–1903), for example, went to Paris at the age of twenty-two to study painting and remained abroad permanently. After a long and stormy career in England, where he was often embroiled in arguments with professional critics, he retired for most of the latter part of his life to France where his talents were recognized and he was hailed as a leading modern painter. The French government bought his *Portrait of the Artist's Mother,* a most unusual honor to be accorded to an American.

Like many of the French painters of this time, Manet and Degas for example, Whistler greatly admired Japanese prints. Certain of their characteristics are reflected in his work. The stress on simple and beautifully designed shapes, and the close range in tone found in these prints are all part of the charm of his *Little Rose of Lyme Regis* (Illustration 248).

250. **THE RACE TRACK** *Ryder*

This snugly capped and picturesque figure, with his long beard so neatly tucked inside his jacket, is the painter of *The Race Track*. The portrait was done by Marsden Hartley (1877–1943), a well-known American painter and friend of the artist.

251. **ALBERT P. RYDER**
Hartley

Another American, Mary Cassatt (1845–1926), went to Paris to study painting and remained there. As a pupil of Degas, she absorbed much of that master's extraordinary ability to organize compositional elements into a design apparently spontaneous and casual. The mother and child themes which were her greatest interest were treated in a sympathetic yet strong way. This artist never allowed over-sweetness or sentimentality to mar her interpretation. Illustration 249 shows how effectively she could arrange two such figures. The angular scheme is relieved by occasional curves; even the striped pattern in the mother's dress plays a definite part in her linear scheme.

Pioneer Painters

At a time when most American artists were following the fresh and exciting paths discovered by Cézanne, Matisse, and other European painters, a New England painter, Albert P. Ryder (1847–1917), was living a hermitlike existence in his dingy studio in New York. Almost entirely self-taught, and oblivious to the work of his contemporaries, both at home and abroad, he did not paint easily or quickly because his technical traning was slight, and he was so painstaking that he worked at intervals on a painting for as long as eighteen years.

Ryder's numerous paintings were based on land and sea subjects. They are the work of a man who knew nature thoroughly, had absorbed her essential characteristics, and subsequently used them as an instrument to convey his dreams and mystic visions. One of his widely known paintings, *The Race Track* (Illustration 250), is a symbolic interpretation of a tragic theme. It was painted after the death of a friend, a waiter who lost his life savings at a race track. The mood is suggested not only by the pale figure of the horse ridden by death and by the snake, symbol of evil, in the foreground, but also by the dramatically barren landscape with its ominous sky.

Ryder was unrecognized during his own lifetime but later was hailed as the first truly American modern painter. During this same period, a contemporary, Winslow Homer (1836–1910), also painted in a way that had many of the characteristics of modern painting. Homer's paintings reveal his interest in his surroundings and his

252. STORM AT THE BAHAMAS *Homer*

What means do you think the artist used to convey such a strong feeling of an impending storm?

253. WHITE HORSE *Bellows*

Even simple, homely themes can be made dramatic when interpreted by an artist as talented as Bellows.

vigorous power in interpreting them. His capabilities are well displayed in his *Storm at The Bahamas* (Illustration 252). Those of you who have worked in watercolor will be especially appreciative of the crisp, fresh, decisive quality of the washes and the simple, undetailed handling of the theme.

Painters of the American Scene

The American scene at the beginning of the twentieth century found many painters, such as Alden Weir (1852–1919) and Childe Hassam (1859–1935) interested in landscape which they painted very much in the manner of the French Impressionists. At this time a younger group of painters, although many of them Paris-trained, united in a vigorous fight to establish native American traditions in art. Included in this group were Robert Henri (1865–1929), Maurice Prendergast (1859–1924), William Glackens (1870–1938), Ernest Lawson (1873–1939), John Sloan (1871–1951), and George Bellows (1882–1925).

Although each was a highly individual artist interested in varying aspects of painting, the group found themselves dubbed the Ashcan School of Painting, a name derived from the fondness some of the members had for painting the backyards of New York's tenements.

Bellows, the youngest and most versatile member of the group, painted many aspects of the American scene, ranging from vigorous "man's world" paintings of prize fights to scenes of the countryside. His *White Horse,* shown in Illustration 253, suggests a haunting, half-remembered farmland caught in a moment just before twilight. It is an assured painting which shows that the artist could go beyond mere reporting to the translation of his theme.

Painting the American scene continues to have endless fascination for regional painters. On the whole, they do a kind of down-to-earth reporting that emphasizes, as in the work of Grant Wood (1892–1942) and John Curry (1897–1946), the sturdiness of rural life in the Middle West and its characteristic environment. Quaintly pictorial aspects of other sections, are to be seen in the work of Doris Lee (1905–   ) and Anna Mary (Grandma) Moses (1860–   ), the astounding primitive who never painted until she was 75 years of age.

254. MAINE COAST *Marin*

In this strong painting, details have been sacrificed to make the total organization more compelling and so convey the artist's message more effectively.

255. PERTAINING TO YACHTS AND YACHTING
Sheeler

The almost mathematical severity of this painting by Charles Sheeler (1893–   ) makes it highly effective.

Painting Loses Its Boundaries

In 1913 an extensive exhibition of painting and sculpture, known as the Armory Show, was displayed in this country, first in New York, then in Chicago and Boston. It included the works of some 300 pre-modern and modern painters from France, Germany, England, Russia, Italy, Spain, and America. It was arranged by a group of young painters here who thought the American public should become aware of the advances made in painting within recent times. The public, as you may well imagine, was either totally unprepared to appreciate or unwilling to understand the work of the moderns, or "madmen" as they were called. They felt that this work was deliberately designed to destroy all traditional standards of painting.

Public enlightenment and recognition came slowly, but it finally arrived. Today our museums, for example, have exhibitions of modern paintings that are attended by thousands of appreciative visitors.

From the days of the Armory Show onward, painting in America gradually joined forces with European painting. While painters naturally continued to work in an individual way and struggled to solve the particular problems in which they were interested, all those who were truly creative recognized the need for a fundamental framework, an underlying structure of design on which to build. In order to understand this idea more fully, consider the work of some of America's best-known moderns.

Paintings of John Marin

John Marin (1870–   ) is considered America's greatest water-colorist. Many professional critics, in fact, are convinced that he is the greatest American-born painter. His highly individual style is so unmistakable that a Marin watercolor could not possibly be mistaken for the work of any other artist.

Nature has always been the favorite source of Marin's inspiration. He has painted again and again the rocks, mountains, skies, seas, and sand to be found on the Maine coast. Just as the Chinese landscape painters searched for and recorded the essential elements of their

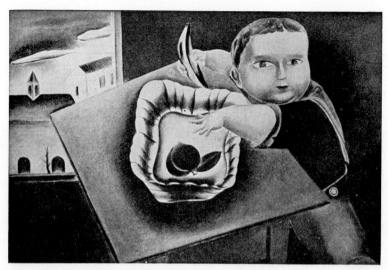

256. BOY STEALING FRUIT *Kuniyoshi*

Distortion has been freely used by the artist to make his composition more interesting and to heighten its dramatic quality.

257. APRIL SHOWERS *Rattner*

There is fascination in discovering how many different people appear in this active painting.

subject, so Marin extracts from nature those forms which will best express his reactions to the whole scene. Notice, for example, in his *Maine Coast* (Illustration 254), that the forms are semi-abstract; that is, they are recognizable even though they have been suggested by the simplest of means. Planes of color have their movements accentuated by dark washes, by brilliant paths of light, and by forcefully indicated line directions. It is interesting to notice how all of these movements lead the eye to the center of the painting. Beginning with the long diagonals in the upper part, which are parallel to the observer, his attention is swept across the top, around the right hand side, and from the lower edge swiftly into the middle and far distance, ending with a shape that vaguely suggests a many-masted schooner. Other diagonals are thrust against these movements; they balance them and add to their vitality and force.

Other Important Painters

America, with her many opportunities for freedom of expression, has naturally attracted foreign-born artists. Their varied strains of race, outlook, and training, when mingled with those of the native-born American painter, have enriched our art to an immeasurable degree. One of these is Yasuo Kuniyoshi (1893–   ), a Japanese-American who came to this country at the age of fifteen. His work is an interesting combination of Oriental and American traditions. You may see this in his *Boy Stealing Fruit,* shown in Illustration 256. Its somewhat self-conscious primitive quality reminds us of primitive American paintings, such as *Henry Gibbs,* which you have seen on page 268. It has, moreover, a sense of humor, for the child's act of sly greediness has been subtly emphasized.

Today the field of painting is so broad that it contains countless painters, each with a particular interest. Abraham Rattner (1895–   ), for example, one of the most powerful painters of our time, is particularly interested in presenting his theme in a multiple view. His *April Showers* (Illustration 257), you will notice, conveys a strong feeling of movement by his device of merging faces, bodies, arms, hands, and umbrellas in an almost kaleiodoscopic pattern. It is clear that he did not attempt to convey the idea that he saw his subject

Paintings such as this may not be pleasant to see but they tell a vivid story of misery and poverty. What do you think the artist's purpose might have been for painting this picture?

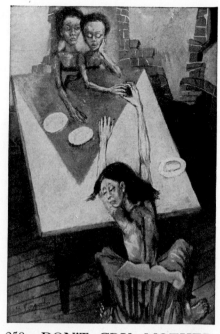

A message may be read into this painting. Do you think it concerns the misfortunes of one man only?

258. **DON'T CRY, MOTHER**
Evergood

259. **THE RED STAIRWAY** *Shahn*

from just one point of view, but that he presented it as though he had walked around, seen and then painted it from many different angles. Notice how he has merged the various heads, for example, and has recombined them to form multiple images of them.

Painters of the Social Scene

Philip Evergood (1901–   ), like Goya and Daumier, whose work you have seen on pages 194 and 202, is known today as a painter of social messages. The disaster, suffering, and dire poverty that countless humans undergo are brought, through the paintings of this artist, to the attention of those far more fortunate.

Don't Cry, Mother (Illustration 258) is a grim, almost bitter painting, deliberate in its intention of conveying how forcefully the artist was moved by his subject. Notice how Evergood distorted the three figures, with their emaciated and lengthened arms and their enlarged heads, and how he gave them expressions of complete despair. These are his most readily apparent ways of heightening the emotions he wished to convey to you.

Another contemporary painter, Ben Shahn (1898–   ), is equally concerned with human suffering and despair. His *Red Stairway,* seen in Illustration 259, shows a cripple laboriously ascending the stairway of a ruined building. Below emerges a figure shouldering a burden, possible fragments of rubble. The entire scene suggests tragedy.

Experimental Painters of Today

In tracing the course of painting from its early days to the twentieth century, you will see that on the whole it has been based on representational subject matter. You can recognize, for example, Bushman and Egyptian figures, understand the meaning of Giotto's religious scenes, Titian's portraits, Constable's landscapes, and Cézanne's still life. They are based on human experiences with which the observer can more or less easily identify himself. Although most observers may not be able to capture them with brush and paint, they can recognize the impulses which led others to do so.

However, the twentieth century has produced abstract paintings that are far more difficult to understand. Their meanings often elude the public; observers feel out of sympathy with, if not downright suspicious of, the painters who produced such work. In this attitude our generation is not unique, for the majority of painters have not been fully appreciated during their lifetime. In some cases, hundreds of years have elapsed before they have been "discovered." Thus although a painter is often a stranger to his own generation, he may be a familiar friend of the next.

The paintings of Stuart Davis (1894–   ) often present a challenge to those who look for a story in paint. Why paint something so unromantic as *Garage Lights* (Illustration 260), you might ask. Read what Davis himself says about his painting:

"In my painting, *Garage Lights,* there was no intention to make a replica of the optical appearance of the place. Instead, its elements of form, color, and space are changed to meet the requirements of a sense of dimensional unity, which develops and becomes complete as I study them. The result is a permanent record of an emotional experience expressed in terms of coherent color-space dimensions."

From this statement you may well realize that painters of semi-abstract or abstract subjects have a definite aim which they choose to express in their own particular way.

Many other painters of your own time are seeking to create paintings which, in content and in method, will be entirely a product of this century. For example, take the work of I. Rice Pereira (1907–   ), to be seen in Illustration 261. By studying it carefully, you will discover what she is interested in expressing. Notice first the number of suspended, framelike shapes, some light and others dark, some apparently solid and others semi-opaque. Their planes intersect, or pierce, one another in such a way that they bring the eye to the centrally placed dark square that establishes the definitely limited depth of her painting.

An additional quality, one rather difficult to realize without seeing the original, is that of transparent light with its corresponding shadows, and the effect of both on the color quality. The artist paints on sheets of glass that have been fixed in successive positions in front of a masonite panel. Some of the glass is transparent and smooth; some has been made opaque and rough by sandblasting. The sheet nearest

260. GARAGE LIGHTS *Davis*

The sharp, clean-cut brilliance of this geometric pattern seems to have been logically derived from the utilitarian, manmade forms selected by the artist.

In addition to her other innovations in painting, this artist has added the idea of viewing a painting from many angles. This composition varies according to the position of the spectator.

261. TRANSFLUENT LINES
Pereira

to the observer is corrugated, as you will see by closely examining the faint vertical lines that indicate its rippling.

As well as the novel use of glass, the artist uses plastic, tempera, and oil paints, and various varnishes and lacquers. Some of these materials have been mixed with sand and other substances which vary their textural effects. In addition, they have been applied with a variety of unconventional tools, as you can see by observing the areas that are crossed by thinly combed lines.

Painting in Mexico

Have you ever heard it said of an artist that "he paints in an ivory tower"? This description, as you probably know, implies that such a painter does not find his inspiration for painting in the actual world in which he lives. Those of you who feel strongly that painting should be based on real life situations rather than on abstract concepts of the physical world will find great satisfaction in the work of many of the modern Mexican painters, for their work is, on the whole, deeply rooted in the life and the traditions of their people.

Mural painting is a much practiced art in Mexico, for the government commissions its painters to decorate the interior walls of public buildings with murals based on the life of the people as the painter himself interprets it. Since Mexican painters naturally get a great deal of satisfaction from producing murals that are constantly seen by thousands of people, they do comparatively little "easel painting," or paintings to be seen occasionally and enjoyed by a few people at a time.

Outstanding among modern Mexican artists are Diego Rivera (1886–   ), Alfaro Siqueiros (1898–   ), and José Orozco (1883–1949). Each of these artists is concerned with the same theme, that of exposing and bettering the lot of the laboring classes, yet each has a highly individual mode of expression. Orozco, for example, painted with the great intensity which has distinguished the work of another equally passionate painter, Vincent Van Gogh. Study Orozco's painting, *Zapatistas* (Illustration 262), which depicts a group of farm laborers and followers of Zapata, a reformer who strove to improve the condition of the worker. Strongly opposed diagonals sug-

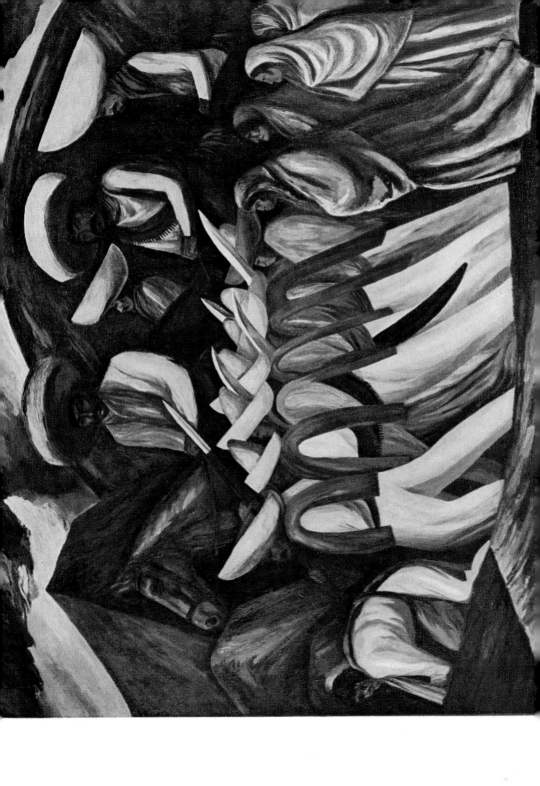

262. **ZAPATISTAS** *Orozco*

gest forceful movement. Hot colors, reds, pinks, yellows, and deep oranges, made intense in certain areas by the use of white, are almost violently opposed by the few but important cool green and blue notes of color. Do you not agree that the entire painting is charged with tremendous vitality?

Painting in Cuba and Brazil

Strongly marked individuality is a characteristic of most Latin Americans. It is not surprising, therefore, to find in the work of many contemporary Cuban painters a vigorous expression of an independent spirit. Notice, for example, how the brilliant light of a tropical country has inspired Carlos Enríquez (1900–   ), a Cuban painter. How effectively he has used this intense light in his *Landscape with Wild Horses* (Illustration 263). Vast, whirling rhythms of light compose the skeleton of this painting. Follow them rapidly with your eye; you cannot help reacting to their stirring movement. Starting in the right hand corner, analyze their force by tracing these light rhythms with your finger. You will then discover how their sweeping curves, in the shape of the letter "s," convey a sensation of perpetual motion.

How different is the *Barber Shop* (Illustration 264) by Cundo Bermudez (1914–   ), another Cuban painter! Here are things characteristic of such a commonplace scene: a barber, his customer, comb, scissors, a barber's chair and pole. Added are elements typical of Cuba, such as floral decorations and a musical instrument. The artist has used all these elements freely, making them large or small, elaborate or simplified, according to his estimate of their importance in his painting. Again you see how the truly creative painter can take a scene of everyday life, intensify it, and make it an instrument of personal expression.

Although it is in the field of modern achitecture that Brazil has particularly distinguished herself, there is also in this South American country a growing awareness of the modern movement in painting. The most important of the Brazilian painters is Candido Portinari (1903–   ) whose work is highly colorful and visually exciting. His *Woman and Children,* seen in Illustration 265, shows his interest

285

263. **LANDSCAPE WITH WILD HORSES** *Enríquez*

264. **BARBER SHOP** *Bermudez*

Free, rapid movements, a marked contrast between the large, wind- and rain-swept landscape and the small, wild horses build a dramatic and highly personal interpretation of an exciting and romantic theme.

An element of humor plays a part in this painter's interpretation of his subject. The two figures are almost identical in profile. One is comfortably relaxed; the other, having momentarily laid aside his guitar, is intent on the performance of his duties.

265. WOMAN AND CHILDREN *Portinari*

Notice how unusually the painter arranged these figures. The large, centrally placed group furnishes a striking contrast to the small, dancing figures that recede into the distance.

in the festivities of the common people. A mood of abandoned merriment which is conveyed by rapidly fluttering rhythms of light and dark, is intensified by the masklike treatment of the six heads.

Meaning of Modern Painting

Just as it is difficult for us to form a well-rounded idea of the character of a person who is close to us, like a member of our immediate family, so it is equally difficult to estimate the full value of the paintings of our contemporaries. Their achievements, naturally, need time to be properly evaluated. That will be accomplished by a later generation. We do know, however, that today there is a host of lively, independent, and highly creative young artists who use painting to develop new concepts of our world, and who do not hesitate to express them in a courageous and forceful way.

14.

Modern Architecture

MANY of you have often heard older people, such as your grandparents, say, "My! How things have changed! Why, I remember when we thought a seven-story building was terribly high, and you know, when I was young, there were only a few houses in our neighborhood. Now it's crowded with tall buildings."

To you, of course, there probably have not been many spectacular changes in the appearance of your neighborhood since you have lived there. But if you were older and had lived in several places, you, too, would be conscious of amazing changes in the appearance not only of your own neighborhood, but also of cities, towns, and even villages throughout America, for within a fifty-year span a vital new art, that of modern architecture, has developed.

You know from your previous study of architecture that builders had long been content simply to vary traditional forms and methods of building. What, then, do you suppose are the factors that brought about such radical changes in the way of building bridges, factories, offices, stores, schools, churches, terminals, houses, and other similar structures?

To begin with, there was, in the late nineteenth and early twentieth centuries, a need for new kinds of buildings. Various discoveries of science had developed ways to manufacture things more cheaply and faster than ever before, and so commerce became an enormous indus-

266. OFFICE, JOHNSON WAX FACTORY *Racine, Wis.*

It is interesting to see glass and reinforced concrete used not only functionally but also as part of a design which repeats its curves even in the office desks and chairs.

267. U.S. FOREST SERVICE BUILDING *Madison, Wis.*

Notice the interesting contrast between the stable horizontal planes of the lower portion of this building and the definitely vertical movements of its upper section. This structure is also well provided with extensive window spaces.

try. Commerce called for expanded factories in which to make things, larger places in which to transact business, and more attractive places in which to sell industrial products.

In the early days of manufacturing, factories and offices were not built for the comfort and the efficiency of workers. They were ugly, dirty, and far from being systematically planned. Light, air, and cleanliness were not thought of as essentials. It is interesting, therefore, to discover that our pioneer modern architects were very much concerned with the relationship between the efficiency of the worker and the physical conditions—light, air, and space—as well as the working facilities which were available to him. Just as the designer of a machine strives to produce one that will be an improvement on previous models by successfully accomplishing more operations in a shorter time, so the modern architect came to think of his building as a machine to be designed so that it would perform its various functions with the highest degree of efficiency. Since he was primarily concerned with the activities to be carried on within the building, he carefully considered the requirements of the interior spaces first. The outward form of the building was then the result of its interior plan, or as the commonly used phrase goes, its form followed its function.

Look at Illustration 266, which shows the office of an industrial plant. See how the architect, Frank Lloyd Wright, consciously planned for the comfort, both practical and esthetic, of the people who work there. The large room is open, airy, and through the use of Pyrex glass tubes in the ceiling, both efficiently and attractively lighted.

It is a heartening sign of the times to find that industrial plants of all kinds are receiving serious architectural consideration. Science and art are together responsible for amazingly efficient and handsome structures, not only one such as the *U.S. Forest Service Building* by Holabird and Root (Illustration 267), but also schools, hospitals, terminals, service stations, banks, and storage buildings, to name but a few. You probably think of a school or a hospital as a rather dreary place, as most of them are indeed. Fast increasing in number, however, are the schools and hospitals, such as those shown in Illustrations 270 and 271, which have been designed in the modern manner, that is, only after the architect has made a careful study of both the functions of the building and the nature of the people who are to use it.

291

Here workers are perilously aloft, setting into place the steel beams which form the framework of a modern skyscraper.

Industrial structures such as this are designed with only one aim in mind, that of efficiency, yet often there is an exciting and even dramatic quality in their purely functional forms that has served to inspire the modern architect.

268. **FRAMEWORK, ESSO BUILDING,**
New York, N.Y.

269. **BAYTOWN REFINERY** *Baytown, Texas*

Design and Materials

One of the important ideas of the pioneers of modern architecture concerned the relation between the design of the building and the materials from which it was constructed. Cast iron and steel, for example, in the late nineteenth century, had been used as reinforcement for stone but the metal was concealed so that the building looked as though it had been built entirely of stone. Louis Sullivan, a revolutionary architect, and more than any other the creator of the modern skyscraper, did not believe in this misleading type of design. He thought that an architect should not attempt to conceal the structure of his building. He believed, in fact, that this very structure, together with the forms dictated by its function, should be a controlling feature of its design. Thus, for example, a building with a structural steel framework would emphasize its skeleton of vertical shafts and horizontal beams. When you realize that countless architects of Sullivan's time were still copying old buildings even though their methods of construction were contemporary, you can better understand the importance of Sullivan's theories. That they greatly influenced future building may be easily seen by referring to Illustration 268, for the vertical and horizontal steel skeleton is clearly visible in the lines of the completed buildings in the background.

The use of steel developed rapidly and produced revolutionary changes in architecture. Thick supporting walls became a thing of the past. With steel construction, walls became merely the outer shell, or covering of a building; they supported no weight. It became possible to make them of almost any material, even glass. Since, with steel construction, each floor carries its own weight, there seemed to be almost no limit to the height to which a building might go, provided that the newly invented elevator could service it adequately.

The Skyscraper

There was, of course, every reason to aim for taller and taller buildings, especially in large, rapidly growing cities. Land there is valuable, with business and commerce heavily concentrated in certain

293

The character of this design is appropriate to a warm, sunny climate. The architects of this school were Guirey and Jones.

The plan of this unconventional little hospital was based upon the needs of the people there. It is an unusually open and airy structure.

270. **PHOENIX UNION HIGH SCHOOL**
Phoenix, Arizona

271. **LEA COUNTY COMMUNITY HOSPITAL** *Hobbs, New Mexico*

Notice that the upper section of this building is reminiscent of the towered Gothic cathedrals of the Middle Ages.

272. WOOLWORTH BUILD-
ING *New, York, N.Y.*

273. DAILY NEWS BUILD-
ING *New York, N.Y.*

The modern architect designs his build-ings to be seen from a distance. However, they are seldom viewed in their entirety by the observer.

of its sections. Thus an era of skyscraper building set in which produced in large cities, such as New York and Chicago, towering buildings that served as many persons as might be found in a small city. See how the architects of the first skyscrapers met the problem of this new kind of design. One of the early skyscrapers was the *Woolworth Building* (Illustration 272), finished in 1913, in downtown New York. Its architect, Cass Gilbert, although designing a twentieth-century building, still clung to the idea that some architectural traditions should be maintained; so he ornamented the building with Gothic details which seem strangely out of keeping with its modern form of construction, not to mention its use and location.

A later skyscraper, the *Daily News Building* (Illustration 273) designed by Raymond Hood, shows how subsequent architects really began to design in terms of modern construction. There is not the slightest hint of the past in this highly efficient building, nor does it have superfluous ornamentation. Notice how the vertical pattern stresses its vertical steel shafts and thus accentuates its height. Another interesting thing to notice about the *Daily News Building* is its slight and beautifully balanced irregularity of contour, created by its setbacks. The setback, as you doubtless know, came to be a part of modern architecture as a result of zoning laws. These laws were created to maintain light and air for other buildings around a skyscraper, and so regulated the amount of land and aerial space a skyscraper could occupy.

The Slab Skyscraper

One of the most interesting experiments in modern building is *Rockefeller Center* (Illustration 274) in New York, the largest privately owned business and entertainment center in the world. Its fifteen buildings occupy an area of more than twelve and one-half acres in the heart of Manhattan. They provide for many different activities, such as entertainment, sports, broadcasting, journalism, and international trade. There are also a wide variety of offices which represent countless world industries, a shopping center, a post office, consulates, many restaurants, a large garage, and two underground shipping rooms.

296

274. ROCKEFELLER CENTER *New York, N.Y.*

For the first time on an extensive scale, *Rockefeller Center* has employed landscaping as decoration for a business center. Countless gardens flourish both on roof tops and on the street level.

275. SECRETARIAT BUILDING, UNITED NATIONS

New York, N.Y.

The slab form presents an interesting contrast to that of the set
back to be seen in the *Daily News Building* at the right.

In form, in color, and in texture, this modern home is closely related both to its site and to the surrounding landscape.

276. **FALLING WATER** *Bear Run, Pa.*

277. **SAVOIE HOUSE** *Poissy, France*

You can look at many buildings from the outside and get quite a good idea how the inside looks. The outer view of this house, however, does not reveal many of its interesting features, such as the second story terrace, the roof garden, and the ramps which have been used instead of stairways.

The original architects for *Rockefeller Center* were Reinhard and Hofmeister; Corbett, Harrison, and MacMurray; and Hood and Fouilhoux. From the first they planned this Center on a large scale and in a new and independent manner. Its buildings were designed as a unit with ample space for plazas, promenades, gardens, and good light and air. Notice that the tall buildings, although they have some setbacks, are essentially slab-like in form. The slab evolved from mathematical calculations designed both to utilize ground and space to best advantage, and to provide adequate light and air in all parts of the building. It is as expressive of modern times as the pyramid was in Egyptian days and the Gothic cathedral in the Middle Ages.

The slab type of building was selected by the international group of architects in charge of the plan for the United Nations as the one most suitable for its restricted seventeen-acre site, since space had to be gained by height. If more than one tall building had been constructed, natural light would have been shut off. The *Secretariat Building, United Nations* (Illustration 275), in New York overlooking the East River, is thirty-nine stories high and provides outside office space for over 4,000 people. The east-west façades are surfaced with blue-green glass in aluminum frames, while the windowless north-south ends are faced with white marble.

Modern Houses

Modern ideas about architecture include the designing of homes well adapted to modern living. Although there are still vast numbers of people who cling to traditional types of homes, such as those in the Colonial style, there is an increasing number of those who, when choosing a home, prefer to have one in the modern style, built with modern methods of construction and with the latest of modern materials.

Frank Lloyd Wright, whose well-planned *Office* you have seen on page 290, is one of the most inventive of the modern architects who are particularly interested in domestic architecture. Characteristic of his houses is an emphasis on horizontals, which he feels relates the house to its site. Study his *Falling Water* (Illustration 276), which was built of rough native stone and smooth reinforced concrete on a

278. SHATTUCK HOUSE *Seattle, Wash.*

Without partitioned spaces, this room is unusually large and well lighted.

279. HAINES HALL HOUSE *Marin County, Calif.*

Extensive use of glass and native redwood produces interesting shadows and transparencies.

rocky ledge of varying levels over a stream. Notice how slabs of concrete project without the conventional end support of pillars. This type of reinforced concrete construction, known as cantilever construction, aids greatly in making the house seem more open and less box-like in character.

The modern style of domestic architecture has made definite headway in Europe, spreading from Austria, Germany, and Holland to France, Belgium, Czechoslovakia, Switzerland, Italy, Scandinavia, and Russia. You have seen the *Tugendhut House* by Mies van der Rohe on page 13 and have noted the simple, clean-cut forms which distinguish the work of this famous architect. Equally interesting and inventive is the work of the Frenchman, Le Corbusier, an architect, painter, and writer, and an acknowledged leader in the modern movement. His *Savoie House* (Illustration 277) has a unique construction, with the outer part of the cubic volume held aloft by slender piers. Thus its inhabitants can look over the countryside and enjoy the view. The upper section is partially open to provide a roof terrace. On the level above there is also a roof garden.

Interiors

The interior of the modern house is basically different from that of the traditional house because of its treatment of interior space. Interior walls in traditional houses fulfill two functions: they help to support the structure and they break up the interior into fixed and permanent areas, such as a living room, a dining room, a library, and a bedroom.

Since, however, in modern methods of construction, interior walls are not needed for support, they may be placed at will or even omitted entirely. Thus a definite feature of the modern house is its open and freely flowing space, and its relatively few fixed flat or even curved partitions. The *Shattuck House* (Illustration 278), designed by Young and Richardson, has a spacious, airy interior with work, entertainment, and conversation areas an unsegregated part of the whole. Notice that the window has been so expanded that it forms an entire wall. This treatment of glass which, as you have previously seen, is characteristic of modern architecture, serves to unite the outdoors and the indoors and to overcome that "shut-in" feeling which often comes from being indoors and apart from sun and fresh air.

The traditional house often has a high porch, well separated from the ground. The modern house, in contrast, generally has a low terrace from which one moves directly to the surrounding lawn or garden. In the delightfully open *Haines Hall House* (Illustration 279), designed by Hillmer and Callister, there seems to be scarcely a break from the interior to the expansive terrace and the surrounding lands.

Problems of City Planning

Those of you who either live in large cities or occasionally visit them, are aware of their disadvantages as well as their advantages. Chief among the former are the difficulties involved in transportation since the city dweller often must travel miles to go to work or school. The conveyances that move as quickly as the subway are so uncomfortably crowded that they are far from being a pleasant mode of travel. Types of conveyance which travel on the surface cannot make their way with any speed because of traffic congestion and the constant stopping for traffic lights. Pedestrians are frequently hampered by this rush of traffic. Impatiently dodging between cars, they make life miserable for the car drivers who, in turn, make walking equally unpleasant for the pedestrian.

Then, too, the city dweller often has a feeling of being "cooped up." He may go all day, or all week, or even all year without seeing green grass and trees, and breathing uncontaminated air. Since city rents are high, he is often forced to live in crowded quarters in an undesirable neighborhood. Many critics of our city life say that the city dweller is a victim of our highly industrialized life. Not until large cities are broken up, or decentralized, and until man can again have some kind of direct contact with nature will he live a healthy, happy, and productive life. However, other critics, similarly concerned with the plight of the city dweller, feel that it is not too late for men of vision to transform cities that grew up unplanned. Little measures will not suffice, they say. Heroic ones will be necessary. To accomplish great improvements, government, business, and the private citizen must coöperate with the city planners to the fullest extent.

Zoning the City

The modern city planner believes that a city should be divided into zones: transportation zones which separate motor from pedestrian traffic; commercial and industrial zones; and residential zones with "green" zones and recreational areas.

Examine what has been done with the first problem area, that of providing transportation zones designed to expedite motor traffic. New York, for example, now has 300 miles of connecting parkways within the metropolitan area which speed traffic to a great degree to and from outlying districts although they have not as yet penetrated the city itself. The design of these parkways eliminates cross traffic almost entirely by a modern system of underpasses. Look at the *Clover Leaf* of the Henry Hudson Parkway, seen in Illustration 280. Science and art, the engineer and the architect together, have solved, along with countless similar problems, that of smooth integration of the various directions and demands of automobile traffic. The mathematical precision of complex lanes for through and for local traffic is a striking contrast to the meandering route of the horse and buggy days of less than a century ago.

The second problem in planning for an improved city, that of the separation of commercial and industrial zones from residential zones, is as difficult to accomplish in the long-established city as it is to create the greatly needed new streets and parks by demolishing all buildings in their path. However, much has been done to control the smoke, dirt, and noise of factories, coal and freight yards, and terminals. In recent years, restrictions have been set up which protect residential areas, as well as river fronts and parkways.

The third problem to be met in order to improve the welfare of the city dweller, that of establishing residential zones with "green" areas, means specifically that all new residential sections must be planned so that the actual dwelling units will cover only a small amount of land, and that the remaining sections will be devoted to parks, playgrounds, and open spaces. Countless cities recently have razed slum districts and have built low-cost multiple dwellings on the same sites. In some cases there has been wise planning that has limited the number and the height of the new dwellings; in other cases, far too many tall buildings have been erected and, as a result, hordes of people are still living in congested areas.

Community Planning

It is, in general, outside the limits of the city proper that you can see some stimulating examples of community planning and building on both a small and a large scale. One such development is *Fresh Meadows* (Illustration 281) on Long Island, New York. Its architects, Voorhees, Walker, Foley, and Smith, broke away from the depressing tradition of uniform rows of houses so alike that owners could scarcely identify their own. Instead, these architects have provided a variety of two-story houses and three-story apartments, to serve varying family requirements. These have been placed in small groups, each with its own play yard, lawns, trees, and terrace gardens. This scheme helps to give the inhabitants of *Fresh Meadows* the feeling of living in a small community rather than an enormous one of 11,000 people. Even the inclusion of two thirteen-story apartment buildings in one corner of the development, which was necessary in order to save park space, has not spoiled the rural atmosphere. With several shopping centers, schools, theaters, a bowling alley, rooms for art activities, over 100 acres of lawns, gardens, and parks, garages, and excellent traffic routes, *Fresh Meadows* seem to have everything that such a development could provide for a happy and healthy existence.

What Plans for the Future?

With the advent of community planning, we realize that the architect, working directly with the engineer and the scientist, is the person whose plans not only affect our esthetic life but also reach the very core of our economic existence, our physical welfare, and our social relationships with our fellow men. Not too long ago, large-scale community planning was unheard of. Today community planning has

280. CLOVER LEAF *New York, N.Y.*

Those of you who are interested in photography will admire this excellent night shot which reveals not only practical but also dramatic qualities.

281. FRESH MEADOWS *Long Island, N.Y.*

The small group of two-story homes at the left and the three-story, terraced apartments at the right comprise a pleasantly open and friendly community.

extended its realm to include regional planning, that is, not only planning particular communities but also seeing each one in relation to the larger community of the city, of the state, and eventually of the entire world.

Much that we hope for in the future lies within the mind of the artist. An eminent writer, Sigfried Giedion, in his book *Space, Time and Architecture,* has expressed this thought so well that it is quoted here for you:

". . . every artist is part of a long line of tradition. When he is a creative spirit, however, it is his function to go forward, beyond the limits of that tradition, to explore what before him no one has known, no one has seen, no one has felt. By means of intuition, imagination, mystical impulse—what you will—he must open up new spheres of the unconscious. These spheres are distinguished from the organization of the outer world in that their essential work is done directly, personally, without interference by any external power. They grow only in liberty, for no command can open the way to the unexplored."

TOPICS FOR DISCUSSION AND THINGS TO DO

CHAPTER 1

Topics for Discussion

1. What examples can you give to illustrate the statement, "The love of art is one of man's strongest instincts"?
2. What are some of the thoughts that man conveys through art?
3. What are some of the qualities every artist must possess?
4. What do you gain through your study of art?
5. What are some of the ways in which art contributes to the welfare and happiness of mankind?

Things To Do

1. Give a definite amount of your leisure and study time to art. Become acquainted with the museums and galleries you can visit. Make a check list of historic sites, notable architecture, and other structures you should be sure to see. Keep your eyes open for new buildings and plans for new developments.
2. Familiarize yourself with the art reference books in your school and local library, as well as the available art magazines.
3. Acquire the habit of reading the articles on art in the daily and Sunday newspaper, and in magazines which devote considerable space to art.
4. Make a collection of clippings from newspapers and magazines of things related to the various fields of art. Keep your collection at hand for use in class discussion.

CHAPTER 2

Topics for Discussion

1. What is meant by the prehistoric period?
2. What primitive forms of building have you actually seen? Describe them to the class.
3. What are some primitive ways of making fire? Did primitive man use fire as an aid in constructing any of his art work?
4. In what do the following specialize: the anthropologist; the archeologist; the philologist; the geologist? How has each contributed to our knowledge of early man?
5. In what age did primitive man become an artist?
6. What are at least two reasons for primitive man's painting?
7. Do you think that primitive man ever painted directly from models? Give reasons for your answer.

309

8. What is concept painting?
9. What are the following: dolmen; tumulus; monolith; obelisk; cromlech?
10. Why are the pyramids considered a symbol of the Egyptian religion? Why is a scarab another appropriate symbol?
11. What is the Great Sphinx of Gizeh? Why does it have the head of a human and the body of an animal? For what purpose was it made? What art qualities does it possess?

Things To Do

1. Visit a Museum of Natural History. Make a study there of early man: his appearance; his weapons, clothes, and types of shelter; the objects he made and decorated. Take careful notes of your findings and illustrate them; report on them to the class.
2. Borrow from your library *Men of the Old Stone Age* by Henry F. Osborn, Scribner, 1918; *The Story of Mankind* by Hendrik Van Loon, Macmillan, 1938, or *The Outline of History* by H. G. Wells, Macmillan, 1920. You will find all three of these books interesting.
3. Two other vivid stories of primitive life are *The Story of Ab* by Stanley Waterloo, Doubleday, 1897, and *First Penthouse Dwellers of America* by Ruth M. Underhill, Augustin, 1938. You will enjoy reading them.

CHAPTER 3

Topics for Discussion

1. Why did the early sculptors create idols?
2. Why were their idols seldom lifelike?
3. Why did early sculptors so often exaggerate the size of the head?
4. What are some of the characteristics of sculpture in wood?
5. What are some of the characteristics of sculpture in stone?
6. Why is it said that Egyptian sculpture has enduring qualities?
7. Why do we know more about Egyptian civilization than we do about that of Mesopotamia?
8. What are the differences between relief and full-round sculpture?
9. Does the sculpture of our times serve the same purposes as it did in early civilizations? Give reasons for your answer.
10. What were the *Seven Wonders of the World?* Where were they to be seen?
11. What do you consider the chief merits of primitive art?

Things To Do

1. Become acquainted with *African Negro Art* by James J. Sweeney, Museum of Modern Art, 1935.
2. Make a special trip to a museum, if possible, to look for examples of primitive and early sculpture.
3. *Digging up the Past* by Sir C. Leonard Wooley, Pelican Books, 1949, is recommended for a first-hand account of the way the archeologist works. You might like to buy a copy for yourself, as it is inexpensive.
4. Read *The Adventures of Odysseus and the Tale of Troy* by Padraic Colum, Macmillan, 1918. It will add greatly to your background of pre-Hellenic art.
5. For related reading on primitive people, you will find *Kon-Tiki* by Thor Heyerdahl, Rand McNally, 1950, and *Four Years in Paradise* by Osa Johnson, J. B. Lippincott, 1944, full of suspense and adventure.

CHAPTER 4

Topics for Discussion

1. Do you know of any sections of the country where native craft processes are still being carried on today? If so, tell the class about them.
2. Do you, a member of your family, or a friend have a special craft hobby? If so, can you describe it to the class? Does this hobby provide a real opportunity to design in materials?
3. Why do many people prefer handmade to machine-made products?
4. Describe the process of making coiled pottery.
5. What things in use today are made by a handweaving process?
6. What things in use today are made by a machine weaving process?
7. What is the meaning of the term nomad? Name some nomad peoples. Why did they live their particular kind of existence? How did this existence affect their art work?
8. Describe and if possible demonstrate the processes of any craft with which you are familiar.
9. What are the following: loom, warp, weft; biscuit, glaze, kiln?

Things To Do

1. Make a list of at least four important Indian tribes in North America. Select one and read about the art work for which it is best known. You will find *Indian Art in the United States* by Frederic H. Douglass and René D'Harnoncourt, Museum of Modern Art, 1941, a useful and interesting reference.

Report your findings to the class, showing, if possible, some reproductions of Indian work.

2. Check with your local museums to see if you may find there some interesting examples of Indian work.

3. Borrow from your library a book on the technique of pottery. Read about the Indian potter's method of decorating pottery and the types of design he used.

4. Borrow from your library *Arts of the South Seas* by Ralph Linton, Paul S. Wingert, and René D'Harnoncourt, Museum of Modern Art, 1946, and *Native Arts of the Pacific Northwest* edited by Robert T. Davis, Stanford University Press, 1949. You will find them interestingly written and well illustrated.

5. Japanese Nō Masks have an unusual history. Read about them in the *Encyclopedia Britannica* to discover what types they represented, how they were made, and how they were used. This information is to be found under "Nō Drama" in the Encyclopedia.

CHAPTER 5

Topics for Discussion

1. Describe a typical Greek temple.
2. Do you think you would like to see our churches and temples as brightly colored as those of Greek days? Give reasons for your answer.
3. What are the qualities that contribute to the beauty of Greek architecture?
4. What were some of the Roman architectural inventions?
5. Why did the Romans erect triumphal arches? Where are similar arches to be seen in cities other than Rome? Why were they erected?
6. What were some of the characteristics of Byzantine architecture? Do you see any similar characteristics in present-day buildings? If possible, name such a building and describe its Byzantine aspects.
7. What is a mosaic? How was it made? Do we use mosaic decoration today?
8. Why did the guild system produce such excellent craftsmen?
9. The period of Gothic architecture has been called the "Age of Aspiration." Can you explain why this term has been used?
10. What are the following: pediment; flying buttress; campanile; elevation plan; ground plan; basilica; apse; transept; clerestory; Greek cross; Latin cross; rose window?

Things To Do

1. Read about the Greek Gods in *Classic Myths by* Charles Gayley, Ginn and Company, 1911.

2. Do some research on the Greek theater and make a report to the class. You will find an account in *The Stage Is Set* by Lee Simonson, Harcourt Brace, 1932, and in the *Encyclopedia Britannica* under "Theatre."

3. Read about miracle and mystery plays in *Marionettes, Masks, and Shadows* by Winifred H. Mills and Louise M. Dunn, Doubleday Doran, 1930.

4. If you are an especially appreciative reader, borrow *Mont-Saint-Michel and Chartres* by Henry Adams, Houghton Mifflin, 1913, from your library. It contains a beautifully written description of the spirit of the Middle Ages.

5. Those of you who are especially interested in architecture will like to become acquainted with a classic in that subject, *History of Architecture on the Comparative Method* by Sir Bannister Fletcher, Scribner, 15th ed., 1950.

6. For a delightful version of the days of Caesar, read *Caesar and Cleopatra* by George Bernard Shaw, Dodd Mead, 1930.

7. Read *Dawn in Lyonnesse* by Mary Ellen Chase, Macmillan, 1938, and *Idylls of the King* by Alfred Lord Tennyson for tales of the days of knights and chivalry.

CHAPTER 6

Topics for Discussion

1. What sculptural qualities were shared by Egyptian and early Greek sculpture? To what kind of sculpture did both progress?

2. What was the goal of the Greek sculptor?

3. How did the finest Greek sculpture reach the Roman Empire?

4. What was the outstanding Roman contribution to the art of sculpture?

5. Can you recount any myths or legends having to do with people or places mentioned in this chapter?

6. What are the differences and similarities in the work of the Greek and the Chinese sculptor?

7. How would a modern sculptor react to the rules the Hindu sculptor was bound to follow?

8. Why is it said that the Gothic sculptor created a Bible in stone?

9. Do you know how to cast an object in plaster or in lead? If so, can you describe these processes to the class?

10. What is numismatics?

Things To Do

1. Do some general supplementary reading in *Art Then and Now* by Kathryn D. Lee and Katherine T. Birchwood, Appleton-Century-Crofts, 1949.

2. Become more familiar with Roman sculpture by looking at *Roman Portraits* by Ludwig Goldsheider, Phaidon Press, 1940.

3. Those of you who are interested in collecting old coins and medals will enjoy doing some research on Roman coins: their history, their design quality, and how they were made.
4. One of the processes used to cast bronze statues is called the lost wax process. Look up this process and explain it to the class. You will find it in the *Encyclopedia Britannica* under "Sculpture Technique." See *Casting* and *Finishing*.
5. For a sympathetic picture of the Chinese people, read *The Good Earth* by Pearl Buck, John Day, 1931.

CHAPTER 7

Topics for Discussion

1. What were Giotto's unique accomplishments in painting?
2. What is meant by primitive painting?
3. Describe the spirit of the Renaissance.
4. Why is it said that Leonardo da Vinci best typifies the spirit of the Renaissance?
5. Compare the work of Leonardo, Michelangelo, and Raphael.
6. What is perspective? How many different kinds of perspective are there?
7. Why did the Renaissance painter become interested in perspective?
8. Why do artists varnish paintings?
9. Has varnish affected the work of the old masters? If so, in what way?
10. Explain: gesso; gouache; oil paint; water color.

Things To Do

1. Look through Chapter 7 and list the artists you think used models for their paintings and those you think did not. Check your list with your neighbor's list and discuss the reasons for your selection.
2. Do some supplementary reading in a *World History of Art* by Sheldon Cheney, The Viking Press, 1946, in *A History of Italian Painting* by Frank J. Mather, Jr., Holt, 1923, and in *Art in the Western World,* by Robb and Garrison, Harper, 1942.
3. Plan to visit your nearest museum in order to see some originals of the masters of painting. Bring back some color reproductions to show your classmates.
4. *Leonardo da Vinci* by Ludwig Goldsheider, Phaidon Press, 1943; *The Paintings of Michelangelo* by Ludwig Goldsheider, Phaidon Press, 1940; and *Michelangelo, a Renaissance Profile* by Leo Lerman, Knopf, 1942, will give you added pleasure in the work of these great artists.

314

5. Read *The Flight of the Dragon* by Lawrence Binyon, Dutton, 1922. You will find it a fascinating study of Chinese art.
6. Become familiar with "Andrea del Sarto," the famous poem by Robert Browning which subtly reveals the personality of that famous painter.

CHAPTER 8

Topics for Discussion

1. What is papyrus? For what was it utilized in Egypt?
2. On what did the scribes of Mesopotamia write? What instrument did they use?
3. What are the following: pictographs; ideographs; cuneiform writing; hieroglyphics; manuscript writing; illumination; calligraphy?
4. The three inventions which revolutioned the Renaissance and helped inaugurate the modern age were the mariner's compass, gunpowder, and the printing press. What were some of the results of these three inventions?
5. Who invented paper? Of what materials is paper now made?
6. Was any kind of printing press in use before the printing of the Gutenberg Bible? If so, when and where?
7. What are the following: type face; folio; monotype; linotype; line cut?

Things To Do

1. Find out about and report on the story of the Rosetta Stone. You will find an account of it both in the *Encyclopedia Britannica* and in *The Story of Mankind* by Van Loon.
2. Visit a printing press and report on your visit to the class.
3. Read the *Canterbury Tales* by Chaucer, translated into modern English verse by Frank E. Hill, Longmans Green, 1931. You will find them delightful.
4. Investigate and make a report on one of the following crafts: silverwork; glass blowing; arms and armor; tapestries and embroideries; lacemaking; or any other craft popular during the Middle Ages or the Renaissance.

CHAPTER 9

Topics for Discussion

1. What is genre painting?
2. What effect did El Greco achieve through the use of distortion?
3. What was Rembrandt's favorite form of lighting? What was the general effect it had on his paintings?
4. What is "still life" painting?

5. What is propaganda painting? Why were Goya and Daumier considered propagandists?
6. In addition to being an excellent painter, Daumier was a cartoonist of note. Do you know of any cartoonists today who might also be considered artists?
7. What were the aims of the Impressionist painters? Name some important Impressionists.
8. Why is it essential to view an Impressionist painting from a distance? Can you explain why both their theories of color and their technique of painting have made this necessary?

Things To Do

1. Add to your background of art by becoming familiar with *The Great Painters* by Edith R. Abbot, Harcourt Brace, 1927, and with the *History of Art* by José Pijoan, Harper, 1927. The latter is especially interesting for his account of Spanish painting.
2. Look through *El Greco* by Ludwig Goldsheider, Phaidon Press, 1938. It has some excellent reproductions of the work of this great painter.
3. Read the *Life and Times of Rembrandt: RvR* by Hendrik Van Loon, Garden City, 1932. It is a lively account of the times of one of the world's greatest painters.
4. *Trilby* by Gerald du Maurier, to be found in *Three Novels,* Pilot Press, 1947, is a romantic novel that you will enjoy reading. It presents a vivid picture of the life of the artist in Paris at the beginning of this century.

CHAPTER 10

Topics for Discussion

1. Why is it said that Renaissance painters were more creative than Renaissance architects?
2. What is unusual about the location of Venice? How was the character of Venetian architecture affected by its location? How was it affected by the character of its builders?
3. Explain how the Colonial architecture of New England, the South, and the Southwest naturally had wide variations in size, in form, in materials and methods of construction.
4. Describe to the class a typical Colonial structure with which you are familiar, such as a southern plantation, a mission church, or a New England sea captain's house. Tell, if you can, a little of the history of its building.
5. Are you familiar with any buildings in this country that are copies of a Greek or Roman temple? If so, where are they located?

6. How many cities or towns in the United States can you think of that have Greek or Roman names? Can you think of some that have English, Dutch, or Indian names?

7. In certain sections of the country, some rather peculiar styles of architecture have developed. How many of you have seen "American Gothic" houses, "Wedding cake" houses, or "Gingerbread" houses? Are you acquainted with any other local style of architecture?

Things To Do

1. Add to your general background of art by doing some supplementary reading in *Art Through the Ages* by Helen Gardner, Harcourt Brace, 3rd ed., 1948.

2. If you wish to know more about a particular period of architecture, read about it in *Architecture Through the Ages* by Talbot Hamlin, Putnam, 1940.

3. Look carefully at some of the public buildings in your community, such as a church, a bank, and a school. Do they show some superficial traces of the architecture of the past? Can you identify the source?

4. For general background reading, *The First Americans* by T. J. Wertenbaker, Macmillan, 1927, will give you interesting information about the first Colonial settlers.

CHAPTER II

Topics for Discussion

1. What is the difference between painting the essence and painting the surface of a subject?

2. Can you state the differences in the general aims of the Impressionists, of the Post Impressionists, and of the Expressionists?

3. Can you name painters for each group?

4. Can you name a modern primitive painter and describe his work?

5. What is Cubism? Do you know of any Cubist painters of today or is Cubism a thing of the past?

6. What is a "collage"?

7. What do you think about Surrealist painting? Those of you who like it might debate its merits with those who do not care for it.

8. Some critics consider Picasso the greatest of all modern painters. Others state that he paints "with his tongue in his cheek." What is your opinion of his work? Give your reasons for it.

9. To what kind of painting are you most strongly attracted? Why?

317

10. It is inevitable that some contemporary painters will be considered "old masters" by future generations. For what painters do you predict that honor?

Things To Do

1. Look over the paintings done by you and your classmates. Do some of them look like "little Picassos," or "little Van Goghs," or like the work of any other well-known painter? Is this a merit or a defect?
2. If possible, go directly to art galleries where modern paintings are being shown. Look especially for those painters who are doing something new and different. Tell the class about what you have seen.
3. Read *Noa-Noa* by Paul Gauguin, tr. by O. F. Theis, Greenberg, 1927, to discover what this artist felt about nature.
4. There are countless good books about modern painters and paintings. Borrow some from your library, possibly including *What Is Modern Painting?* by Alfred H. Barr, Museum of Modern Art, 1943; *The Story of Modern Art* by Sheldon Cheney, Viking, 1944; and *They Taught Themselves* by Sidney Janis, Reynal and Hitchcock, 1944.
5. Begin to collect an art library. The publications of the Museum of Modern Art are uniformly good as are those of the Phaidon Press. Also recommended are the small Pelican Books, the Penguin Books, and the Mentor books on art.

CHAPTER 12

Topics for Discussion

1. Most authorities consider Michelangelo the greatest sculptor of the Western World. Do you agree with them, or do you have another candidate for that honor? Explain the reasons for your choice.
2. What are some of the problems of carving in stone? What implements does the stone carver use? Does he usually make a small model to go by?
3. Have you noticed that few modern buildings have sculptural ornament or have sculpture as a part of their general plan? Why is this so? Is the modern architect making a mistake in disregarding the age-old relationship between architecture and sculpture? Debate this point with your classmates.
4. What are the following: plasticine; terra cotta; armature; mould; cast; bronze; patina?
5. Do you think that the modern sculptor, in his search for new forms of expression, is departing too radically from the enduring traditions of sculpture? Give specific examples to illustrate your point of view.
6. Explain to your classmates the theory of the mobile. Compare it with static

sculpture. What has the introduction of the element of time added to the art of sculpture?

Things To Do

1. Read *Zorach Explains Sculpture* by William Zorach, American Artists Group, 1947, for a glimpse into the many practical problems of sculpture.
2. Visit available museums and galleries where modern sculpture is to be seen. Observe the wide variety of subject matter and of individual interpretation, as well as that of media and technique.
3. Look at *The Sculptures of Michelangelo* by Ludwig Goldscheider, Phaidon Press, 1940, to see more of the work of this sculptor.
4. You will find it interesting to look through *Contemporary American Sculpture* edited by C. Ludwig Brummé, Crown, 1948, for a survey of the work of American sculptors.

CHAPTER 13

Topics for Discussion

1. It has been said that painters are inspired either by the realm of the imagination, the realm of the intellect, or the realm of the visible world. Explain this statement. What painter or painters can you mention who have been inspired by each of these sources?
2. On what substances other than canvas do artists paint?
3. What different kinds of paint do they use?
4. Do they ever combine different kinds of paint in one painting?
5. What service do you think the painter performs for mankind?
6. Why is it that many people say they do not care for modern art? Do you think that the people of the Renaissance felt that way about the art of their times? Support your opinion by concrete examples.
7. Why is it that an artist is often unappreciated in his own times yet highly praised by following generations?
8. The painter of *Don't Cry, Mother* believes that "the role of the artist in society has always been and always will be to express the life of his day." Debate this statement with your classmates.

Things To Do

1. Read *Art in America* by Susan La Follette, Harper, 1930, and *Art in America* by Holger Cahill and Alfred Barr, Jr., Halcyon House, 1939.
2. Study your own paintings to see if they reveal aims similar to any of the paintings you have seen in this chapter.

3. Collect reproductions of modern paintings and bring them to class for discussion. See if you can explain what you think each artist is trying to express.

CHAPTER 14

Topics for Discussion

1. What is the underlying principle of steel-cage construction which makes tall buildings and non-supporting walls possible?
2. What is cantilever construction?
3. What things would you consider essential to the plan of a modern high school? Does your school seem to you ideal in plan? How would you improve it?
4. Where and why did the skyscraper develop?
5. What are zoning laws? Why were they necessary?
6. What are some of the problems connected with modern city life?
7. Do you know of any communities where some of these problems have been solved successfully? Illustrate by definite references to various phases of their planning.

Things To Do

1. Does your neighborhood need a recreational area, such as a park with playgrounds, or a community center for sports and theater? If so, plan one and discuss your ideas with the class. Your teacher can probably tell you what civic groups would be interested in hearing about and in seeing your plans.
2. Make a study of the newest office building or factory in your neighborhood, or of one you find illustrated in a magazine. Make some large sketches of its floor plan and other interesting features, and give an illustrated talk about them in class.
3. Form a group to draw up plans for an ideal school. Refer to such magazines as the *Architectural Forum, The Magazine of Building* and the *Architectural Record* to see how architects present their plans.
4. Select a work area, such as a kitchen, a studio, or a modern workshop for various crafts. List the functions to be performed and the equipment needed. Draw plans which you think would lead to an efficient and comfortable arrangement.
5. Borrow from your library *Rameses to Rockefeller* by Charles H. Whitaker, to read an interesting survey of the development of architecture. For further reading on the background of modern architecture, become acquainted with *Space, Time and Architecture* by Sigfried Giedion, Harvard University Press, 1949. Although you may find some of the reading difficult, the illustrations will show you vividly how modern architecture developed.
6. Plan how you can continue your investigation of your heritage of art. You will find it a deep and abiding source of pleasure and enlightenment.

INDEX

Actor's Mask (Klee), 246, 247

Adoration of the Magi (da Fabriano), 149, 150

Adoration of the Magi (Giotto), 139, 140

Affection (Zorach), 257, 258

Albert P. Ryder (Hartley), 272

Amiens, Cathedral of, Doorway, 104, 105

Anatomy Lesson (Rembrandt), 197

Angel, Notre Dame de Chartres, 134, 135

Annunciation (Martini), 140, 141

April Showers (Rattner), 278, 279

Archer, 114, 115

Architecture: American Colonial, 219–222; Baroque, 215–217; Byzantine, 89–95; Early Christian, 88–91; Egyptian, 23–35; Eighteenth-Century American, 225–227; Gothic, 100–109, 213, 227; Greek, 80–83; Later American, 227–228; Maya, 54; Medieval, 96; modern, 289–306; Mohammedan, 93–95; primitive, 17–21; Renaissance, 211–219, 225; Roman, 83–88; Romanesque, 96–100; Spanish-American, 222–225

Articulated Dance Mask, 74, 75

Balzac (Rodin), 251, 252, 257

Bamboo in the Wind (Wei Chû), 174, 175

Bar at the Folies Bergère (Manet), 206, 207

Barber Shop (Bermudez), 285, 286

Barbizon School, 203

Barlach, Ernst, 253, 254

Basilica, 88

Basketry, 56, 58, 59

Bath (Cassatt), 270, 273

Baths of Caracalla, 86, 88

Bawon Temple, 128, 129

Baytown Refinery, 292

Beaded Moccasins, 68, 69

Beckman, Max, 237

Belling, Rudolf, 263

Bellini, Gentile, 157, 158

Bellini, Giovanni, 157, 158

Bellows, George, 274, 275

Bermudez, Cundo, 285, 286

Birth of Aphrodite, 110, 115

Block Book, Page, 176

Blue Boy (Gainsborough), 199, 200

Boat Model, 69, 71

Bodhisattva, 124, 127

Bodhisattva on a Double Lotus Leaf, 126, 127

Book of the Dead, 33

Book of Hours, 169

Book of Kells, Initial Letter in, 166, 169; *Page* in, 166, 169

Botticelli, Sandro, 147, 148, 149

Boucher, François, 201

Boulevard des Italiens (Pissarro), 206, 207

Boy Stealing Fruit (Kuniyoshi), 278, 279

Brahma, 129, 130

Brancusi, Constantin, 253, 254, 261

Braque, Georges, 240, 241

Breughel the Elder, 185, 186

Bri-Bri King's House, 16

Brunelleschi, Filippo, 213

Buckskin Dress, 68, 69

Buddha, 128

Ca d'Oro, 212, 215

Caernarvon Castle, 96, 97

Caesar, Portrait of, 120, 121

i

Calder, Alexander, 266, 267
Calligraphy, 169, 173
Canterbury, Cathedral of, 108
Canterbury Tales, Page, 177, 179
Caracol Tower, 53, 54, 129
Carcassonne, 98
Card Players (Cézanne), facing 229, 230
Caslon, William, 177
Cassatt, Mary, 270, 273
Cathedrals and Churches: Amiens, 104, 105; Canterbury, 108; Chartres, 101, 102, 103, 104, 132, 133; Florence, 210, 211, 213; Havana, 222, 223; Mont St. Michel, 96, 97; Notre Dame, 102, 105; Pisa, 100, 101; Rheims, 105, 106; St. Apollinare in Classe, 89, 90, 139; St. Apollinare Nuevo, 139; St. Francis, 139; St. Mark, 94, 95, 156; St. Paul's, 218, 219, 227; St. Paul's Outside the Walls, 89; St. Peter's, 214, 215, 219, 227; St. Trophime, 99, 100; Ste. Chapelle, 105, 107, 108; Salisbury, 108, 109, 219; San Francisco, 222, 223; San José y San Miguel de Aguayo, 224, 225; San Xavier, 224, 225; Santa Sophia, 91, 92, 95, 213; Sistine Chapel, 154; Wells, 108, 109, 219; Westminster Abbey, 108
Catherine Howard (Holbein), 188, 189
Cave paintings, 18, 19
Ceramic Jar, 60, 61
Cézanne, Paul, facing 229, 229, 230, 231, 233, 235, 241, 247, 273, 281
Chagall, Marc, 245
Chardin, Jean-Baptiste, 201, 202
Charioteer of Delphi, 114, 115
Chartres, Cathedral of, 102, 103; Northern Portal of, 132, 133; Plan of, 101; Rose Window in, 104
Child's Painting, 21, 22
Choir Book, Page, 169, 171
Cimabue, 137, 139
Circus Girls (Gross), 7, 8
City (Grippe), 255, 256
City (Léger), 12, 13
Classicists, 203
Cliff Palace, 24

Clover Leaf, 303, 305
Coiled Basket, 56, 59
Colleoni (Verrocchio), 248, 249, 259
Colosseum, 86, 87
Constable, John, 199, 200, 201, 281
Coral Reef Caves, 16
Corinthian order, 81, 85, 87, 211
Corot, Camille, 203
Cosden Head (Hepworth), 262
Country Road by Night (Van Gogh), 232, 233
Crying Woman (Salerno), 257, 258
Cubism, 233
Cubists, 241–243
Cuneiform, 47, 162, 164
Curry, John, 275

Da Fabriano, Gentile, 149, 150
Daily News Building, 295, 296
Dalí, Salvador, 244, 245
Dancing Girl, 117, 118
Dancing Siva, 131, 132
Daumier, Honoré, 202, 203, 281
David, Jacques, 203
Da Vinci, Leonardo, 145, 151–154, 156, 215
Davis, Stuart, 282, 283
De Chirico, Giorgio, 245
De Hooch, Pieter, 197
De Segonzac, André, 236
De Vlaminck, Maurice, 236
Degas, Edgar, 204, 205, 271, 273
Delacroix, Eugène, 203
Della Francesca, Piero, 144, 147
Delphic Sybil (Michelangelo), 154, 155
Derain, André, 236
Diana Fastening Her Cape, 117, 118
Discus Thrower (Myron), 118
Dlugosz, Louis, 261, 263
Doge Leonardo Loredano (Bellini), 157, 158
Dolmen, 23
Don't Cry, Mother (Evergood), 280, 281
Doric order, 81, 87
Duchamp, Marcel, 241, 265
Dufy, Raoul, 236
Dürer, Albrecht, 181, 182, 188, 189

Echaurren, Roberto Matta, 245
Effigy Vase, 62
El Castillo, 34, 54
El Greco, 10, 190–193, 230
Embroidery, 68, 69
Enríquez, Carlos, 285, 286
Ernst, Max, 245
Esso Building, Framework, 292
Evergood, Philip, 280, 281
Execution of the Madrileños (Goya), 194, 195
Experimental painting, 281–284
Expressionists, 236–239, 245

Falling Water, 298, 299
Family Group (Moore), 261, 262
Figure (Lipchitz), 255, 256
Fish Effigy Mask, 75, 76
Flight into Egypt (Fra Angelico), 142, 143
Florence, Cathedral of, 210, 211, 213
Fra Angelico, 4, 6, 142, 143, 149
Fra Filippo Lippi, 146, 147, 149
Fresh Meadows, 304, 305

Gabo, Naum, 261, 264, 265
Gainsborough, Thomas, 199, 200
Gallery of Mirrors, 216, 217
Garage Lights (Davis), 282, 283
Gaudier-Brzeska, Henri, 253
Gauguin, Paul, 234, 235, 239
Genre painting, 183
Géricault, Théodore, 203
Gilbert, Cass, 296
Giotto, 137–140, 141, 142, 156, 213, 229, 247, 259, 281
Giovanni Arnolfini and His Wife (Van Eyck), 183, 184
Girl in Pink (Modigliani), *facing* 237, 237
Glackens, William, 275
Gleizes, Albert, 241
Gourmet (Picasso), *facing* 1, 6
Goya, Francisco, 193, 194, 195, 203, 281
Gozzoli, Benozzo, 149, 150
Greek alphabet, 167
Grippe, Peter, 255, 256
Gris, Juan, 240, 241

Gross, Chaim, 7, 8
Guilds, 100
Gutenberg Bible, Page, 177, 178
Gutenberg, Johannes, 175, 177, 178

Haines Hall House, 300, 302
Hals, Frans, 197
Hampstead Heath with a Rainbow (Constable), 200, 201
Hanging Mobile (Calder), 266, 267
Hanging Mobile in Motion (Calder), 266, 267
Harp of Queen Shub-ad, 71, 73
Hartley, Marsden, 272
Hassam, Childe, 275
Hatshepsut, Queen, 29, 30, 42–43, 45, 54, 251
Havana, Cathedral of, 222, 223
Head, 39, 40
Head (Belling), 263
Head (Cypriote), 50, 51, 52
Head (Modigliani), 10, 11, 43
Head of Athena, 116, 253
Head of a Maize God, 53, 54
Head of a Young Girl (Maillol), 252, 253
Head of a Young Man, 116, 118
Henri, Robert, 275
Henry (Dlugosz), 261, 263
Henry Gibbs (*anon.*) 268, 269, 279
Hepworth, Barbara, 262
Hera of Samos, 110, 112
Hicks, Edward, 268, 269
Hieroglyphics, 164, 165
Holbein, Hans, 188, 189
Holy Family (El Greco), 190, 191
Home Post, 72
Homer, Winslow, 273–274, 275
Hood, Raymond, 296
Horse and Rider, 70
Horse and Rider (Marini), 259, 260
Hours of the Virgin, Page, 171, 173
Hypostyle Hall, Temple of Amon, Model of, 31, 33

Ideographs, 173
Impressionists, 205, 207, 229, 275
Infanta Margarita (Velázquez), 193, 194

Ingres, Jean, 203
Inner Coffin of Tutankhamen, 26, 27
Inscriptions, Cylinder Seals, 162, 164
Ionic order, 81, 87

Jefferson, Thomas, 225, 227
John Whipple House, 221, 222
Jones, Inigo, 219
Journey of the Magi (Sassetta), *facing* 141, 141
Journey of the Three Kings (Gozzoli), 149, 150

Kali with Cymbals, 131, 132
Kandinsky, Wassily, 239, 243, 244, 245
Katchina Dolls, 77, 78
King Ashurbanipal and His Queen, 48, 49
Kist, 23
Klee, Paul, 239, 246, 247
Kokoschka, Oscar, 237, 239, 253
Kolbe, Georg, 253
Koran, Page, 172, 173
Korwar, 36
Kuniyoshi, Yasuo, 278, 279

La Mousmé (Van Gogh), *facing* 233, 233
La Pietà, Detail (Michelangelo), 248, 251
Landscape (Tung Yüan), 160, 161
Landscape with Wild Horses (Enríquez), 285, 286
Lao Tse on a Water Buffalo, 124, 125
Lawrence, Sir Thomas, 199
Lawson, Ernest, 275
Le Corbusier, 301
Lea County Community Hospital, 294
Lee, Doris, 275
Léger, Fernand, 12, 13, 241
Lehmbruck, Wilhelm, 251, 253
Les fauves, 236
Libyan Desert paintings, 20
Light Form (Kandinsky), 243, 244, 245
Linear Construction, Variation (Gabo), 261, 264, 265
Lipchitz, Jacques, 255, 256
Little Rose of Lyme Regis (Whistler), 270, 271

Lorenzo de' Medici (Michelangelo), 250, 251
Louis XIV, 217
Luncheon of the Boating Party (Renoir), 207, 208, 209

Mme. Charpentier and Her Children (Renoir), 4, 5
Madonna Adoring the Child (Fra Filippo Lippi), 146, 147, 149
Madonna and Child, 136, 139
Madonna of the Goldfinch (Raphael), 155, 156
Maillol, Aristide, 252, 253
Maine Coast (Marin), 276, 277, 279
Manet, Edouard, 206, 207, 271
Manuscript of the Gospels, Cover, 168, 169
Manuscript (Persian), 172, 173
Manuscripts, Medieval, 168, 169, 170, 171, 173; Persian, 172, 173
Marin, John, 276, 277, 279
Marini, Marino, 259, 260
Martini, Simone, 140, 141, 142
Masaccio, 144, 145, 147
Mask (African), 41, 43
Mask of Saiyatsha, 77, 78
Masson, André, 245
Mastaba, 25
Matisse, Henri, *facing* 236, 236, 273
Medici-Riccardi Palace, 212, 213
Metzinger, Jean, 241
Michelangelo, 3, 145, 154–155, 156, 215, 248, 249, 250, 251, 261
Millet, Jean-François, 203
Minor arts: basketry, 56, 58–59; embroidery, 68, 69; manuscripts, 168–173; pottery, 60–63; printing, 175–179, 182; prints, 175; weaving, 63–69; woodcarving, 69–78
Miracle of the Holy Cross (Bellini), 157, 158
Miró, Joan, 245, 246, 247
Miss Expanding Universe (Brancusi), 253, 254, 261
Mobiles, 265–267
Modigliani, Amadeo, 10, 11, 43, *facing* 237, 237

Mona Lisa, Detail (Da Vinci), 153, 154
Monet, Claude, 207, 229
Mont St. Michel, 96, 97
Mont Saint-Victoire, 230, 231
Monticello, 227
Moore, Henry, 261, 262
Mosaic, St. Apollinare in Classe, 90, 91
Mosaics, 90, 91, 93, 139
Moses, 3, 5, 154, 251
Moses, Anna Mary (Grandma), 241, 275
Mount Vernon, 221, 225
Munch, Edvard, 237
Mural painting, 21, 22
My Ch'i, 160
Myron, 118

National Capitol, 226, 227
Nativity (Fra Angelico), 4, 6
Neo-Impressionists, 209
Night Watch (Rembrandt), 197
Nobleman Hunting, 32, 33, 35
Nofretete, Queen, 44, 45
Nolde, Emil, 237
Non-objective painting, 243
Notre Dame, Cathedral of, 102, 105

Offering Bearer, 69, 70
Office, Johnson Wax factory, 290, 291
Orozco, José, *facing* 284, 284

Painted Box, Section of, 31
Painting: American, 269–284; Brazilian,
    285, 287–288; Chinese, 159–161,
    230, 277; Cuban, 285, 286; Dutch,
    195–199; Egyptian, 33, 35; English,
    199–201; Flemish, 183–188; French,
    201–204, 205–209; German, 188;
    Italian, 137–159; Maya, 35; Mexican,
    284–285; modern, 229–247; primi-
    tive, 18–21, 142, 239, 241, 269, 275,
    279; Spanish, 188, 190–195
Palace of Versailles, 216, 217
Palladio, 219
Pantheon, 84, 85, 87, 89, 91, 95, 213
Paradise, Detail (Fra Angelico), 142, 143
Parthenon, 81, 82, 83, 118
Pazzi Chapel, 210, 213

Peaceable Kingdom (Hicks), 241, 268,
    269
Peasant Dance (Breughel), 185, 186
People in the Night (Miró), 246, 247
Pereira, I. Rice, 282, 283
Persistence of Memory (Dalí), 244, 245
Pertaining to Yachts and Yachting
    (Sheeler), 276
Phidias, 118
Phoenician alphabet, 167
Phoenix Union High School, 294
Picabia, Francia, 241
Picasso, Pablo, *facing* 1, 6, 159, 241, 242,
    243
Pictographs, 164
Picture writing, 163
Pierrot (Rouault), *following* 236, 237
Pippin, Horace, 241
Pisa, Cathedral of, 100, 101
Pissarro, Camille, 206, 207, 229
Playing Cards, 176
Polyclitus, 118
Pont du Gard, 84, 85
Porch of the Maidens, 82
Porte des Allemandes, 98
Portinari, Candido, 285, 287
Portrait (Van der Weyden), 185, 186
Portrait of the Artist's Mother (Whis-
    tler), 271
Portrait of Dr. Tietze and His Wife
    (Kokoschka), 238, 239
Portrait of a Maya Astronomer, 54, 55
Post-Impressionists, 209
Potlatch Dish, 74, 75
Pottery, 60–63
Pottery Drum Jar, 62
Pottery Jugs, 60
Praxiteles, 118
Prendergast, Maurice, 275
Priest with Dove, 51, 52
Print Shop, 179
Printing, 175–179, 182
Prints, 175
Pyramid of Sahure, Model of, 28, 29
Pyramids: *Great Pyramid*, 27; *Sahure*,
    28, 29

v

Race Track (Ryder), 272, 273
Rain in the Jungle (Rousseau), 238, 239
Ramses II, 44, 45
Raphael, 155, 156, 215
Rattner, Abraham, 278, 279
RCA Building, 3, 5
Red Stairway (Shahn), 280, 281
Redon, Odilon, 237, facing 239
Rehearsal of Ballet on Stage (Degas), 204, 205
Rembrandt van Rijn, 196, 197
Renoir, Pierre, 4, 207, 208, 209
Reynolds, Sir Joshua, 199
Rheims, Cathedral of, 105, 106
Rivera, Diego, 284
Rock painting, 19, 20
Rockefeller Center, 296, 297
Rodin, Auguste, 251, 252, 257
Roman alphabet, 167, 169
Romanticists, 203
Rosetta Stone, 167
Rouault, Georges, following 236, 237
Rousseau, Henri, 238, 239, 269
Rousseau, Théodore, 203
Rox, Henry, 259, 260
Rubens, Peter Paul, 185, 187, 188
Ryder, Albert P., 272, 273

St. Apollinare in Classe, 89, 90, 139
St. Apollinare Nuevo, 139
St. Eustace (Dürer), 181, 182
St. Francis, Church of, 139
St. Mark, Cathedral of, 94, 95, 156
St. Paul's Cathedral, 218, 219, 227
St. Paul's Outside the Walls, 89
St. Peter's Cathedral, exterior of, 214, 215, 219, 227; interior of, 214
St. Trophime, Church of, 99, 100; Cloisters of, 99
Ste. Chapelle, 105, 107, 108
Salerno, Charles, 257, 258
Salisbury, Cathedral of, 108, 109, 219
San Francisco, 222, 223
San José y San Miguel de Aguayo, Mission of, 224, 225
San Xavier, Mission of, 224, 225
Santa Sophia, exterior, 91, 92, 95, 213; Interior, 91, 92

Sassetta, facing 141, 141, 142
Savoie House, 298, 301
Saying Grace (Chardin), 201, 202
Schöngauer, Martin, 180, 182
Sculpture: Chinese, 122–127; Cypriote, 50–52; Egyptian, 42, 43–45; Etruscan, 118–120; Gothic, 132–135; Greek, 112–118; Hindu, 127–132; Maya, 52–55; Mesopotamian, 45–49; Modern, 252–267; primitive, 37–43; Renaissance, 249–251; Roman, 118–120, 121
Seacoast Maya Village, 34, 35
Seated White Man, 76
Secretariat Building, United Nations, 297, 299
Self-portrait (Dürer), 189
Seurat, Georges, 208, 209
Shahn, Ben, 280, 281
Shattuck House, 300, 301
Sheeler, Charles, 276
Shepherds of the Nativity, 134, 135
Shub-ad, Queen, 73
Singing Man (Barlach), 253, 254
Siqueiros, Alfaro, 284
Sisley, Alfred, 207
Sistine Chapel, 154
Sloan, John, 275
Soul Bird, 39, 40
Sphinx of Gizeh, 28
Statuette of a Bear, 122, 125
Statuette of a Horse, 113, 115
Stele of Senu, 165
Still Life with Fruit Dish (Cézanne), 230, 231
Still Life: Le Journal (Gris), 240
Still Life: The Table (Braque) 240, 241, 243
Stone Pipe, 38
Stonehenge, 23, 24
Storm at the Bahamas (Homer), 274, 275
Striding Warrior, 119, 120
Strozzi Child (Titian), facing 158, 158
Sullivan, Louis, 293
Sumerian Priest, 46, 47, 73
Sunday on Grande Jatte Island (Seurat), 208, 209

Surrealists, 245–247
Suzanne Fourmont (Rubens), 185, 187

Taj Mahal, 93, 94
Temple of Amon, 31, 33, 81, 87
Temple of Queen Hatshepsut, Model of, 29, 30
Temple of Ramses II, 29, 30
Temple of Warriors, 34, 35
Temples: Amon, 31, 33, 81, 87; Bawon, 128, 129; Caracol Tower, 53, 54, 129; El Castillo, 34, 54; Hatshepsut, 29, 30; Pantheon, 84, 87, 89, 91, 95, 213; Parthenon, 82, 83, 118; Ramses II, 29, 30; Warriors, 34, 35
Temptation of St. Anthony (Schöngauer), 180, 182
Ter Borch, Gerard, 197
Textile, 64
Three Geisha (Utamaro), 204, 205
Three Kings, 136, 139
Three Musicians (Picasso), 242, 243
Tiger by Waterfall (My Ch'i), 160, 161
Tiki, 38, 39
Titian, 145, facing 158, 158, 159, 281
Totem Pole, 72, 73
Transfluent Lines (Pereira), 283
Tribute Bearers, 48, 49
Tribute Money, Detail (Masaccio), 144, 145
Tugendhut House, 13, 301
Tumulus, 23
Tung Yüan, 160, 161
Twined Basket, 56

United States Treasury Building, 227
University of Virginia, 227
Uprising (Daumier), 202, 203
U.S. Forest Service Building, 290, 291
Utamaro, Kitagawa, 204, 205

Van Eyck, Jan, 183, 184, 185
Van Gogh, Vincent, 232, facing 233, 233, 235, 239, 253, 284
Van der Rohe, Mies, 301
Van Ruisdael, Jacob, 197
Van der Weyden, Rogier, 185, 186

Vase of Flowers (Redon), 237, facing 239
Vase with Poppies (Matisse), facing 236, 236
Velázquez, Diego, 185, 193, 194
Venus de Milo, 118
Vermeer, Jan, 197, 198, 199, 201
Verrocchio, Andrea, 248, 249
View of Toledo (El Greco), 191, 192, 193
Virgin and Child with St. Anne (Da Vinci), 151, 152, 154, 156
Virgin Enthroned, 138
Virgin, Infant Jesus, and St. John (Botticelli), 148, 149
Visit of the Queen of Sheba (Della Francesca), 144, 147
Vitruvius, 213

War God, 36, 39
Washington, George, 225
Watteau, Antoine, 201
Weaving, 63–69
Wei Chû, 174
Weir, Alden, 275
Wells Cathedral, Interior, 108, 109, 219
Westminster Abbey, 108
Whistler, James McNeil, 270, 271
White Horse (Bellows), 274, 275
White Horse (Gauguin), 234, 235
Windmill Psalter, Page, 169, 170, 177
Wine Vessel, 122, 123
Winged Being, 46
Woman and Children (Portinari), 285, 287
Woman of the Old Testament, 8
Woman Weighing Gold (Vermeer), 198, 199, 201
Wood, Grant, 275
Woodcarving, 69–78
Woolworth Building, 295, 296
Woven Bag, 66
Woven Blanket, 65, 67
Woven Shoulder Blanket, 65, 67
Wren, Sir Christopher, 219
Wright, Frank Lloyd, 291, 299
Writing: calligraphy, 169, 173; cuneiform, 47, 162, 164; Greek alphabet,

167; hieroglyphics, 164, 165; ideographs, 173; Phoenician alphabet, 167; pictographs, 164; picture writing, 163; Roman alphabet, 167, 169
Writing: Pictograph to Cuneiform, 162, 163–164

Young Girl at a Half-Open Door (Rembrandt), 196, 197
Young Monk (Rox), 259, 260

Zapatistas (Orozco), *facing* 284, 284
Ziggurat, 47, 49
Zorach, William, 257, 258